BURN RATE

Also by Michael Wolff

White Kids

*Where We Stand: Can America Make It in the Global
Race for Wealth, Health, and Happiness?*
(with Peter Rutten and Chip Bayers)

BURN RATE

*How I Survived the Gold Rush
Years on the Internet*

Michael Wolff

Weidenfeld & Nicolson
LONDON

First published in Great Britain in 1998
by Weidenfeld & Nicolson

Published in association with Simon & Schuster,
1230 Avenue of Americas, New York, NY 10020, USA

A CIP catalogue record for this book is available
from the British Library.

ISBN 0 297 84261 7

Printed in Great Britain by
Clays Ltd, St Ives plc

Weidenfeld & Nicolson
The Orion Publishing Group Ltd
Orion House
5 Upper Saint Martin's Lane
London, WC2H 9EA

For Our Children

Elizabeth, Susanna, and Steven

"How many people have you got on staff now?"

"Over seventy," I say with pride, even though I realize that each person is another parcel the boat cannot handle.

"What's your burn rate?"

"All in, a half million a month or so," I shrug.

"Rest in peace, baby."

Contents

Preface

While I have spent most of my career as a practicing journalist, I have also dabbled in various entrepreneurial schemes. Through those efforts, I became an early participant in the growth of the Internet industry. This put me near the center of a business that, I believe, will transform the time we live in. In other words, a great story fell into my lap.

The company whose fortunes are here described—first called Michael Wolff & Company, Inc., and then, after a round of investor financing, Wolff New Media LLC—started in 1990 with three employees. Its business was to develop ideas for books, magazines, and television. For several years the company hummed along in a contented and profitable manner. Then, in a two-year period beginning in 1994, when the company extended its activities, as well as its definition of media, to the Internet, both its revenues and personnel expanded almost twentyfold. Its respectable profits turned to dramatic losses, and it attracted the sudden and persistent attention of bankers, venture capitalists, the press, competitors, and potential acquirers.

The Internet, because it is a new industry making itself up as it goes along, is particularly susceptible to the art of the spin. Those of us in the industry want the world to think the best of us. Optimism is our bank account; fantasy is our product; press releases are our good name. My hope now is to write a sort of anti–press release: What the people actually said and thought and accomplished.

Most often in the business world, one is bound by client confidentiality or by nondisclosure agreements or by the desire to stay employed and to do another deal. I am, at this time, bound by none of those things.

While I have (perhaps even convincingly) run a business, raised capital, and sold air with the best of them, I never did break myself of the habits of my writer's career. And so at conference tables, board meetings, and industry gatherings, while others were scribbling to-do lists on their legal pads, I found myself recording observations and jotting down telltale lines of dialogue on mine.

This story weaves through the growth years of the Internet industry between 1994 and 1997, but it is most specifically about the six-month period in 1996 during which I was shuttling back and forth between the East Coast and the West Coast trying to raise the money and make the deals that I hoped would let my company survive its burn rate—the money a company spends each month exceeding its revenues.

The story is, for the most part, my own. But having started early in the Internet business and grown with the industry, I hope I can offer the reader a coherent picture of how the Internet industry came into being virtually overnight and how it came so quickly to the center stage of American life. Still, as you will see, the view presented here of the Internet business is uniquely my own. I take exclusive responsibility for its errors of omission and commission.

I have stayed as close to the truth as I remember it or have a record of it. Because there were hundreds of meetings that took place in the time frame of this story, I have obviously omitted many and, I am sure, inadvertently condensed some. In general, I have changed the names of neither the individuals nor the businesses that play principal roles in this story or important roles in the industry; I have, however, in some instances changed or omitted the names of individuals who, though they play curious and instructive roles, are not principal players in this tale or in the Internet business.

This is, however, a story. No doubt my memory has at moments exaggerated foibles and sometimes simplified the line between cause and effect. I am confident, however, that my memory has not distorted the truth. In the end, as a businessman, I might have wished that this story had turned out differently; as a writer, I couldn't ask for anything more. It happened like this.

MICHAEL WOLFF
mwolff@burnrate.com

BURN RATE

Chapter One

A Diamond As Big As the Ritz

August 1996

I am a reluctant participant in a conference of CEOs of information and technology companies being held at the Ritz in Laguna Beach, one of the poshest in the Ritz chain. I'm embarrassed by my hunger for affection and approval, preferably in the form of another round of financing for my company. Powerful forces are represented here—principals of venture capital funds and managers of corporate strategic investment pools; these are ordinary men and women with extraordinary powers, who, if they so desired, could let me sleep through the night.

But who am I to be singled out? Most of my fellow CEOs at the conference are up all night too, disturbed not just by earnings that are down or market issues that need to be addressed but by a countdown, measured in weeks, of how much cash they have left. We are the leaders of an industry without income.

Some of the entrepreneurs here, though in similar *extremis,* hold themselves with striking poise and equanimity, while others buttonhole the venture capitalists, demanding their attention and delivering, in the verdant Ritz hallways, heated sales pitches. In the end, who will be left standing—the hot and bothered or the cool?

It seems like high school all over again. The VCs are upperclassmen, study hall proctors, varsity athletes. A casual word or familiar gesture from any one of them can confer status, meaning, value. To be ignored is to not exist. The stakes are as high as they were in high school: existence itself.

Attendance at this particular conference has already conferred status.

In the technology industry you could (and people do) attend conferences on a weekly basis, but this one has a track record of deals lined up, of good action in the halls, of hot faces in the crowd.

It was not my idea to come to the conference. I would have preferred to stay home, reticently, or modestly, or insecurely, but the lead investor in our company, a young man with large cyber ambitions, thought we both should make an appearance. "This is where we can make something happen," he theorized. "It's all in the halls. We'll just stand in the halls. I'll introduce you to who I know. You'll introduce me to who you know. It'll be very cool. You'll be great."

But the day before our departure, he bailed: "We'll go to the next one together."

I am grateful to be here on my own.

What fuels the emotions of these conferences, and this industry, is change. What is taken for granted today will be a joke tomorrow. All technology, as they say, is transitional. This rate of turnover, of obsolescence, makes it possible for people with heart and imagination, but without capital or experience, to make themselves into moguls within months instead of over the span of a career. All it takes is "the nod," the gesture (in the form of a minority investment) that acknowledges the prescience, the genius, or just the cleverness of the new kid on the block.

I am painfully aware that my lovely, wonderful company, which publishes some of the coolest guides to the Net and maintains one of the most lavish sites on the Web and has grown from four to seventy people in little more than two years, has seven weeks before it will crash and burn without new investment. So much depends on my ability to now attract the attention of one of these Big Men On Campus: not only next month's payroll but growth, expansion, dominance, and my chance to walk away with enough wealth to support generations to come. (This is not a long-term plan, but one meant to be accomplished, ideally, by next year's meeting at the Ritz.)

The desperation in the air here is perfectly complemented by the thrill of seeing several faces desperate at this time last year (some who a year ago did not have dreams large enough to make them desperate) now elevated, esteemed, and valued.

Tall and handsome, with prep school straight hair, Halsey Minor, the thirty-one-year-old CEO of CNet, a company that produces a cable show and a Web site about computers, takes the podium in the Ritz's oversized reception room, otherwise used for the cream of Orange County's weddings and bar mitzvahs. Minor has a net worth, in negotiable securities, of $40 million. In comparison, my own paper worth of $5.4 million seems crabbed and amateurish, especially considering that my credit cards are all maxed out and I'm sucking cash from every ATM in Orange County.

Two years ago Halsey Minor was an executive recruiter. Between making cold calls on behalf of larger corporations to executives at other corporations, he had an idea to create a television show about computers. That idea led directly to another idea: a site on the Internet all about computers. Duh.

What allows Halsey to get rich on the obvious? Capital? Tenacity? Timing? The Halsey Minor performance is stellar and intimidating. He's the head boy. His confidence and certainty are extreme. Unusual, you might think, because we are part of an industry so young, so unformed, so not real, that we're not even sure who should pay whom yet. Fact of the matter, there is no real money yet to be paid with. The question is not, How do we sell more of what we have to sell? or How do we reach more people? or How do we produce products more cheaply? but What is the economic basis for existing? Who is buying? Who is selling?

Of course, this is the opportunity, too. Truer moguls, more seasoned entrepreneurs, vaster sums of capital have left the territory wide open to eccentrics and opportunists—and freelance writers like me.

Take a computer, send information through it—hell, send all the information ever recorded through it. And then what? What is your business model? is the salutation in almost all conversations about this newest medium. What is the economic justification for what you do? What is the value proposition? How will you convince people to pay you more than you're spending? If the universe of information is now free, who will pay for your insights, wit, pith, truth?

When will we invent the game shows, soap operas, variety shows, newscasts, and sitcoms—not to mention the art—of this new medium? Is this like 1947 in the television business (meaning another six years before a mass market emerges)? Or are we in a year like 1953, on the verge of changing the nation? Or is it like 1971 in the cable business or—a horrible thought—1985 in a business known as videotext, a precursor to the digital information business that sucked up hundreds of millions of dollars from a galaxy of major media companies before evaporating.

Halsey Minor, in an open-collared striped shirt, is not anxiety ridden. At the heart of his confidence, of course, is his company's $200 million market value on $4 million in revenues. His presentation today deals with the conundrum of the CPM, or cost per thousand, model of advertising. If BMW, say, is paying $25 per thousand "impressions" or page views on the Web (an impression is registered when an individual Web viewer clicks to an individual "page" of a Web site)—a rate similar to what BMW would pay for space in a consumer magazine—we (Web site proprietors) are penalized if we only deliver one hundred people. But what if one of those one hundred people will definitely buy a car? The CPM model encourages us to build larger, more costly, less efficient audiences, while digital technology allows us to build an ever more targeted, economical, buyer-positioned audience.

Although the argument that the CPM model has no place in a wired world has some elegance, no one takes it all that seriously. No products have disappeared off America's supermarket shelves because of the Internet. Few cars have left their showrooms (cars are a commodity that many people believe is especially suitable for Internet sales), no commercial fads have been created, and no buying habits have shifted as a result of the Internet. There is no empirical evidence whatsoever that advertising works (i.e., gets you more and costs you less) on the Internet. But that is not the issue. The point is that if advertising works—a carefully minimized big *if*—it is likely to work for Halsey Minor and CNet.

"I've got thirty-nine million dollars in the bank, and my competitors don't. I've got people coming to me who were previously thinking of going public and are now offering to sell their businesses to me. I always hoped the door would close right after us," Halsey told *Red Herring*, a magazine that covers Internet financings.

There is a hierarchy here of companies that have made it out through the public portal with big war chests in the bank, companies that have secured the first round or two of professional financing, and companies that are little more than an idea. It does not matter that not one of these companies—funded or not—is profitable. The hierarchy, the aristocracy, depends on being first.

Land, as in most aristocracies, is the measure. Not trade. Who has the resources to claim the most valuable property—occupy space through the promotion of brands, the building of name recognition, the creation of an identity—is the name of the game. Conquer first, reap later.

The names are already building household recognition: Yahoo! *Wired*. Netscape.

Names as powerful now as the Dumont Network, a major player in the earliest days of television, and the Kaypro computer, at the top of the PC business in the early 1980s, in their day.

"We may not know all the winners, but we certainly know some of them," says Halsey Minor with a uniquely satisfied grin. "Questions?"

A tall, crane-like woman unfolds from the audience.

"Oh, Suzanne. Suzanne, be kind," says the conference moderator, an Internet industry journalist.

The sense that everyone knows everyone here is, for those who feel they know no one, painful. And while I feel that way—unrecognized and unknown—I do know Suzanne. She's a magazine editor who has recently acquired the digital faith. While sitting with her in the Harvard Club one day in the late 1980s, I told her that personal computers would connect us all and replace media as we know it and that we would all be in the computer business before we turned forty. I was teasing, of course.

"Considering," Suzanne says to Halsey Minor as she puts on large glasses and looks down at some notes she has scribbled, "that almost every company here is dependent on the capital markets rather than a customer base, and considering that the capital markets have turned cold to new technology companies over the last forty-five days, can you talk a little about the future of this industry?"

"And your point?" Minor gives a short laugh, a snort.

At the long tables with laptop power cords, I am seated next to a dwarf in a wheelchair, a bizarre counterpoint to the disembodied digital future. A reporter for one of the industry trade magazines, he has been offering, *sotto voce*, a running commentary on the digital aristocracy. At first his whispering seemed unruly and bitter to me, but I am secretly starting to appreciate it. "Where do you think Halsey Minor will be in five years? Is greatness within his grasp? I can't decide," he says.

"Couldn't begin to guess," I say, hearing and regretting my envy.

"How long do you guys have left?" He asks pointedly, merrily, about my business.

"Well," I respond cautiously, "we're not unsatisfied with our model."

"Come on."

"Really, we're in fairly good shape."

"How many people have you got on staff now?"

"Over seventy," I say with pride, even though I realize that each person is another parcel the boat cannot handle.

"What's your burn rate?"

"All in, a half million a month or so," I shrug.

"Rest in peace, baby."

"It's not so bad, honestly."

He practically hoots at the next presenter. "Do you know this guy? Have you heard about him? Life is so unfair."

On the podium the stage hands are making a quick adjustment to the presentation laptop while Seth Godin, a thin, sharp-featured, prematurely bald thirty-five-year-old, one of the new impresarios of the industry, chats amiably with Halsey Minor. A year ago, Godin had written me a note about people and business interests we had in common and followed it up with a call and an invitation to lunch. He wanted to know whom I knew, wanted to know what paths I had crossed and with what inspiration I had carved my business out of whole cloth. He would have taken any crumb. I was unforthcoming, however, and uncharitable.

Now, with an idea to create game shows using e-mail over the Internet, he has nailed down $4 million in VC financing and is in a position to play Mark Todson, television's greatest game show impresario, to Halsey Minor's William Paley, the founder of CBS.

Godin and I had run into each other earlier in the day. Disturbingly, he told me how many people said we looked alike. What's worse, he lectured me on money-raising skills, from which I inferred that his venture capital sources, whom I'd met and petitioned at some length, had found me less than inspiring. "You're so laid back," he said. "You're not selling enough. Hey, where's the passion? That's what people are ponying up for. Passion. They have to know that you are just so hot for it."

What today's presenters have in common is that they are considered "content," as opposed to technology, people. They represent the ideas and concepts and formats that will draw people to this new medium. They will provide the reason ordinary people, not just "early adopters" or technology professionals, will want to make the Internet part of their lives. They represent a notion, too, that Content is King, possessing value that the medium will keep bidding higher and higher prices for. From content will come the hits, the *Lucys*, the *Star Treks*, the *Seinfelds*, of this new medium.

This view of content, with its royal status, is part of the television bias through which most people understand the Internet; a not dissimilar bias, perhaps, to when movies were thought to be a form of theater, and television a form of radio. It's what I certainly have believed. The Internet is an expanded, heightened, energized form of media, an incredible new mechanism by which to send a coherent message to the world.

"Do you know how bad these ideas are?" whispers my new friend beside me. "Think about this for a second. Games by e-mail. Pathetic! Delusional!"

Candace Carpenter, now taking the podium and hugging Halsey Minor, is another of the Internet's first generation of programming whizzes (programming in the television, rather than the software, sense). A former executive at QVC, Time Warner, and ABC, her company, iVillage, is one of the best-funded content companies in the Internet business. She has been heralded as the first example of a seasoned media executive crossing over into the Internet space, and iVillage has in fact structured itself as an independent production company, creating shows for network broadcast. Its network is America Online (AOL), which, along with the Silicon Valley venture group Kleiner Perkins Caufield & Byers, has invested more than $12 million in the company. The first "show" produced by iVillage is called Parent Soup—a place, an environment, a channel, for parents on the Internet.

Carpenter, a stylish, blond fifty-something living with her husband and daughter in Manhattan on Park Avenue, is far from the computer company start-up type. She's very New York, the Californians say. She professes little interest in technology but possesses, as anyone can see, remarkable sales talents and tenacity. She understood that if you wanted to talk to AOL, you had to go to Vienna, Virginia. You had to show up, present yourself, hang around, get people familiar with your face, then wander the halls. It was America's greatest dysfunctional company, after all. So you had to intervene, confront it.

There's something appealing, scattered, Annie Hall–like about Carpenter. She plays with her hair and speaks in a tumble of enthusiasms, of contrary impulses, all of them passionate. What the Internet is to her—"This thing, this incredible thing, totally beyond comprehension, totally beyond what anyone would have dreamed up if someone was dreaming of this"—is, well, she can only really relate it to her experience as a recovering alcoholic in AA, to how the whole 12-step dynamic works.

In fact, although iVillage had invested heavily in the creation of traditional magazine and television-like content for Parent Soup, envisioning the product as a cross between a special interest magazine and a targeted cable channel, that approach has now been abandoned. Creating original and traditional content was expensive, and it isn't what users want, anyway. Users are happier creating their own content. They don't want to hear the experts, they want to hear themselves. It is just this incredible cacophony of voices, of user-created content, Carpenter says breathlessly. What's more, the users will do all the work—for free! This, she says, is a viable business model.

It pains me. I am motivated by the opposite impulse—away from the cacophony, looking for the symphony. While I obviously have no quarrel with people getting together to chew the fat in chat rooms across the Internet, it is not a process that I necessarily bring value to.

I am looking forward to Time, Inc., editor in chief Norm Pearlstine's remarks, because he is likely to represent a voice for journalism—sentences, paragraphs, order, punctuation, point of view—in this new medium.

"You should get Time to buy you," offers my new friend, as Pearlstine shakes hands with his new media counterparts. "They might as well. They're going to buy something. They obviously don't know how to do it themselves."

"Not impossible, I suppose. We know the people at Time Warner, of course. We were the original consultants on Pathfinder." (Pathfinder is the multi-million dollar Time Warner Internet site.)

"Something to be proud of," he laughs.

Pearlstine's manner at the podium, along with his dark suit and pallid complexion, suggests a higher level of mission and seriousness than that of the other presenters. He seems purposely to eschew the relaxed, casual dress and the bonhomie of the cyber world.

But instead of endorsing the principles of journalistic objectivity and smart analysis and emphasizing the importance of good writing, Pearlstine gives a speech that seems to be about defending and protecting Time. With its bureaus around the world and its journalistic standards, Time stands over here and the riffraff and anarchy of the Internet stands over there. In the end, what will people pay for? What do people always pay for? Consistency, quality, reliability. Sure it's nice to go to someone's house for dinner, but you wouldn't pay for it; it isn't Le Cirque.

"An industry of metaphors," interjects my companion.

The real conflict, however, Pearlstine continues, is not between Time and the do-it-yourselfers of the Internet but between Time Warner and Microsoft.

"The truth can now be told," says my friend.

Microsoft clearly has the capital to compete as a media organization, but does it have the credibility, the integrity, the temperament to function at the forefront of today's events and popular culture? Pearlstine wants to know.

I am worried about this myself. Anybody who has ever visited the "campus" in Redmond ought to be worried, I am thinking.

On the other hand, a kind of counterintuitive logic says that Time Warner will not be trounced by Microsoft but that both Time Warner and Microsoft will be trounced by some as-yet-unidentified new force. The thinking is that the old, because it is already committed to a direction and a bias and an infrastructure and a set of tools, can never produce the new and that the new will invariably lay waste to the old.

One of the hottest new companies at the conference is Boston-based Firefly. Now its two twenty-something founders follow Pearlstine to the podium. Firefly has been applying various data-matching technologies to musical tastes. For example, a person, X, represented by a digital marker, might indicate an interest in the rock group Jane's Addiction and theoretical physics and could therefore be matched with Y, a person whose digital marker indicates similar preferences. The goal is to establish enough markers that the system can inform you that you, although you might not know it, are an inevitable Jane's Addiction fan. Firefly, on the basis of this technology, has succeeded, in its last round of financing, in raising its value to something like $200 million—without yet having recorded any revenues.

While virtually everyone at the conference is devising some strategy to include personalization in what they are doing, I am staying a skeptic.

I believe we are approaching our job in a *more* personalized way. We have writers and editors performing the old-fashioned task of describing what might be interesting to a reader. I believe the connections between people and their interests are going to have to be made the traditional way—by reviewers, critics, commentators. Software will not be able to tell me if I will like a movie or a rock group or the person who liked the movie or the rock group that I liked.

On the other hand, I feel ill-tempered, crabbed, old. Am I putting an undue emphasis on words and literacy?

I go looking for Norm Pearlstine (in his fifties, he is about the oldest person in the crowd) after the Firefly presentation and catch him during the midafternoon break. I circle first, then double back, observing, moving onto the fringe of his conversation. Pouncing.

Pearlstine looks at me as I would look at a petitioner. Distractedly. Eyes roving. Moving further away from the vortex of my enthusiasm. It is incumbent on me to suck him in. Hold him. Make the connection. But this is hard to do. He seems glum, distracted, even depressed.

Pearlstine had left the editor's job at the *Wall Street Journal* with the notion of building a group of information age media companies based on technology. With investors at the ready, he set out in early 1994 to read business plans and interview technology's next wave of entrepreneurs. What he had in mind were large databases, corporate systems, business-to-business information models. But he kept getting business plans about the Internet; they surrounded him like flies. It was annoying. For one thing, Pearlstine had never been on the Internet. Nor had anyone he knew been on the Internet. For another, the way the Internet was being described—a free system available to everybody—didn't make any sense, certainly not to someone who was trying to *sell* information. It was a relief for Pearlstine when he went to Time Warner, back to real media.

Now, as much as he tried to minimize Time Warner's new media problem—it wasn't even a rounding error on their balance sheet, but it was a public relations headache—it kept returning, kept growing. It was Pearlstine's problem again.

Was it possible that the Internet, an information distribution system maybe as revolutionary as the printing press, could threaten *Time*'s basic business (remember the way television leveled *Life*)? Conversely, was it possible that the Internet posed an opportunity that the world's largest media company, with the best-known information brand names, was ideally positioned to take advantage of? Was it possible that Norm Pearlstine was the man best positioned to lead the information revolution? Or was it likely that Time Warner's continual losses on its Internet activities would give Pearlstine a big black eye?

"Have the technologists ever run the medium?" I prompt Pearlstine. "If so, not for very long, right? The movie business. What did those guys know about literally making movies? Radio. Television. I don't see Microsoft really going the distance here."

"No?"

"Seriously," I press, "do you think Microsoft is really interested in speaking to America? I mean, who is the messenger here? We're the messengers. Not those guys, hey?"

"They're very bright people in Redmond."

"Oh, I don't know. Do you really think so?" I scoff. "They're engineers, marketing people. They're all from the middle of the country somewhere. They're not from the East Coast. That doesn't mean they're not bright, of course, but it probably means that they're not, well, media savvy."

Straining, I lose him. Pearlstine excuses himself with a minimum of politeness, backing away from me and the other entrepreneurs who want Time Warner's ear.

"I've been working the room for you," says my friend, sliding up beside me in his wheelchair.

"I hope you're doing better than I'm doing."

"Buck up. Have you spoken to any of the search engine people?"

Search engines—Yahoo, Infoseek, Alta Vista, and Excite among them—are the software designed to index and catalogue the hundreds of millions of pages of digital information now accessible with a personal computer and a modem (soon enough, it appears, the entirety of man's recorded knowledge will be reachable with a PC and a modem).

"Infoseek is looking for content."

"They want it for cheap," I say bitterly.

"But they want it."

In the Internet bull market, Infoseek had banked more than $40 million dollars from the unsuspecting public.

Six months before the conference at the Ritz, Robin Johnson, Infoseek's CEO, and I had sparred over the future of the industry. I argued that given the Internet's growth—100 new pages of information generated every fifth of a second—and the increasing sophistication of his product's ability to search out this information, the consumer with an idle query would be dead by surfeit. Enter the word *Paris;* get back six hundred thousand matches.

What was needed, I said, was discrimination, discernment, point of view, taste.

"Content," said Johnson.

He argued that content was like oxygen—necessary but plentiful and free. There was a glut, he said. In his analysis of content's value, it would receive a few modest cents on every dollar received.

Now, those cents sound pretty good to me.

I quicken my pace through the function rooms and halls at the Ritz. I don't want to lose the opportunity to casually run into Johnson. I move through the lounge looking in back-to-back stuffed chairs, then through the cappuccino bar, and around the palm trees by the pool. Finally, on the cocktail verandah on a precipice overlooking the Pacific I find him huddled with an America Online executive.

If AOL and Microsoft are the superpowers of this industry, then a company like Infoseek is France. A company like mine is an ethnic minority in the Sudan. This is a good way to look at the field of play—alliances, spheres of influence, trading relationships, ideological partners, geopolitical partners (New York versus the Silicon Valley peninsula).

"Robin!" I exclaim with warmth and surprise.

Now I can move in. I can ask to join, presume to join. They will not say go away. They will accept me—dislike me, perhaps, but . . .

"Please. Don't let me interrupt," I hear myself say. "I'll be around. I'm on the red-eye."

"Okay." Wan smile from Robin.

I continue on, walking suavely, slowly, gracefully, moving in a physically dignified manner around the cocktail tables on the verandah overlooking the Pacific. I believe for a few seconds that I have accomplished something, that the stars have aligned nicely. This turns quickly into a tumult of regret and indecision. So close, but now what? My main impulse had been to get away and not, as a good salesman would have done, to stay, to press, to insinuate, to worm, to do the unsubtle, the heavy-handed, the uncouth.

"Did you find him? Why are you back so soon? Go back," orders my friend, doing a wheelie and looking up at me from his chair.

"We're going to try to meet later."

"Yeah, sure."

I shrug.

"Hey, you can do this, you know. You're nearly a name. The *Wall Street Journal* writes about you."

"Twice."

"Well, you're my hero."

"I really hate this part, looking for money."

"No one has ever gotten rich without begging."

"I thought that was 'no one has ever gotten rich without stealing.'"

"No. Sucking. No one has ever gotten rich without sucking. This is Silicon Valley. That great sucking sound you hear is the sound of . . ."

The patio, with its several bars and their rows and rows of Perrier and earnest groups of cyber politicians debating the next big thing, was now being transformed around us by the falling light, the musicians tuning their instruments, and the sudden flutter of table cloths. The wardrobe change to light jackets and little black dresses completed the transformation to a swanky soirée.

What was I doing here?

For entrepreneurs (or unemployables) the Internet offered one of the most startling opportunities since—actually, has there been anything to match it? The cost of entry was minimal, the required knowledge base was so idiosyncratic that few could claim a meaningful head start, and there was little or no competition, regulation, or conventional wisdom. It was ground zero: no rules, no religion, no canon, no bullshit. It was startup time. If all else failed, you could still have the satisfaction of having been there; it was like Hollywood in the teens or Detroit in the twenties. A new American industry was being born.

If you were in the media business—the book business, the magazine business, the television industry, the movies, advertising, newspapers, radio—the Internet offered every opportunity to do it yourself and do it right. You could defy the pace, the shibboleths, the dead wood, and the underlying economic models of those businesses and produce and distribute content on some altogether new basis.

The Internet was going to be an incredibly sweet revenge.

Because nobody who had a real job got it.

Get in on the ground floor. I could hear the admonition of my immigrant forebears: "You've got to get in on the ground floor."

Cell phones are used at cocktail parties on the West Coast like cigarettes were once used—as a social prop, an excuse to step back for a moment, an opportunity to regroup in a crowd. I use mine to call my wife, who is also my lawyer and my on-again, off-again CFO. She is eager for results.

"Yes, I've made some valuable connections, I suppose."

"Well, anything likely?"

"You have to develop relationships."

"We don't have time to develop relationships. We have seven weeks, then we can't make payroll."

The tension between us hangs on that date. It was a big surprise for her, I think, to discover that she had married an entrepreneur. Entrepreneurial uncertainties combined with lawyerly precision against the backdrop of already ridiculously pressured lives (and three children) opened up whole new areas of marital sensitivity.

"Yes, I know. It isn't something that you have to keep telling me."

"I'm not sure about that. I'm not exactly sure you get it."

"I get it. What do you think?"

"Sometimes I wonder."

"I can't really talk about this now."

"You can never talk about it."

"Listen, I'll see you in the morning."

I go looking for my friend and wheel him into the banquet hall.

Barry Diller, the former head of Paramount, Fox, and QVC, is due to give the after dinner speech. Diller is a big draw for this crowd. Not only did his "fuck you, I do it my way" countenance make him a kind of patron saint of entrepreneurs, but in many ways the new interpretation of what qualifies as media began with Diller's acquisition of QVC. QVC provided a model—the transaction model—for the kind of programming that might be effective through computer networks. I once interviewed Diller for the *New York Times Magazine,* and he threatened me with professional and bodily harm ("I don't think you understand I would kill you," he grinned) if I revealed anything about his personal life. But I assumed he had mellowed.

"I know Barry," I say to my friend as we go to our table.

"Shit. You should say hi to him."

"Oh no."

"You should. I mean this is a man who knows about this shit. Fuck, he invented the Simpsons and the movie of the week. The man knows a thing or two about inventing media." My friend wheels back from the table and casts his stunted arm over the banquet guests. "Look at them eat, all the honchos of this industry. Hardly a one has ever run a business. Months ago everyone here was either on an entirely different career track or was a failure at their chosen profession. What do you think the average age of the average cyber CEO is? Twenty-seven? You don't think that this isn't a little worrisome? You don't think that Barry isn't saying, 'What the fuck?'"

I look at Diller, one of the most successful media executives of our time, sitting in the midst of two hundred executives who have given themselves a mandate to create an altogether new advertising, programming, and communications medium with which to usher in the new millennium.

"I'll do it," I nod. "I'm going to speak to him."

"You want the chair?" my friend offers. "Sometimes it helps."

Fifteen years before, I had fearfully sat with Diller beside his pool in Coldwater Canyon in Beverly Hills while he spun out a sinisterly brilliant, graphic, and brutal analysis of the entertainment business. He swore me to secrecy then and I cannot remember the details now but I remember being overwhelmed by his mastery of the whole business, of all the pieces—the New York piece, the L.A. piece, the personalities. You couldn't mention someone without him putting his finger on their weak spot. It was breathtaking. I suspected then that if you wanted not just to run something but to shape it, mold it, remake it, you had to aspire to become like Diller—fevered, Kurtz-like. In my most manic phases I thought, Well, I can do that.

"Barry?" I bow slightly. "Michael Wolff."

"Oh yeah. Yeah. Hey, man."

He is the don.

"I'm in the Internet business now."

He had once been the youngest of the young turks, but his neck had turned to crepe. "Tough business."

"Well, it brings together a lot of things that I've been interested in, I guess. Content. Technology. Distribution. What's your feeling? Do you think you'll be moving more in the direction of the Net?" I tried to control my urge to fawn.

"Sure."

"I guess everybody is. I mean . . . I guess I've been lucky, getting in on the ground floor."

"Yes, if you're still standing in the end," said Diller affably. "Nice to see you. Stay in touch."

Others closed in on him.

"Now wasn't that worth it?" asked my friend with only slight mockery. "How many times do you think you'll just casually happen to mention about when you were speaking to Barry in Laguna?"

"Are we that small-time?"

"Hell no, this is big-time. You're among the most important people in the most important industry in America. It's going to change the way we communicate, it's going to change the way we learn, the way we have fun. It's going to change the entire economy. Haven't you been listening?"

"Do you believe that?"

"Sure. Don't you?"

I did. But, frankly, the air of unreality was large, too. It had happened so quickly. Where other industries developed over decades, the Internet industry had popped into being overnight. Who was prepared for it? Not corporate America, not the technology business, not the media industry, and, above all, not the people who suddenly had to create profitable businesses. That's why there were these conferences. Relationships that in other industries would be formed over the course of a career had to be put into place and cemented over a weekend in this business. The pace of technological development didn't allow for long lunches and the 6:15 to Scarsdale. This was not a game of golf.

I run into Infoseek's Robin Johnson at the airport. He's getting the red-eye, too. Twice a week he gets on a plane on the West Coast at 10:00 P.M. and gets off on the East Coast at 6:00 A.M. He looks terrible, with deep circles under his eyes and puffy skin.

"Maybe we should be talking," he considers.

"Anytime," I say eagerly.

"We're averaging under three impressions per visit. I wonder if we gave them some content, if we gave them something to read, could we get them to stay a little longer," he says, speaking of content as though it were something like Ritalin.

This was the bottom line. He sold every impression—every click—for approximately $.02. If we could supply the reason for his users to click again, content would be triumphant.

"No question," I say. "Guarantee, I can double your click rate." This is selling, I think. Express no doubts. Whatever they want, tell them you can double it. But it makes sense, too. Tell a few jokes, mention a few celebrities, provide a little intelligent comment, people will hang around a while longer, obviously.

"Do you think?" He puts his hand out and steadies himself on my shoulder. "Our share price is in the toilet. The analysts are all over us. Our board wants a profitable first quarter."

"We can absolutely help you with this! This is what we do. We hold people's attention. We talk to them. We build a relationship with them. They'll never want to leave you." We go down the boarding ramp together and enter the plane. It's lucky, I think, that I have enough miles for an upgrade to first class so I can use this flight to seal a deal, but Robin, clutching his garment bag, turns toward coach. "I'm used to it," he says, looking through the curtains at the full cabin. "I'm looking for Gates," he adds. Bill Gates in coach is one of the industry's enduring myths.

"I feel guilty."

"No, no. You content people need your pampering. We're software. Applications. Clean code. We don't need creature comforts. This is a revolution."

Chapter Two

How It Got to Be
a Wired World

I had limited interest in the stock market. Other than my own paltry net worth, which grew suspiciously in various mutual funds, I had never felt much of a personal connection to the subtleties or the personalities of the securities industry. Having lived through the market's collapse in 1987, and having experienced nothing more than some enjoyment at the tremors of anxiety on the Upper East Side and the generally lower real estate prices, I had become even more convinced that the market had little to do with me.

Even after the public offering in August 1995 of shares in Netscape, the Web browser maker with less earnings than my own company, created overnight one of the most valuable corporations in the country, it was still a while before I actually began to understand that people who said "That could be you" were halfway serious. When the college kids out in the Valley started to go public in late '95 and early '96, the same ones whose burritos I'd paid for just a few months before—Joe Kraus, a Stanford student whose company, Excite, went public in the spring, kept sticking me with the bill—I reluctantly started to pay attention. People—investment bankers, venture capitalists, industry busybodies—were saying, "You won't be able to compete if you don't go public. You need a war chest. Excite has forty million dollars in the bank so it can compete with Yahoo, which has sixty million dollars in the bank from its IPO. What do you have?"

Hmm. My argument that we made money and they did not was not a persuasive one. That other companies now had enough money to buy up the waterfront property while I operated a hot dog stand seemed to be the basic perspective.

But it wasn't until Wired, with its magazine and Web operations, announced it would go public that I really paid attention. It was, for one thing, a business philosophically and temperamentally near to our own. It wasn't a software business. It was a media business. Content. Not code. What's more, Wired's founder, Louis Rossetto, was someone I certainly would have voted among the least likely to succeed, and here he was soon to be worth more than $70 million.

While envious, I was happy, too. Everyone seemed to agree that all boats would rise along with the SS Wired.

But then in July 1996, just as we, and many others like us, were interviewing underwriters and organizing mezzanine rounds and soliciting bridge loans, all in an effort to create the kind of financial story that the bankers said the Street was eager to hear, something went wrong.

Wired failed to price. Whatever that meant.

Its IPO was withdrawn.

The company that had almost single-handedly articulated the need and desire for a digital revolution (or, at the very least, a new way of thinking about technology, namely, as a point of view, a social analysis, an economic strategy, rather than just a product launch) was being turned back from the promised land.

With that, the shares of all other cyber start-ups shuddered and fell. Other offerings failed. Still others found reasons to conveniently delay going public.

"What does this mean?" I asked one of our bankers.

"It means the market is saying something."

"What?"

"That is not necessarily clear. It may be saying that the jig is up, that the Internet is a joke, or it may be saying just that it needs time to digest what it has already consumed or it may just be saying that your friend Louis is a flake."

The stock market, which I heretofore had no interest in at all, was suddenly the oracle in my life.

"What do we do?" I asked our bankers.

"We wait to see if confidence builds."

"And if it doesn't?"

"I'd tell your friend Louis he better get an offer out there toot goddamn sweet."

I was working on a catch᷉l of book projects and film deals and magazine ideas in 1988, living on the Upper West Side of Manhattan with two children under the age of five, and largely indifferent to digital technology and the personal computer when I received a phone call from a partner in my father-in-law's law firm. My father-in-law, a lion of Wall Street, humored my various endeavors with contacts and corporate finance advice ("Always do it through a limited partnership"). In return, I would sometimes have to pretend to take an interest in his firm's other entrepreneurial (read *nonpaying*) clients with quirky business ideas. This partner, who specialized in the publishing business, had been visited by a relative of a law school classmate who had an idea to start a magazine. In a polite brush-off, this relative of the law school classmate was passed on to me.

And so one afternoon in the late spring, I opened my door to a Christlike figure with dramatic hair and a rucksack over his shoulder.

He was much too old to be hawking hopeless ventures, I thought. Still, his age made him slightly more interesting—and slightly more frightening.

He was living in Amsterdam. He had gotten there by a circuitous route, beginning at Columbia University in 1968, by way of Italy, Paris, Afghanistan, and soft-core filmmaking. In Amsterdam he was editing a small-circulation computer trade magazine.

He had watery eyes, a caring, "I have been hurt" voice, and an otherworldly patience. He would not only listen to whatever you had to say, he would wait until you had something to say.

You had to coax him to talk. Then, however, the fever increased to delirium:

We had to start thinking of how computers could serve the interests of the culture, of how computers were transforming the culture! The real news wasn't about numbers crunching, it was about word crunching. Words—how we manipulated them, reproduced them, stored them, combined them—this was all changing. This was the revolution, because now computing would involve everybody, not just scientists, engineers, and accountants. Computing was for writers, artists, musicians, for the people who created the culture. Computing had always been seen as procedure, process, method. But that was all wrong. You had to see it as a medium itself, which of course altered the terms of the expression itself. McLuhan! The Macintosh. Desktop publishing. Not only will print be produced more efficiently, but the whole idea of what print is, what print could be, was going to change; books and magazines, via the computer, were going to be something that we would never have thought of before. Imagine that type is mutable, plastic, expressive, nonlinear. Man. Imagine that the photograph, formerly a representation of a single instance in time, is now fluid, in motion, expressive as a painting. Imagine. We are no longer wed to gross units; expression is broken down into data, bits, atoms.

He wanted to spread this message. He wanted to bring his magazine, his Amsterdam-based, two-or-three-thousand-circulation magazine, called *Language Technology,* to America. What did I think of that? What did I think would be involved with that? Perhaps he should change the magazine's name for the American audience. He made me look at the magazine. What did I think?

I thought he was a lost soul.

Still, I had begun to discover the startling powers of the Macintosh for myself. The mysteries and costs of layout and format and page production had kept writers down on the farm for a long time; type was a weird, authoritarian aspect of a writer's trade. But more or less normal, technically maladroit people could take a Mac for a spin and start to imagine the possibilities, conceive the lifestyle, that would result from being in this driver's seat.

Even if I recognized that there was something to what he was saying, that there was a sexiness to the Mac, it never occurred to me that this person from the margins of our time (forgotten in time, he seemed) could succeed at anything. But I was kind.

I advised him on the hegemony of computer magazines in America (all of the successful ones were product based), on the capital requirements of start-up publishing businesses, on newsstand versus subscription revenue, on investor prospects, on advertising sales methods. In short, my advice was to go back to Amsterdam.

After another beer, I left him on Broadway, rucksack over his shoulder.

But he had an unexpected persistence. He had accepted me and signed me up. I would hear from him, be kept informed by him, as though I were part of the board of directors of a new movement. Almost a year later, continuing to be kind (and not, I suppose, immune to his flattery and attention), I called him on my way through Amsterdam on the trail of money for a new project I had going.

He met me at the airport. His otherworldly dreaminess had been replaced by a new intensity, even franticness. He sensed, I think, that a revolution that I was unaware had started might pass him by. He had converted his magazine into a new iteration, now called *Electric Word.* He made me sit in an Amsterdam coffee shop and page through all of the issues. It still had a turgidness, a trade magazine sense of minutia, gray pages, and homemade design, but personalities were emerging, too. You could meet Nicholas Negroponte, who ran MIT's Media Lab; Paul Brainerd, the president of Aldus, the company that was reinventing type; Ted Nelson, one of the first philosophers of hypertext; Andrew Seybold, who was inventing desktop publishing; and Richard Saul Wurman, a designer who had focused his skills not on graphics but on information. All would become, in a few years' time, founding members of the *digerati*.

He waited, patiently, for my opinion.

"This is better than the last one you showed me. It's an improvement," I said.

"What should we do with it? How can we get circulation in the U.S.?"

"Hmm. I'm not sure, actually, how realistic that is. I don't know. Perhaps there might be a specialty distributor."

"Could you get those names? I would appreciate that. I would appreciate that very much," he said, softly, as if these names were the secret and the ticket.

"I can probably get you some names. But you should not look at this as anything too significant. I don't see the market as being large for something like this," I said apologetically.

There was a clatter, then, through the door of the coffee shop, bringing in a light from the gray weather—a young woman with a Holly Golightly animation and brightness who slid in beside him. She was as much as fifteen years his junior. Where he was somber and pained, she bubbled—if not necessarily with sincerity, then certainly with energy and enthusiasm.

"This is my girlfriend," he said, "Jane." One would certainly not have written him with a girlfriend. "She's going to be selling advertising for the magazine. I thought you could tell her some of the things she should be doing."

I was embarrassed for them, and grateful to be in Europe where no one I knew might see me.

Jane came to eager attention, poised with pen and pad. "I want to get liquor and car ads!"

She was a startlingly good-looking American girl from Kentucky, footloose in Europe. She had dabbled in fashion in Paris before being swept into the cold and damp of Amsterdam by—by what? I certainly speculated on the passion here: the passion of the love affair or the passions of the digital revolution he had aroused in her. These passions strained credulity. She was as young and fey and comely as he was old and burdened and humorless.

It was a moment of pure futility. Me, a magazine writer who knew paltry little about selling advertising, explaining it to two people who had no hope of comprehending what little commercial sense I might have inadvertently achieved, two people sitting in a coffee house by the side of a canal in Amsterdam who were in another world, anyway.

Still. He was so unflappable in his focus. Not even an incredibly pretty girl could make him look sideways. He had gotten her to see through his eyes. She did not notice his weird, discomfiting intensity.

His proposal was to bring together all the potentially liberating ways technology was going to create new communities, new kinds of entertainment, new means of communicating, and bring about a shift in the power paradigm, decentralized, on a human scale, in a magazine that would speak beyond nerds, MIS directors, and computer hobbyists. It would be called *Millennium,* a kind of *Rolling Stone* for technology. Its mission was to do what *Rolling Stone* did in the 1960s—become the voice of a new age and articulate the inchoate. Everything is changing. Whether we want it to change or not, it is going to change. People are going to need help. They are going to need help understanding these massive social and cultural shifts brought about by the fevered pace of technological development and commercialization.

To talk about *Rolling Stone* in the context of creating and planning a new magazine was as real as assuming you would finance it with lottery winnings. *Rolling Stone,* an unlikely crystallization of the commercial and cultural, happened by chance, by fluke, by mistake. *Playboy* was like that, too.

Which would therefore have to mean that Louis Rossetto, this middle-aged man living his expatriate life while fantasizing about how he could be at the center of a new American era, would have to turn himself into Jann Wenner or Hugh Hefner and do for computers what Wenner did for rock and roll and Hefner did for sex to realize his dream. One might as well set out to be Gandhi.

It was 1990. As tanks rolled across Kuwait, the office where I rented space on lower Fifth Avenue in Manhattan was home to the death screams of some of the hottest media success stories of the 1980s.

On several cavernous open floors (a work style that would become *de rigueur* when this neighborhood turned into Silicon Alley) you could find offices of the magazines *Psychology Today, Mother Earth News,* and *Smart*—all getting ready to go out of business.

These magazines—this *old* media—collapsed over a period of two or three months, first with cleaning and bathroom supplies eliminated, then outgoing service on the telephones suspended, then elevator access curtailed, then lights cut off. Total demise was signaled by the arrival of the repo man, who in an on-the-spot transaction sold me enough Macintoshes to put me into the desktop publishing business.

For me, the urgency was not the future and what it would look like and who would lead us to it but what could I do with these Macintoshes?

Now, it didn't take much for me to realize that information was flowing at a new speed. My idea was that with the Macintosh and its preternatural page design capabilities, you could repackage lots of this overflow of data for the ordinary reader. The charts, graphs, maps, and other tools to display quantitative information visually had always been expensive treats in books. Suddenly, it was a cinch to make ugly data pretty. I had lots of ideas for how to take this explosion of data and make a spiffy new kind of book with a Macintosh.

Even though it was true that the world was awash in this massive new Niagara of data, the cost of getting to this data was still large, still a luxury of wealthy corporations. The monopoly held by the data giants—Lexis/Nexis, Dialog—was a bitter pill for the information hungry. You knew the information was out there; you knew that database technology rendered it retrievable, sortable, and searchable. Too bad you couldn't afford it.

But I had a friend: Stanley. Stan the man. Weird Stan. We had gone to high school together. He had taken the scenic route, through Morocco and India to end up as a data guru in the health care industry. Having achieved a high level of corporate responsibility and anxiety, Stan was now on his second round of dropping out and had retreated to an isolated northern island, from which he consulted on complex data algorithms.

To my complaint in late '91 about the high cost of information, he had said, "The Internet, man."

"The—?"

"You'll be able to get a lot of what you're looking for, free."

"Free?"

"I jack into a community college with a password I got from a waitress who's taking a few courses."

"Free?"

"Dig it. You'll see. I'll get you in."

My introduction, at this moment, was part of a critical mass matrix then in progress. How many people knew about the Internet in late 1991? More than five thousand but possibly less than twenty-five thousand. Possibly less than ten thousand! Now how many people have to know about something for it to be in the *New York Times,* mentioned by Jay Leno, understood by my mother? What is the process of going from the arcane to the commonplace?

It begins with the sudden sense on the part of people who know (even if it was just yesterday that they found out) that they have a piece of knowledge before others and that simply possessing this knowledge is worth something—bragging rights, business opportunities, new erotic possibilities—and grows because even if you're the millionth or the ten millionth person to learn, you know that there are millions behind you who will have to make the arduous climb up the curve. And it feels so very good to have already gone over the top, to know what others do not yet know.

It took me a while to realize that the Internet could possibly be a professional opportunity. It was hard to make the conceptual leap from simple data communication, in which one computer communicates with another computer via modem (a relationship that almost always ended in breakup and despair), to a network wherein a modem connected you to unlimited numbers of other machines and other users and nearly infinite data resources. It was not so apparent that this was not only an information and communications technology but, potentially, a new kind of media. This would be the conceptual leap that virtually everyone would stumble over.

Some, however, would stumble sooner and get up faster.

Louis Rossetto and Jane Metcalfe arrived in our offices on lower Fifth Avenue. Louis brooded while Jane collected telephone numbers and worked the phones.

"There's something wrong with him," said my wife, Alison, after a dinner at our house that continued on long after a reasonable bedtime—not because we were so engaged but simply because Louis wouldn't get up and go home.

"He's a little impacted," I allowed.

"He doesn't even listen."

"A different drummer."

"No. Really. It's odd. You seem to find him interesting but—"

"Not interesting. Unusual."

"He's not unusual. He's out to lunch. You can't introduce him to anybody. What will they think?"

"You don't think it's sort of an interesting idea?"

"You have to express an idea before it can be interesting."

"It's sort of a fuck-you idea. Fuck the media. Fuck the technology industry. Fuck computer magazines. Fuck everybody."

"Well, that comes through."

"Too much?"

If against all odds, and all signals to the contrary, a person maintains, without any waffling, an unproductive stance, perhaps it's inevitable that they begin to earn a begrudging respect.

Louis had a frighteningly singular point of view, which, in the face of a variety of social and economic pressures, he kept.

He continued revising his business plan. And he kept calling people. If you didn't want to help him or speak further to him, you had to give him another name to get him to let go of you. The little humiliations that dissuade most people from pressing on did not affect or even register with him. It was eerie.

Rejection, in fact, did something beneficial for Louis. Instead of being diminished by it, it somehow ennobled him. It stiffened his carriage, extended his neck, focused his eyes. He became handsome. Extraordinary-looking, in a way.

And he—or Jane, at his instruction—kept dialing.

They began to find themselves in two parallel discussions: one with a disparate group of technologists in Boston and on the West Coast and the other with traditional New York media types. The first group (many of whom had been slavishly profiled in Louis's magazine *Electric Word*)—including Mitch Kapor, who created Lotus; Nicholas Negroponte, from the Media Lab; and John Perry Barlow, former Grateful Dead crony and technology sage—greeted Louis's plan for a magazine about the new digital culture with respect and incremental support (one introduction begat another). What did they have to lose? They had all been, to some degree, shut out of the mainstream media, which was New York centered and which did not understand technology. What's more, many of them had been shut out of the main currents of the technology industry, which, more and more, was coalescing around a few companies. On the other hand, they were wealthy, entrepreneurial, and flattered by the notion of a magazine that would express their point of view—that technology was not merely business but a kind of salvation, too!

The second group, the media professionals, was much less open to Louis Rossetto and his idea for what he was now calling, without apparent irony, "the least boring computer magazine." The New York pros were embarrassed for him—not even for him but for their colleagues and friends who introduced Louis to them.

I certainly cringed.

Louis held his business plan as a kind of grail. It didn't matter to him that his estimates of advertising pages or of newsstand sell-through or of circulation expectations were wildly out of line with anything magazine professionals had ever experienced with a new publication.

He continued to deliver his intense, heated rationale and justification for this new magazine about the culture and the meaning of technology and filtered all possible objections and impediments to his plans.

Louis didn't smile.

He didn't dress appropriately.

He would have seemed disturbed were it not for Jane's enthusiasm and wholesomeness and constant presence at his side.

It was a hard sell:

Technology is cool. Technology is at the forefront of a cultural revolution. Technology is a key component of entertainment. There are personalities associated with technology who are sexy, compelling, fashionable. Technology is a business opportunity not just for the mathematically inclined but for us all. The fact that these ideas seem obvious now is the *Wired* magazine monument. Then, in '90, '91, and '92, when Louis was wandering around New York, they were ludicrous.

Louis and Jane left the unmoved media community in New York and relocated to San Francisco. With a Macintosh, access to a color copier, and the aid of an art director who specialized in corporate annual reports (the magazine's first issue would bear a striking resemblance to the first postmerger Time Warner annual report), they created their prototype of a magazine celebrating synergy, technology, globalization, media, and smart people who recognize the future before others. With a dangerously small amount of money, all of it garnered from outside traditional media circles, they went to work on the first issue.

Back in New York, their acquaintances spoke with concern about this extreme behavior. At the same time, we all took solace in knowing that new parameters of failure were being established. It certainly seemed fair to conclude that while you might fail, you would never fail as bizarrely as Louis was in the process of failing.

The parallel development then in progress was an effort by the National Science Foundation (NSF), a federal agency, to get out of the increasingly costly business of subsidizing an academic computing infrastructure growing like kudzu. In 1990 an understanding was put in place among the NSF, private carriers maintaining the system's fiber-optic backbone (including the regional Bell companies and certain of the long distance carriers), key academic facilities, and the ad hoc associations that had grown up around the network. The deal? The NSF would withdraw funding over a two-year period and allow commercial use of the infrastructure. The *com* domain was added to *org* and *gov* and *edu*. The network was ready to be opened to the general population.

It was not clear to anyone, even the digitally advanced, what this meant. It was a policymaker's administrative tinkering. It could easily have meant nothing. It didn't change the network per se. It didn't enhance the technology. It was, however, one of those things, those moments, those convergences that change everything. It gave focus and form and purpose to the digital revolution.

Louis foresaw the digital revolution without foreseeing the growth of the Internet, just as Hugh Hefner foresaw the sexual revolution without foreseeing the Pill. Each saw the desire without seeing the invention. They were the beneficiaries, you might say, of smart luck rather than dumb luck.

But after a while, they, the self-styled pioneers, "got it," as Louis took to delineating. They understood what the opening of the network meant, as opposed to virtually all major media organizations and established technology companies, who did not get it.

Getting it was no easy process.

You had to understand the nature of a computer network, you had to understand that machines could exist in a community, and you had to understand the nature of a WAN (or wide area network), wherein the infrastructure had no geographic bounds.

Then you had to appreciate that WANs had come into existence on a relatively ad hoc basis that allowed almost anyone to "jack" into them and therefore become part of this extended and extending community.

This system allowed its users to communicate with any other individual on the network, store or retrieve large amounts of digital information, and get access to all or portions of any other computer attached to the network.

It was nearly impossible to describe or explain the significance of this network to those who had not experienced it for themselves. But prior to 1992 the opportunities for having such an experience were almost nonexistent outside of academic or scientific circles.

By 1992 the new NSF rules had begun to foster a bedroom industry in local ISPs (Internet Service Providers). Panix, one of two Internet providers in New York City, operated out of an apartment on Manhattan's Upper West Side. The World (in Boston), one of the largest ISPs in the country, and The Well (in San Francisco), one of the seminal establishments in the digital culture, had little more than a few thousand members between them.

The 1992 Internet experience was a hybrid between a closed bulletin board service (my modem calls your modem, which allows our two machines to communicate with each other) and access to the greater worldwide network. Access tended to be incremental. E-mail was the first step. Then the user might petition for access to the network's other protocols, like telnet (the ability to work another computer on the network), FTP (the ability to move files across the network), IRC (the ability to join real-time conversations), and gopher (a way to search for information stored on various connected computers).

Through most of 1992 and 1993, it would have been unlikely, if not impossible, for a consumer without arcane computer skills to arrange access to the Internet.

That meant, among other things, that large portions of the business population that might otherwise take an interest in this technology could not. While the required skill sets were not especially complex, they were, nevertheless, eccentric. The system, or access to the system, tended to favor trial and error; it demanded a hobbyist's interest and hours. If you were an executive who'd gotten wind of this network, it was unlikely that you'd know whom to call to try it. There would be no reason for your MIS director to have a clue. Later, in 1994 or 1995, if you were really trying, you'd find someone's son, who, motivated by technical acumen and the possibilities of pornography, could hook you up.

Several other forces in 1992, though, were helping to articulate the concept of information flow, personal computers, and an online world:

The "information highway" metaphor was born. Uttered in 1991 by Al Gore, it had nothing to do, per se, with the Internet. It had to do with fiber optics, or the relatively cheap transmission of data over new fiber networks. Even this notion got mixed into something more tangible, the five-hundred-station cable dial.

Then there was Prodigy, the online service owned by IBM and Sears. By spending millions on national advertising, Prodigy explained to America the concept of receiving certain information, services, and entertainment through a personal computer. Prodigy proved, albeit on an economically catastrophic basis, that there was, in 1992, a million-plus audience interested in such fare. Behind Prodigy, there was CompuServe, owned by H&R Block, with nearly 1 million members; then GEnie, owned by GE, with approximately 200,000 members; and then America Online, in the vicinity of 150,000, and Delphi, with something like 100,000 members.

The online services had no relationship to the Internet—in fact, they represented the exact opposite model. Online services were closed networks. In 1992 and 1993 however, this was too subtle a point for executives of those companies and for investors, analysts, and most of the technology community.

Out in San Francisco, Louis Rossetto and Jane Metcalfe launched the first issue of their magazine, now called *Wired,* in January 1993. It would have been reasonable to expect this effort to go unnoticed. The venture did not have the necessary capital to promote itself. It did not have access to all-important distribution channels. Its management had scant publishing experience.

What happened?

How is it possible to achieve the exposure, the recognition, the understanding that producers of other products pay millions more to achieve?

What siren song was sung?

The country was coming out of a recession, the recovery being led by the technology sector, an industry made up of young men looking for a positive identity. Computer programmers were like bond salesman in the 1980s; they were looking to turn themselves into Masters of the Universe. Windows was spreading the Mac ethic—computers did cool things! What's more, *Wired* magazine was a product designed as an artifact—it wasn't just a magazine, it was a statement.

The zeitgeist was in play.

Climb on board.

I had the advantage of being in New York, which at that moment was a dumb town technologically speaking. It had paltry few technology businesses, virtually no technology research facilities, and scant technology talent. The media industry—centered in New York and including magazine publishing, book publishing, television, newspapers, radio, and advertising—did not see itself as a technology-driven business. There was a software industry and a media industry. To the extent that they might someday intersect, the media industry believed itself to be sitting pretty because Content was King. The one technology bet (or new media bet) that was being made by the traditional media was on CD-ROMs. CD-ROMs were easy to understand for publishing companies. They were physical units sold through retail outlets or direct channels.

My idea, in early 1993, for the Internet was a New York–type of idea, a media idea. It wasn't about technology. It was about entertainment and service.

A guide to the Net. *NetGuide.* That was a concept.

People in the publishing business who had not tried the Internet—and no one had—could get enthusiastic about that!

It was so clean and pure and self-explanatory and just right sounding that even I started to believe in it, even though (a) precious few people could get onto the Internet, (b) most of those who did could not make it work anyway, and (c) if you could get on and if you could make it work, all you'd find were pages and pages of computer text.

But the notion of this medium—being able to access all the world's libraries, to post a message and have unknown people read it, to send e-mail—bred a contagious enthusiasm. You wanted it to be more than it was. The early days of television were a powerful fantasy and impetus. Inventing a new medium was the kind of opportunity you never thought you'd have. More than anything you could do, more than any endeavor you could undertake—politics, business, technology—inventing a new mass medium would impact the world we live in.

NetGuide appeared in book form in January 1994, little more than six months after the release of the first web browser and the beginnings of the World Wide Web. *NetGuide* contained more than two thousand reviews of various offerings on the Internet. It also contained an offer for fifteen free hours online, an 800-number, and an offer of assistance ("no question too dumb").

Other than the stray Nazi who phones at 3 A.M., I know how difficult it is to get America to call you up.

The first call came on January 2. "Hello? Is this the Internet?" Forty thousand more calls came into our six-man company over the next few months.

<hr />

The zeitgeist, though, is an unreliable business partner.

Jann Wenner, with *Rolling Stone,* created a magazine that made its readers feel that every other reader was hipper and druggier and had a better record collection than you. Hugh Hefner created a magazine that made you feel that everyone else was having sex but you. And Louis Rossetto, in *Wired,* created perhaps the most exclusive (or excluding) magazine of all. Its challenge was, Do you get it? *Can* you get it? Can you even follow the type on this page, you linear so-and-so?

In addition to articulating the interests and style of a digital mind-set and demographic group, Louis also articulated a marketing approach. What you were buying, what you felt compelled to buy, was the notion that Louis, and the rapidly growing *Wired* magazine staff, knew more than you knew. They understood something that you didn't understand. They had a feeling for the future, which you didn't have. The fact that this knowledge basis was not profit producing was judged to be irrelevant by the marketplace. You had to understand the future, you had to step into the future, you had to be part of the future before you could make a buck off of it—or so the market seemed to be saying.

This became, first for Wired, and then pretty much for every other Internet-associated business, the basic economic model. You are as valuable as your vision.

Louis and Jane (subtly transformed from Parisian gamine to Bay Area power babe—flowing hair became tight cropped, long skirts became short, swaddled arms became bare and muscular) returned to New York to deal with the issue of a growing staff, exploding ambitions, and an ever-widening shortfall of cash. With a circulation of under one hundred thousand, large portions of which were unpaid, they began to look for new investors. They told potential investors that they believed the four-issue-old *Wired* was worth $20 million. In other words, if you invested $1 million, Louis and Jane would give you 5 percent of the Wired company. The discrepancy between the value they placed on the business and the value that a traditional financial analysis would place on a magazine with *Wired's* revenues was approximately 20 to 1.

"It's not even something that you can pretend to take seriously," said Christopher Meigher, who had just left one of the top posts at Time Warner to start a magazine investment fund.

But Louis was unwavering. Evidently, doubt was not in his emotional makeup. There's something compelling about someone who can't see or even sense doubt. Such certainty sells.

"Louis will never compromise," said Jane, proudly. It was a stance that was thrilling to her. To me, too, I confess. It was playing chicken on a grand, and financially tantalizing, scale. It was heroic. It was.

Condé Nast, the magazine arm (*Vogue, Vanity Fair,* the *New Yorker, Glamour, Brides,* etc.) of Advance Communications, which includes one of the largest national newspaper chains, cable stations, and, until recently, Random House, sat down with Louis. Condé Nast had few, if any, technology resources. The media industry in general had shown only a limited interest in how personal computers fit into the editorial (aka the "content") business.

Condé Nast invested $3 million for 15 percent of Wired.

The investment had a fascinating ripple effect. It meant Wired could stay in business and pursue its ambitions. It validated *Wired* magazine and Wired's business plan ("I certainly wish we had bought it," said Walter Isaacson, in retrospect, from Time's fabled thirty-fourth floor). And it contributed to making "validation" a part of every other money-losing cyber business. If you could find a "name company" to give you money, then the fact that you were losing money was okay.

The way the Wired enterprise began to grow was awe inspiring. The awe came from the realization that such transformations are, apparently, possible. Louis could go from lost soul to fearless mogul, Jane from ditziness to great stature in the publishing and advertising industries—all in a year and a half!

"You know," said someone in our office who went out to Wired for a visit, "it feels more like a cult than a business."

This appraisal was only partially negative. To achieve cult status in your business life, that is, to have sucked people in to your thinking and aspirations and sense of identity and working style, often makes a lot of business sense.

Wired was speaking to people. And people were really listening. In February 1994 we placed an ad (gratis) in Wired for our book NetGuide. Not only was the response astounding, but it was global: for as much as a year afterward that single ad was causing people around the world to call us up.

I think I can accurately trace Louis's motivations in the cyber business. In the beginning he wanted to come to the U.S. from what had turned into, no doubt, something of a godforsaken exile in cold and small-time Amsterdam. No one would have hired him, so he had to come with an idea of his own. His idea for a magazine about technology and culture was taken up by a group of wealthy technologists and futurists, a community in which he was comfortable (and there weren't too many communities Louis would be comfortable in). When Wired started to work, Louis began to believe that he was, more than just putting out a magazine, bringing the components of a new philosophy together in a way that no one had before. That he was, really, performing a public service. This was not about getting rich. In fact, when you're as exposed as Louis was, at such emotional and financial risk (few entrepreneurs ever really are, except the crazy and bankrupt ones), you're mostly concerned with downside rather than upside, survival rather than, as the bankers say, "exit strategy." But then there's this other group that jumps into the picture—the people in it for the money. They've gotten into the business, at least in part, because Louis and Wired articulated the need and demonstrated the market for the Internet and digital products. These people, and they tend to be primarily professional moneymakers—for instance the venture capital firm Kleiner Perkins Caufield & Byers, which backed Netscape and Excite, or Sequoia Capital, which backed Yahoo—got to the money sooner than Louis did. They began to develop their strategies for getting to the money in early 1995, just at the time Wired was swelling to a vast cult proportion (I saw a thousand people, at least, in a downtown San Francisco ballroom writhing together at Wired's second anniversary party in the kind of sexual and electric atmosphere older Bay Area denizens were likening to the age of the Fillmore) and passing two hundred, on its way to three hundred, employees. At this time, in fact, Louis was still, in many ways, anti–*the business*. He was still a critic. He was still the judge, and he was not very free with his approval.

Louis was late out of the gate by the time he started to focus on the possibility of vast cyber riches. The IPOs had been going for a year already: first the hardware infrastructure IPOs, then the software IPOs, then the search engine IPOs. They'd gone out or they were in place to go.

Because Louis was motivated by a sense of mission and truth and certainty and superiority, his plan for Wired's embrace by the public was, well, operatic.

The stage was certainly set. Goldman Sachs, the Rolls Royce of the Street, was the underwriter. Wired was the most recognizable brand name in cyberspace. In addition to Condé Nast, Wired's investors now included WPP, the world's largest advertising agency, and Burda, the big German publisher. What's more, if, as some investors were starting to suspect, valuations were now being derived from multiples of losses, well then, Wired's losses were as large as any in the business—to date, more than $40 million! Goldman and Wired set a value of $450 million for the company, nearly twenty times the value it would have had if it had not been an Internet-related business, that is, if it had been just a hot magazine. At that price Louis would have been worth, personally, $70 million. That irked a lot of people.

There was something, people said, about Louis, something that started to make investors feel that he was rubbing it in their faces. Reports were coming from the Wired road show—presentations before financial analysts, brokerages, funds, and other groups that make a successful IPO— suggesting that Louis's hauteur and hubris were in full flower.

"He wears sneakers," people said.

The sneakers were just the symbol, of course, of wider-ranging annoying attitudes. If Louis were twenty-four and wearing sneakers, that would be one thing. But Louis was forty-six and wearing sneakers. He was as old as the average fund manager, who was not wearing sneakers.

More damaging, people started to say Wired wasn't really an Internet business. It was the magazine business, the publishing business. It was content. It wasn't software. A money-losing software business with a good brand name and the chance to be number one in its category could be worth twenty times its revenues. A money-losing content business, even one with a good brand name and chance to be number one in its category was maybe, on a fine day, worth one times its revenues.

Still, it wasn't just one of those things that didn't work, that didn't manage to "price," to find investors willing to pay what Louis was asking. Rather, the possibility that Goldman Sachs would fail to complete a high-profile IPO was so remote that Wired's withdrawn offering had to be a bellwether moment in the history of the Internet.

The signal was not necessarily clear—did it mean that the Internet was over or just that content companies were screwed? Or was it just the inevitable development that hubris would be humbled?—but it was loud.

Through the summer Wired got ready to do another offer. This time cooler heads were in charge, more realistic goals were set. This time Louis only wanted $250 million.

Again, Wired hung over my head. If it "went out" successfully, then it would be good weather for our business; if not, it meant big storm clouds.

"Well, what happens, hypothetically," I asked our investment banker, "if Wired doesn't get out the second time around?"

"You don't want to know," our banker said. "You really don't."

Chapter Three

The Board Meeting

The cyber newsroom in our offices on Madison Avenue and Fifty-third Street—in fifteen thousand square feet of prime real estate that I'd bartered for Web advertising space (of which we had unlimited amounts)—was similar to a conventional newsroom except that it was out-fitted in T-1 lines and staffed by people, most well under the age of twenty-five, with baseball caps and dramatic piercings.

At the head of the newsroom was a large, glassed-in conference room which created a zoo effect when bankers and investors arrived, the staff curiously eyeing the suits and the suits amused by the staff. Each group was slightly threatened by the other but satisfied that barriers existed and precautions had been taken to keep them apart.

In August, shortly after I returned from the conference in Laguna Beach, the board and its advisors gathered in relative good humor for our monthly meeting around the long table in the glass conference room. Fancy sandwiches were provided.

There were, however, reasons to feel less than sanguine. Our new elec-tronic products were three months behind schedule and well over budget. As the balance sheet stood now, we would not be able to make next month's payroll.

Six months earlier, the investors at the table had provided more than $4 million to the company to finance an aggressive business plan. According to this plan, we would take their money and spend it as fast as possible to build brand, gain position, stake out beachfront property in this new cyber landscape. And then we would cash in. We would provoke, as the bankers described it, a "liquidity event," turning our equity from a dreamed-of value into a river of cash.

It was the belief of the board that our company, with revenues of slightly more than $1 million and losses of about $3 million, was worth, in a down moment, at least $60 million. If we could hit the market right, match ourselves with a buyer with, in banking terminology, a real "hard-on" (or, conversely, a buyer who had "gotten pregnant"), we'd get over $100 million.

The fact that we would run out of money within six weeks, while of nagging concern to me, was a situation against which the bankers believed they could apply a "corporate finance solution." This might involve a "bridge," a loan until the next investment came in, a "mezzanine fix," investors brought in before the company goes public, or a "country club round," money from individual fat cats.

If I could only have banked this rich new lexicon, a kind of poetry of money in motion, I would be a rich man.

The presiding poet was Robert B. Machinist, the president of Patricof & Co., one of an elite group of investment banking and venture capital firms in Manhattan. While he and I had, in an unlikely intersection, gone to college together, our paths had diverged in substantive and comic ways. He had achieved an air of fabulousness, with a kind of hollandaise richness, even Robert Maxwell ripeness; he wore bespoke suits and had a large stride and a fleshy imperious face with Robert McNamara slicked-back hair. He was a sportsman (racing cars), a paterfamilias (of four!), and a philanthropist (the largest giver, by a factor of ten, in our college class, his name was on the letterhead of scientific institutes). To me, he stood at the pinnacle of his life and times and was certainly one of the most confident and dominant individuals I'd ever met.

He was accompanied, always, by his factotum, a boyish banker in significantly cheaper suits who worked the calculator and yawned widely and helplessly when he was not performing a ciphering task. (The factotum had spent his early career at Drexel Burnham and would often compare cyber deals to Drexel transactions: "This is really nothing, you know.")

The factotum, in turn, was most always accompanied by his own factotum, one or another of a group of hardworking women in even cheaper suits.

Joining the board meeting for the first time was our company's new executive vice president (EVP) for marketing, a buttoned-down Wharton classmate of the senior factotum, who had been brought by the bankers to the world of new media from a career in packaged goods marketing at

Procter & Gamble. He was part of the plan to bring professional management into our company and to the Internet. Certainly, the mention of
P&G, as unrelated to the Internet and cyber world as any business could
be, seemed to have a salubrious effect on the investment community;
even Microsoft was hiring P&G men. It was no secret to anyone, apparently, that marketing was the secret.

Taking his seat, too, at the conference table was the investor. He was
brought into the deal by the bankers as dumb money, to supply the additional funds we needed to flip the company, or trade up to a different class
of professional investor.

The investor, a young man named Jon Rubin, a wire-thin, almost femi-
nized JFK Jr. look-alike, had been raised between New York, the Colony
in Malibu, and Washington, D.C., where he continued to maintain resi-
dences. His father, Miles Rubin, who controlled a large part of the designer blue jeans market, was a major Democratic Party power whose
name surfaced and disappeared in the Clinton campaign fund-raising reports.

Rubin junior had made several investments in Internet companies and
showed up at the important conferences. One of his other companies,
First Virtual Holdings, offered an online payment method. Used frequently by online pornography vendors, First Virtual, with revenues less
than our own, was planning to go public before the end of the year. Rubin
seemed hungry to be a part of this new industry.

Rubin was accompanied by his technology advisor, an intense, praeto-
rian-guard type in a T-shirt. ("I'm not here to interrupt," the advisor
would often interrupt, "I'm here to help.")

Rubin, while being played for a fool, I suspected, by the bankers ("If
you don't know who the fool is in a deal, it's you," they cautioned merrily),
was working hard to get his head around this new era of communication
and technology. He was not, however, detail oriented, and I was mindful
that while the bankers' plan seemed to be for Rubin to put an additional
round of capital into the deal, there was no precise commitment from Rubin regarding our impending cash crisis.

Board meetings were much more relaxed than I thought they'd be.
There was a strong sense of self-congratulation. We had achieved something, and our primary job was to get the company's name in the paper. A
recurring issue, in fact, was our lack of success in finding a public relations
firm (or, really, my reluctance to pay for one). There was now a proposal
before us from an agency in San Francisco that was said to be as tied into
the industry as any, an agency that was notable for the fact that all its employees wore identical dress, creating a slightly unnerving Heaven's Gate

effect. They proposed to take us on as a client (they rejected, they claimed, most potential clients) for $40,000 per month.

"I don't think we ought to be shortsighted about this," urged Rubin. "The value of this company is going to be based on its level of recognition. I'd like to move that we hire them."

I was rather curious to find out how famous I'd get for $40,000 per month.

I reported, with perhaps more enthusiasm than my short conversation in the red-eye departure lounge with Robin Johnson, the CEO of Infoseek, deserved, how much Infoseek wanted to "partner" with us on the content side. "In essence, they will be our distribution partner. They'll be like the network and we'll be like the creator of the show. There's going to be distribution and there's going to be content. The search engines are going to be distribution. They have all this traffic. Now they have to feed it."

It was intellectually challenging that part of the job was to imagine how the business would work, but it was also alarming to realize that the theories of how the business model for the Internet would come together changed in fundamental ways as often as every other month.

We digested, along with the mozzarella and tomato and arugula sandwiches, the monthly financial report.

Jon Rubin, flipping impatiently through the spreadsheets, seemed only slightly annoyed by what we were politely calling "the cash flow reality." He was much more agitated by his technology advisor's concern about how we risked missing out on the move toward personalization features—the ability of software to know what you want and make choices for you. Firefly's stratospheric valuation was rankling and inspiring to everyone at the table.

The technology advisor ("I'm not here to express an opinion, I'm here to help facilitate options") made a presentation about how we might approximate what Firefly was doing.

He clearly believed that personalization was the future and that critical writing was the past. There was a strong utopian emphasis to his approach—the randomness of human relationships could now be ordered.

I was not unmindful that this debate allowed us to avoid the issue that we had spent all of our money.

"Is that where people think we should be going?" Rubin wondered. "Will personalization be hot next month, too? It is cool though. It's really cool."

"But we're not a technology company, we're a content company," I insisted, weakly, because, in fact, I was getting tempted by the magic. I mean, what if you could run an algorithm and find your true love?

"It is so cool. Have you tried any of this shit?" Rubin asked Bob Machinist (but rhetorically, because the bankers did not use computers). "But do we want to develop a proprietary technology which can be knocked out by someone else's version of the same technology? Can we support that?" Rubin asked, looking to his technology advisor.

"Can we afford not to support that?" asked the technology advisor.

"Let's agree to do it. Issue the press release," said Bob Machinist. "But let's not spend the money. Let's see if there's really heat here first."

Most discussions about technology seemed to have three components: what would win in the distant future, what *should* win in the future, and, finally, what would prevail tomorrow.

The first component was the VHS-or-Betamax debate. On the basis of that bet, empires would grow—or not.

The next was infinitely more theoretical and had to do with, well, right and wrong, in a sense. We were inventing a new medium. The universe of information would be available to everyone. How could we make this information useful? How could we help turn it into knowledge?

And the third component, independent of the first two, was how we, the people at the table, could make as much money as fast as possible— even if that meant doing what we knew to be wrong or futile.

In each of these discussions, I had some self-interest.

Running a business with three employees, then seven, then fifteen, then thirty, forty, fifty, sixty, seventy—new neighborhoods of desks every week, a whole city—I started to dream of being a great business story, of building something that was smart and sound and for the ages.

As a journalist, I found the prospect of defining a new medium, of being Murrow or Luce, pretty heady, too.

But the most powerful of these interests—my upbringing and personal codes to the contrary—was the prospect of making millions quick. Of making more money than you ever dreamed of. Of making the kind of money that would allow you to do all the things you ever dreamed of doing without the bastards getting you down. Fuck-you money. The sweetest lucre.

This dream beyond dreams seemed best personified in my former classmate, who in school was someone I took no notice of but who was now larger than life. Ten years after graduation, during one of my first entrepreneurial forays, I was urged by other classmates to "go see him." Or Him. Machinist's success was already a legend—the Manhattan townhouse, the uniformed house help, the German-speaking wife and children, the racing cars. I went modestly, without jacket and tie or song and dance, hoping—assuming—that my lack of affect, my disdain for the world of high finance, would be as mysterious and compelling to him as his riches were to me.

It was a perfunctory meeting. Machinist was clipped, curt, and uncomprehending. He got me out ASAP. I understood, too. Shown the door, I got it. He was for real. He wasn't playing at this. The hairy, sniveling prep school boy had become an imperial liege. And that office! With its dining rooms, wall-size brand-name SoHo paintings, fresh flowers, and uniformed servants. It meant business on a global scale. Everyone who worked for him was serious; they all meant business. They all *believed* in business.

Over the years I tried but seldom succeeded in getting Machinist on the phone. When occasionally he did relent, it was almost impossible to talk to him. Our sentences didn't meet. There was always a disconnect. In part it was the money vocabulary, which I admired without comprehending, and in part I don't think he could quite find a context for my small-time enterprises. A hundred thousand dollars was my dream, a hundred million was his. Still, I could drop his name. I could hint that he might be involved with one of my schemes.

And then . . .

One Monday morning in October 1994, the Banker rose at his country estate in Greenwich and his uniformed servants brought him his cappuccino, his fresh-squeezed, and his *Wall Street Journal* and there, disturbing his breakfast, he found me and my Internet activities as the featured story.

Because publicity is the currency of our time, it is not unreasonable to assume that there is a Darwinian capitalistic earning process to such riches. Even people who should know better (even those for whom manipulations of the press are a daily accomplishment) are almost always impressed, or rankled, by someone else's publicity. Even though we know nine times out of ten that the fix is in, we somehow can't help regarding rich people as having earned their money, or publicity hounds as deserving their fame.

In short order I received a formal letter from Bob Machinist, handwritten, in fountain pen, on personal letterhead. (He would later ask my advice on a book he thought he was especially suited to write—how to compose a letter for every occasion, including letters of condolence, letters of recommendation, letters to take over companies. Then, too, he was eager to have his wife write a cookbook; "a Jewish Martha Stewart" he saw her as.) It was a letter conferring high respect on my acumen and vision but sounding a clear cautionary note, too. An opportunity, offered to few people in a lifetime, had knocked on my door. I should look carefully at all that would be required to seize it.

"You can be a big swinging dick for a few days, or realize an enormous amount of money for you and your family. I'm suggesting that you can create a capital base for generations to come," he said in a follow-up phone call.

It was a surprise to me that when you get your name prominently in the newspaper, people call you up. All kinds of people. People who want you on television. People who want to make you business propositions. People from deep in your past. No one is bashful. Of all the many people who contacted me and solicited me after the *Journal* article—I could speak to business roundtables, I could have the article encased in *faux* mahogany, I could contribute to numerous worthy causes, I could fill my dance card with financial firms up and down the West Coast—I was most helplessly drawn to my former classmate, Robert Machinist.

It was the dynastic sense of capital which he offered that turned me on. My children and theirs born alight, aloft.

"We could get you out with five to ten million dollars right away," he explained when we met in his office. "But that's not, clearly, where you want to be. I know lots of guys who have sold out for ten million who are the walking dead. You have a family. You live in Manhattan. You don't want to risk the public schools. I know your nut. You need at least fifteen million dollars—an after-tax net of eight, which would produce a fixed income of four hundred thousand dollars a year, if you didn't make a big real estate purchase—to make ends meet. Our minimum goal is to get you out inside of eighteen months with thirty million dollars. That would provide you with the leverage to go on to other enterprises. We'll play that against the opportunity to smack this way out of the park. I'm willing to share with you my personal goal which is to do a public offering north of two hundred million dollars."

"Okay," I nodded.

It was wonderful talk. It was a way of looking at the world in which impediments to the most overachieving daydreams—own a newspaper, perhaps a movie studio, become William Paley, Rupert Murdoch, Bill Gates—are just procedural hurdles, a series of capital requirements, that's all.

Put aside the inconvenient facts that I had never run a business with more than six employees, that I knew scant little about technology development, that I liked to sleep late in the morning and play with my children in the afternoon.

It was the age of the entrepreneur. It was the age of the visionary. Ideas, concepts, constructs, theories, perspectives, perceptions, points of view—all had value if they were sweeping enough, grand enough, beguiling enough. The great, quick fortunes were all about imagining the future.

In addition, bankers are highly competitive. The New York banking boutiques were losing out on the technology spoils. It was the Netscape factor. In order to achieve immortality in your profession as a banker, you had to turn an idea into a colossus and do it within a season or two. Out in Menlo Park, the financiers at Kleiner Perkins had had a disproportionate number of home runs. Here in New York, the financiers weren't getting their bite of the cyber apple.

But that was because New York didn't have the right raw materials to work with . . . until now.

"I'm fortunate enough not to have to do anything at all. Those people out there," Machinist said, waving to the firm's corridors of offices, "have to move the stones. I have the luxury of just being able to think about what makes the world tick, and how to make the cash register ring." He was very pleased with himself. He stretched his neck and stroked it.

"Really," he said, "this is a beautiful moment for you. You just need to crystallize your thinking. I'm going to help you do that, you lucky man."

The uniformed office person came in with a tray of cappuccinos.

"You are where everyone wants to be," Machinist said, standing. "You've heard about the right place and the right time. Well, here. Now. This is it. You're on it." He seemed poised to skip around his office.

What had to be accomplished was a course of financial engineering, according to Machinist. We needed the resources and wherewithal to build brand, to take the industry space, and to hire a management team that could speak to the Street.

Over the next several months, Machinist provided a series of management consultants to consider our business and to suggest the ways we might position ourselves to raise the capital we'd need to transform ourselves into a mighty business machine.

Once a week, I'd meet him for a cappuccino (he had a machine at every port) in his hideaway library. In a Socratic process, we tried to imagine the future. It was a future in which Content was King, technology was a transparent and low-priced commodity, and basic media principles ruled. On one hand there was a revenue stream that came from marketing partnerships, whether in the form of traditional advertising, direct sales, or sponsorship underwriting. On the other hand, a revenue stream that derived from content replication—how many times could you sell the same information? Advertising was good, but content replication was gold. Consider, for example, the music business.

Yes. Yes!

All right. Quietly now . . . what if the replication is achievable at no cost?!

But . . . haven't we given control over this replication process to the consumer? Anybody can do it. If anybody can do it, then who will pay for it?

That's the missing link! The consumer *wants* to pay! Nobody wants what's free! This is the entertainment business! Do you want to listen to U2 or to your sister playing the piano?

Personally, I found a strong point of view enormously energizing, especially when it was taking a contrarian stand. On the West Coast, the *Wired* disciples believed information wanted to be free; here in New York, Machinist blissfully believed information wanted to be paid for.

It was only mildly disquieting that Machinist knew nothing about technology. "I have people in all the time. We hold classes. Do you think anyone goes?" The firm's senior technology analyst, a portly young man who appeared fifteen years older than his real age, was openly disdainful of the Net. "I would not have time to use it, now would I?"

This hauteur was nothing, though, compared to what I endured when I was brought before the firm's most senior partner, whose enthusiasm for the project, or lack thereof, would determine the size of the firm's financial commitment to us.

Nearing retirement, Alan Patricof was an A-list name gracing museum walls and benefit committees and Democratic causes. He was arguably among a handful of financiers who had shaped modern venture capital investing (having made many prescient technology and media bets), gaining a vast personal fortune and the animus of almost everyone who had worked with him in the process.

In fact, the Patricof firm had been one of the early investors in America Online ("We were the early money in AOL," Machinist would say, stating his technology bona fides), although Alan Patricof had bickered with AOL management incessantly and the firm had gotten out of the deal as soon as it could.

From a distance, there was something appealing about Patricof's eccentricities and cragginess (and crankiness), his rumpled suits (although I suspected those suits were as costly as a car), his fulminating, his deep, penetrating scowls. If the alternative was California and its techno-VCs (homogenized sharpies who spoke the language of engineers), then New York and its worldly, intellectual class of financiers, whose perspective went back a tad longer than the advent of personal computers, looked pretty good to me.

Except when you got up close. There, the senior partner resembled a mental patient. Perhaps it was the unsettling notion of newer and newer technologies, of being confronted with a world over which he had no knowledge and hence no control, that threw him into some kind of chemical brainstorm.

"Net-scape! Net-com! Net-guide! What's the difference? What's the difference? What's the difference?"

"Alan, please," calmed Machinist. "These are entirely different—"

"So shoot me. I don't get it. So shoot me. Shoot me!"

"Alan, let's just look—"

"I've seen a computer. I've seen a computer. What do you want to show me a computer for?"

A demonstration of the Internet, its capabilities, and prototypes of our products had been carefully choreographed, but Patricof snatched the mouse from my hand, waving it in the air in one of those eye–hand disconnects. "It doesn't work! It doesn't work! It doesn't work!"

"Who can use it? Who can use it? Who can use it?

"Where's the money? Where's the money? Where's the money? You're gonna sell advertising? Advertising? I know about selling advertising? Has anyone ever tried to sell advertising? It's hard to sell advertising. You can't just sell advertising."

"Alan, people sell advertising on the Internet," explained his partner.

"Yeh! Yeh! Yeh! Fine! You're going to do what you want, so do what you want!"

Over the years I have asked many people for money—small-time five-figure and low-six-figure sums. But so few people not related to me have ever given me money for my various projects that I have never given much thought to the nature, the motivations, the personality of capital. Except to realize that there is nothing more improbable than successfully raising money for a noncreditworthy venture. And while I was not doing anything different from what I had done before except now I was doing it on or in the vicinity of the Internet, suddenly there were some very serious check writers (distinguished by Machinist from another tier in the money-raising business: investors who were once, or more, removed from the capital source) sitting down and looking me in the eye.

We wanted $5 million to spend against an almost entirely imaginary revenue stream. What's more, we wanted this $5 million to constitute a relatively small part of our business, less than a third, for sure.

Remember, please, that I had spent almost the entirety of my career working at home at the kitchen table. I should have been able to understand this laying on of millions as interesting drama or clever farce and to watch attentively, but such balance and objectivity is hard to sustain in real life.

Almost immediately, disbelief becomes absolute certainty. I thought I not only deserved what I was about to get but that I was being cheated out of more. Equally so, an investor, who is agreeing to pay sums not grounded in any logic whatsoever, believes—must believe—that he is cheating the entrepreneur out of the value that is rightfully his.

After surveying the field of capital, Machinist zeroed in on our Investor, who represented not only check-writing capabilities but who had "an incredible hard-on. He definitely wants to be a big swinging dick."

At twenty-eight our Investor, using family funds, was dabbling in a variety of diverse businesses: helping the Clintons raise money, publishing inspirational books, selling steaks through the mail, developing microtransaction systems for the Internet. He was thinking about making an investment in *OUT,* the upscale gay magazine, an association that was creating a minor disturbance among the folks at Patricof. "I actually hear he goes out with models," said Machinist.

Models were worrisome to me. "If he's a coke head in a limo, we probably ought to know."

"And if he is, then what? The question is, Is it cheap money or expensive money? not Is it responsible money? That's not our problem," said Machinist, cutting me off at my naïveté. "He's the good-looking son of a garmento, and he's going to capitalize your business at approximately twenty times its book value. Period. End of story. That isn't what you want? Tell me. Just tell me. You are the client. Would I prefer Michael Eisner's money? There's the phone. I'm sure Michael is waiting. Right now, we take this kid's money because it's there, it's cheap, it's stupid. We won't have to do a huge due-dilly song and dance, which, quite honestly, you couldn't perform. You run this business out of your checkbook! But it's your business. Call it. Call it," demanded Machinist, looming over me in his blue chalk-stripe Jermyn Street suit ("Dress British, think Yiddish," he once mirthfully explained; indeed, there were no gentiles in his bank).

"No, no. "

"Actually, I hear he goes out with Drew Barrymore."

In fact, Machinist was very pleased with himself. He was embarking on a financial strategy for catapulting our business to the heights of valuation—fairy-tale multiples of revenues—that was not dissimilar to taking a rock group up the charts. He was David Geffen, or Brian Epstein, or the Colonel himself. At times, I thought of him, with his dominating physical presence, as closer to Suge Knight, the menacing despot of Death Row Records. The process was about creating legitimacy, building image, spinning a story that would roll into a juggernaut.

All investors are means to an end. But certain types of investors—ours among them—are a means to a better investor. This notion would not have insulted our investor. He understood that his money was supposed to be used to enhance the attributes of the company in such a way as to make it more attractive to a class of more professional, more businesslike, investors, who would pay a premium for such an enhanced enterprise.

There is an implicit contradiction, however, in this model. There is the assumption that by putting his money in early, prior to a company increasing in value, our type of investor is smarter than the professional class of investors; equally, there is the assumption that he is too dumb to know any better.

The professional investor possesses amounts of dispassion and caution because the money he has to invest is most often not his alone (he's a professional and knows better, after all). If he invests unwisely, he'll lose his job.

Whereas our type of investor can invest in our type of company on the basis of good vibes or a good mood. He is not accountable. He can do what he wants, when he wants, wearing what he wants, behaving the way he wants. He is both childlike in his whims and parental in his control.

The fact that our investor was a young man whose wealth and resources flowed from his father tended to reinforce the unbusinesslike nature of the roles and relationships. We were embroiled in family issues and interpersonal conflicts and generational rivalries.

"This is the definition of opportunity," explained Machinist. "In ordinary business terms, who would ever invest in this company? According to the information in front of us, there is no way for this company to be profitable, ever. This is the proposition you're offering: 'Give me five million dollars, and I'll spend it.' Not likely. But not impossible if what you're saying is: 'Give me five million dollars, and I'll make you a different sort of person—cooler, smarter, sexier.'"

The transaction with the investor is, then, by another name, a Faustian bargain. Taking money is not just a business exchange; it has broader implications and immensely more complicated strings. Even beyond a simple Faustian bargain, the investor wants not only my soul, but his own. He wants a reason for being.

⚎

Our mission was to be out of here before we knew if the business was a hit or a flop. "We don't want to be around when it's time to find out if you can really sell advertising on the Internet," Rubin had said to me when we were discussing the terms of his investment in our company.

"I'm actually very confident about how online advertising is going to work."

"I respect your confidence," he said, with a commanding cynicism that gave him sudden stature, "but I'm not prepared to take that risk. We're going to let AOL or AT&T or a Baby Bell or TCI or the American public take that risk."

"Okay."

He struck me as, well, an opportunist. He was a young man who'd arrived on the scene just in time to take advantage of a situation. I understood, of course, that in business terms this is a laudable strategy and that opportunism is an admirable character trait. And I was relatively confident that as a good entrepreneur, I could balance my visceral dislike with my longer-term goals.

Still, if you telescoped in on the personalities I had now surrounded myself with, I certainly had the sense that I was not going to get a lot of sympathy if I woke up with fleas.

There was Machinist, whose manic grandiosity had suddenly filled my bank account with millions of unearned dollars. There were his functionaries, swarming all over our business as though it were a strategic industry beachhead (instead of the more or less profitable way that I passed my time). There was Rubin, a playboy investor (using his father's money, no less) who seemed to genuinely believe he could multiply his money five or ten times in a couple of months. And there were his people, the world's great experts in whatever they were supposed to be expert in by virtue of their association with him (he had a direct marketing expert who created and placed $50,000 worth of ads for us—embarrassing inflight-magazine-looking ads—that yielded $4,000 in sales), including his technology advisor, who sat in our office day in and day out, sphinxlike and oracular, and his lawyer, an angry, threatening, almost antisocial fly in the ointment ("If Jesse gets out of hand, let me know," Rubin said).

And then, of course, I had to deal with myself. I had become the passive capitalist. I was letting riches (or theoretical riches) just happen to me. I did not know enough to contribute much to this multiplying of value, and I was too human or greedy or entrepreneurial or fascinated to object. So I tried to do just what I'd always done, paying as little attention as possible to the fact that my staff of six was growing tenfold.

"These are bad guys," said Alison bluntly and enigmatically. I did not think she was making just a business point.

"Are you speaking as my attorney or as my wife?"

I don't think she was entirely sure. "I'm speaking as your advisor."

"As my business advisor or as my moral advisor?"

"I'm not your moral advisor."

"Listen—"

"Yes?"

"Let's not pretend otherwise—"

"All right."

"This is a get-rich-quick scheme. I can't stand your disapproval. If it's not something you can accept, let's walk away."

"These people don't have your best interest in mind, is what I'm saying."

"They don't have to. We share the same economic interest."

Her eyes narrowed. "Is that what they say?"

"Yes," I acknowledge sheepishly. It was something they say in the venture capital brochures. "Listen, if they can manage to do whatever they do, however they do it, and we can come away with enough money not to have to worry about mortgages, tuitions, vacations, parking garages—"

Her silence was a powerful judgment, which I chose to ignore.

Like those in a criminal conspiracy, I imagine, the relationships between partners in a speculative business—that is, one without real performance measurements and actual day-to-day business goals but one waiting for lightning to strike—change situationally and with perceptions of greater and lesser risk. So it went with me and my investors. Is it happening or is it not happening? Are people getting wise to us or are they even stupider than we thought? Oh shit, it's the cops! We teetered back and forth between confidence and blame.

When it was good, when my name was in the newspapers, when the stock market was enthusiastic about the Internet, when some other company like ours managed an impressive con, then we were a tight bunch, expansive in our regard for each other, dining in the Eurotrash cafés on East Fifty-fourth Street, considering our vast good fortune at having found ourselves in the cyber business.

When it was bad, when I couldn't beg a mention in the press, when the stock market lost billions in Internet value, when other companies like ours began to tank, we were two-bit punks, bickering, nasty, volatile, potentially violent (at least verbally so).

For Machinist, if everything went well, we'd take the company public. That was the most ambitious scenario. That was hundred-million-dollar territory. Going public for a financier was like an election for a politician. Sure you could be appointed to a position of vast influence—secretary of state, the Supreme Court—but it was not the same as winning an election. One wanted the public's acclaim and love.

In some sense, Jon Rubin was more modest. He was wary of hundreds of millions. That seemed to him to be flying too close to the sun. Fifty million was where he was comfortable. He had a calculated plan, too. He wanted our company to be bought by @Home, the company founded by TCI, the cable giant, and Kleiner Perkins to bring the Internet into America's homes via cable television wires. It was a plan he had spent a lot of time thinking about.

The plan went this way: William Randolph Hearst III ("Will"), who had been running the *San Francisco Enquirer,* left his family's publishing empire to become a partner in the venture capital firm Kleiner Perkins. Will Hearst had tried to strike out on his own before, notably when he started *Outside* magazine with Jann Wenner, twenty or so years earlier. Going to Kleiner was smart because Kleiner was arguably the most powerful and most lucrative financial concern in the Bay Area; it was on its way to being for the 1990s something like what Drexel Burnham was to the 1980s. Kleiner and its senior partner John Doerr were creating wealth nearly on the level that Drexel and Michael Milken had created wealth ten years before. More and more, Doerr was thought to be a combination of Milken and agent extraordinaire Michael Ovitz (before Ovitz went to Disney, no doubt a cautionary tale for Doerr, who often seemed to toy with the notion of becoming a CEO); that is, Doerr was a financier, fixer, networker, guru, all-around string puller.

The company @Home was a classic Doerr creation. It wasn't so much a good idea or a bad idea (it would work depending on how much money was spent); rather, it was, like an Ovitz blockbuster, so full of stars that it would be big even if it was bad. You had TCI, representing an almost unstoppable force in the cable industry; you had Kleiner, one of technology's finest imprimaturs; and you had Will Hearst, who was, well, a Hearst.

At *Outside,* Will Hearst had gotten to know Roger Black, who in the intervening years had designed and redesigned virtually every significant publication in the country. Roger, with a little critical interpretation, had designed the printed world. Recently, and somewhat audaciously, he had recast himself as a Web designer. Will Hearst brought Roger to @Home to oversee the look and feel and design of the new service.

Roger was the nexus.

While considering an investment in *OUT,* the upscale gay magazine, Jon Rubin had befriended Michael Goff, the twenty-nine-year-old founder and publishing whiz kid. Goff, who had previously been Black's assistant and protégé, introduced Rubin to Black. In a kind of Kismet, or by the measure of two degrees of separation in the cyber business, Black and Goff and I had shared offices once and worked on a magazine project together.

The myriad permutations of who worked for whom and knew whom in what previous life were becoming the Krazy Glue of the cyber business.

My connection to Roger Black was then, I suspect, the deciding vote in Rubin's decision to invest his money with us. Rubin believed that from him to me to Roger Black to Will Hearst he had forged the path to a transaction with @Home. The final step, the one that would be of highest value to him, was the step to John Doerr. Obviously, this made sense. If you were going to be in this business, one of your main activities had to be figuring out how to get to know Doerr. I was actually depressed not to have thought of this myself; not to have thought of John Doerr and not to have thought that my connection to Roger Black could be parlayed into gun range of Doerr made me question, once again, my drive and hunter's instincts.

Unfortunately, the two major variables in business (and life), personality and timing, played against Rubin's plan.

It's a tricky proposition using someone as a bridge or conduit. Roger himself had built a complex network of business relationships based on a particular kind of elegance and charm and disinclination to take much of anything seriously. In other words, it was hard to pin him down. My own opinion was that Roger's sense of social artifices and strategic subtleties was a New York kind of thing that didn't play so well in the relatively flat-footed world of Silicon Valley engineers.

Also, Jon Rubin was much too literal in what he wanted out of Roger. Jon Rubin wanted the deal, but he couldn't keep up the banter. He grew too insistent; he snarled at Roger once too often.

"Better be careful about crossing Rubin," Roger said *sotto voce* to me, "or you'll never wear designer jeans in this town again."

"Roger doesn't come through on what he promises," Rubin, son of the Polo jeans kingpin, said with a kind of surly disappointment.

"Roger is more textured, more nuanced, more about long-term relationships," I tried to explain.

But Rubin held Roger against me.

Then, in the fall of 1996 TCI let it be known that it wasn't doing any more Internet investments. TCI, in a very rapid turnaround, had gone from deep believer in the industry to major sourpuss. The fact that John Malone, TCI's chairman, no longer believed in the Internet was, for a moment, nothing less than terrifying. It would come to pass, however, that the Internet would rise, John Malone would begin to fall, and by spring @Home would have the most successful IPO of nearly any company ever. But few people are constitutionally able to think two seasons ahead. Jon Rubin, like everyone, did not want to wait.

During the months I was spending his money, I tried to be attentive to Rubin's mood swings. The pendulum went from omnipotence (a playboy-ish "I've got the world by a string" omnipotence) to an agitated paranoia ("Is there anyone who is not trying to take my money?").

In the arch of our board meeting, Rubin went through a transition from young man of artless charm to caged animal pacing behind the conference table. As he impatiently tried to determine the right technology strategy, he became annoyed that no answer was clear.

I had yet to see him last for an entire meeting. For one thing, details—and especially details on top of details—crushed him. For another, he smoked, and after an hour he was jumpy and distracted.

"Okay," he said, coming to attention. "I'll put another five hundred thousand dollars on the table."

"Do you want to do it as a loan or on the same equity terms?" asked the factotum, calculator at his side.

"I'd like to do it on somewhat better terms," said Machinist.

"Fine," Rubin said, as though with equanimity. "Make me a proposal. I'm on my way to the airport. You can reach me tomorrow in L.A. at the Bel Air Hotel."

Chapter Four

The Art of the Deal

"Industries get organized in essentially logical ways," Machinist expounded as we sat in his office reviewing the opportunities of the Internet age some four months before I was due to run out of cash. "What appears to be random is usually not. Monopolies are formed, brands created, behaviors defined, and consumers habituated as a reasonable expression of a variety of market forces."

In the beginning, there was the battle for the home page. The thinking was that people would elect a home page—that is, set their browser to open to the same Web page every time they logged onto the Internet—from a wide range of high-profile, well-advertised, nicely hyped sites, like Pathfinder or HotWired or, we hoped, our site, Your Personal Net.

"What do you have for your home page?" Net people asked each other for a while (a while in the Internet business being a month or two), believing that your home page would be a personal statement, like what paper you took when New York had a multitude of dailies.

But Netscape launched its browser late in 1994 and achieved "ubiquity" by making its software available free to everyone online. It was razor blade marketing: give away the razor and sell the blades. In an accidental turn of fortune, users neglected to pick their own home page. Instead, they passively opened to Netscape's site (www.netscape.com), a page offering nothing but an advertisement for Netscape. This page quickly became the most visited site on the Net. Helpfully, Netscape pointed users to some of the indexes of Web sites, like Yahoo, a search site particularly favored by programmers and college students. There were other search sites that Netscape started to inadvertently promote, like Web Crawler and Lycos. These sites were hobbies, obsessions, academic exercises. But with a sudden torrent of Netscape-provided traffic, these search engines became the business.

This is what Machinist was saying. Invariably, somebody is smart enough and opportunistic enough and powerful enough to set up a system that monopolizes control of the audience. Consolidate TV stations and create a network; gain a cable franchise from a local government and cement a monopoly; use your muscle at the newsstand and elbow everybody else off the shelves.

Honestly, I didn't think it would happen this way in cyberspace. Why would you line up and follow the leader on the Web? You had absolute freedom. There were no price barriers, there were no technology hurdles (well, almost none). You didn't have to wait thirty years for a fourth network. You didn't need your town wired for cable.

I was in some sort of denial.

Machinist sat back then and closed his eyes for a moment.

"There are too many players," he said, concentrating, as we analyzed the search engine business. "Who's number one?"

"Yahoo."

"Number two?"

"Excite, probably."

"Three?"

"Not clear. Magellan. Lycos. Infoseek."

"Hmm . . . differences?"

"Between them? Minor. Negligible."

"Show me."

I gave a brief demonstration of search engines. On the basis of my ten-minute demo Machinist would complete his analysis and arrive at his conclusions.

"All right. All right. Hmm . . ." He closed his eyes again. "I'm waiting for an inspiration."

I found myself believing that there were classic business structures and business patterns that explained the seemingly random direction of the Internet. And that Machinist understood them. And that they would yield to his interpretation, as well as to his command.

Still, his attention span was not long, and his concentration, while possibly deep at a given moment, moved on quickly to other opportunities and dramas. He could easily forget entire conversations.

But he didn't forget this one. Machinist (who had offices in London,

Paris, and Zurich) returned from his next trip to Europe with a brainstorm. He came with tales of a deal that involved oil, areas of the former Soviet Union, a pipeline route, and Kevin Maxwell, the oft-prosecuted son of Robert Maxwell, the English press baron who had intimidated critics, bamboozled bankers, and looted hundreds of millions from his employees' pension funds before taking his final dive in the Mediterranean Sea.

Machinist and Maxwell *fils,* it seemed, had come to an understanding not only about oil but about the Internet, too.

"He has a search engine," Machinist said, slightly annoyed that some- one else in his circle would have an Internet company.

"Yes, Magellan," I said.

In some sense, Magellan was the most interesting of the search engines. It had put a rating system in place, it offered some site reviews, and it qualified sites for children. Given the sheer volume of places to go on the Web, a credible and trustworthy rating system would not only do the user a big favor but could potentially achieve a Good Housekeeping or Miche- lin kind of authority and value. Magellan's technology was pretty good technology, too. Whereas other search engines went through a lumbering digestive process, Magellan spit back its results in a fairly rapid fire.

"It's not bad," I said. "But it's totally controlled by the Maxwells."

"The Maxwells have always been very smart about the information busi- ness," Machinist offered. "Lehman," said Machinist, referring to the Wall Street underwriter and brokerage firm, "is prepared to take the company out at one hundred and fifty million dollars."

I shook my head. "How could anyone do business with the Maxwells?" I laughed.

⸱⸱⸱

"Can you be over here in twenty minutes?" Machinist was saying into the speaker phone. "David Hayden is in my office." The order would not have been more crisp if it were the Prince of Wales.

I put on the emergency tie I kept in my desk and jogged the few blocks around to the Patricof offices on Park Avenue and Fifty-seventh Street.

Machinist caught me on the way in. I knew that look. I could see my fortune in his eyes.

"I've done all the foreplay," he said.

Hayden was on the phone in the study off of Machinist's main office. His conversation sounded important. I thought I could hear major busi- ness moves.

David Hayden was in his early forties, casually (but expensively) dressed and distinguished by an electric, almost Don King, hairstyle, with spoors shooting straight up and out into the cosmos. He had a Hollywood ease and confidence, with good Italian leather luggage by his side.

He was the husband of Isabel Maxwell, one of Robert Maxwell's twin daughters. I tried to imagine the complexities of having married a child of one of the most significant crooks of the epoch. If you regarded Maxwell and his crimes as just somehow larger than life, perhaps it was something that you could deal with, make use of even, dine out on.

Hayden finished his conversation and we greeted each other with an intimacy created not only by shared business interests but by the embrace of the Patricof offices.

"Most often Michael and I pass just ahead or just behind one another," he said to Machinist.

Six months before, my company had been close to forging an alliance with AT&T. It was a deal that, at least in my imagination, would have put our content in the same relative position that IBM put Bill Gates's DOS. But then, just like that, AT&T stopped returning our calls. Magellan had underpriced us and gotten the deal.

"I want you guys to talk," Machinist said, closing the door to the inner sanctum as he left. "Take as long as you want. You can sit here all day. Then we'll see if there's a mutuality of interest." He said "mutuality" by rolling the syllables the way the British say "sexuality," and quietly left us alone.

"Bob is brilliant, isn't he?" Hayden said.

"Yes," I nodded.

"I'm not sure there's anything as important as having smart and powerful financial advisors. And you have a personal relationship with Bob?"

"Yes. We went to school together."

"I think we've been hampered by not having a strong relationship with an important venture player."

"It's been an invaluable relationship for us. But I doubt seriously that you've been harmed. You've done very, very well." I smiled.

He smiled. "Let me try to give you a sense of the ways we've been moving and where we want to be and the kind of timetable we're on." Hayden spoke quietly now, without salesmanship, without posture.

"This business, as you know, the search engine business, when it started to get serious last summer, many people suddenly started to see a way to funnel the Net's traffic."

He told a story I was deeply familiar with. In the retelling we bonded.

Netscape, during 1995, had inadvertently "aggregated" the largest numbers of users. Then, also inadvertently, it passed that mass of users to the search engines. In an advertising-driven world, the search engines, therefore, owned the main revenue opportunity.

Yahoo, started in a dorm room by two Stanford undergraduates, announced in the spring of 1995 that, with a significant investment from Sequoia Capital, it would "go commercial" (i.e., instead of being a dorm room hobby, it would now be a real business), a move briefly interpreted as an affront to the Net community, which regarded Yahoo as more or less owned by the Net (it was, after all, just a list of sites, with most entries sent in by people on the Net).

Meanwhile, Kleiner Perkins, the largest Internet VC specialist, invested in a competing search technology. Backing other Stanford undergrads who'd developed a librarian-type data search protocol, Kleiner began to rapidly aid its client company, called Architext but soon to be Excite, and to position it as an alternative to Yahoo.

In the fall of 1995, Netscape, understanding that it was giving away one of its own assets—that is, the eyeballs that it inadvertently had come to own, if only for a single click—and that it was giving this patrimony to enterprises that would profit off of Netscape's inadvertent windfall, levied a tax. It offered search engines a headliner position on its home page for a twelve-month period for $5 million.

It was at this moment that the business coalesced. It separated the amateurs and dreamers from the professionals—Yahoo, Excite, Magellan, Infoseek, and Lycos from those who thought $5 million was an absurd amount. Within a short time, the search engines were realizing twenty million and more impressions a month from their $5 million Netscape deal. At $.02 per impression that's $400,000 per month. (And on closer inspection, it wasn't really $5 million per year, but $3 million in cash and another $2 million in advertising credits.) In other words, there was a business here, sort of, maybe, almost—the possibility of $4.8 million in revenue against a cash cost of $3 million. At least there was a clearer business model here than anywhere else on the Net.

Yahoo's IPO went out in April 1996. The eager public valued a company with $1.4 million in revenues for the prior twelve months at $1 billion. Magellan, which had not only its own Netscape deal but deals with AT&T and Time's Pathfinder, had a chance to be the next search engine to go out. Indeed, Robertson Stephens in San Francisco, perhaps the most eminent of the high-tech underwriters, was willing to lead the Magellan IPO.

David Hayden told a story as believable as any: Magellan turns to Robertson Stephens, which agrees to underwrite Magellan's IPO. Robertson Stephens, though, has significant connections to Kleiner Perkins, which suddenly starts to rush to get Excite out (a year later, the Excite people would still be marveling at the thunderbolt that took them from start-up mode to well-funded juggernaut). So Robertson Stephens dumps Magellan and leads the highly successful Excite IPO. (In fact, Excite completes its IPO in April 1996, a week before Yahoo completes its IPO.)

David Hayden shrugged.

I was impressed that he had handled the purported Robertson Stephens betrayal with what seemed to be a certain grace under pressure.

Now, as impressively, he had put it together again. Lehman was ready to take Magellan out in six to eight weeks. The S-1, that magical, rite-of-passage document necessary to sell shares to the public, was almost completed.

The next step was to close on another round of financing—called the mezzanine round, or the "mezz" round—prior to the IPO. This round would include players like Ameritech, GTE, and other big-name technology and telecommunications companies and would value the company at $75 million to $100 million.

Lehman believed that with those name strategic investors in place it could sell the company to the public for double that value.

So what was our company to Magellan or Magellan to us? What was this conversation about? Where was it heading? I had no idea, no sense of where we fit in. I did have a dull ache that I was missing out yet again on another really big score.

But then, just then, Machinist rejoined us. And he told us that, coincidentally, Alan Patricof, the firm's fevered senior partner, was at that moment talking to a counterpart at Lehman. I shifted my attention to Hayden, looking for a sign that perhaps he had overstated Lehman's interest in leading a Magellan IPO. I had become quite sensitive to signs of hedging, restating, or damage control. I had found, during my few years in cyberspace, that misrepresentations, especially when it came to numbers, were the rule and that my own, which kept me up at night, were small potatoes compared to most. But Hayden was not covering or qualifying. He seemed very comfortable with what Lehman might have to say to Alan Patricof.

"Alan says they're very enthusiastic. They would be, of course," Machinist said, giving a small back of the hand to underwriters.

"Listen," Hayden said, "I wouldn't mind at all if you used your relationship to feel them out on their true sense of how the market will value us."

"They've indicated one-fifty?" Machinist clarified.

"As high as two hundred, in fact," Hayden confirmed.

"Let me see what Alan can find out." Machinist looked at his watch. "Should we have lunch?"

"Let me tell you what I think," said Machinist to Hayden after we had settled at the table in the partners' dining room and the uniformed waiter had served the appetizer and poured the sparkling water, iced teas, or diet sodas. "Yahoo is the four-hundred-pound gorilla that you have to beat. The way to do that seems to be self-evident: combine topflight technology, which Magellan has, with the gold standard content that Wolff New Media has. Magellan has put in place key alliances with ISPs, Wolff has millions of books in the marketplace ready to move consumers from the aisles of Borders and Barnes & Noble onto the Net," he said. "And, if I'm not mistaken, your revenue base and our revenue base would together make us the largest of the search engines. One more thing, which I think will have a special appeal, particularly on the Street, is that if you put these two companies together, you unite West Coast and East Coast, Silicon Valley and Manhattan, technology and software development, with content and marketing."

Hayden was taking this under consideration. I sympathized with him. It was a lot to be handed. It bordered on a hard sell. I wondered if Machinist hadn't overstepped. Hayden chewed long and carefully.

"We have," Hayden said as he swallowed, "a two-step process in front of us—to close on our mezz round and then to go into our quiet period and complete the IPO. Obviously, a business combination with you presents attractive possibilities. I think the whole deal might become much more interesting to Lehman if they think they're looking at a three-hundred-million-dollar offer."

Machinist's body moved at that moment. It was a subtle repositioning. As an animal to affection. I had heard what Machinist had heard. We would have put the value of our company, on the most optimistic day of the year, at no more than half the value of Magellan, but if Lehman was taking them out at $150 and Hayden had just speculated that a combined company could go out at $300 million, then he had set our value at equal to his company's value.

"But I'm reluctant to slow down the process. If we combined, we'd have to redo the mezz round offer and S-1. I'm certainly not philosophically opposed to that in any way, I'm just concerned about the practicalities at this point."

"Let's put aside for a moment how we achieve the procedural goals and see if we have a two-plus-two business equation that can make five," suggested Machinist.

"Let me add another element which I think gives you guys an undeniable level of strength," said Hayden. "That's the Patricof involvement."

I was surprised to hear the pyramid acknowledged so openly: we were sitting on Patricof's shoulders; we were more valuable simply because Patricof said we were more valuable.

"Obviously, I think it would strengthen the overall position of the deal if Patricof came in," Hayden analyzed.

"We're totally committed to this company," Machinist said (meaning my company). "We're in now and we intend to be in later. Whether this deal works out or the next deal, we'll be a part of it, I hope an important part. If this company continues to operate independently, that's also a strategy we're prepared to support."

Hayden nodded. He was impressed. I think I seemed to him—and to myself—to be a chosen child. A rich man's son. The world is as it is, and I was fortunate enough to have been born into the manor house. I had vast reserves here of support and strength.

"The notion, then, is to merge you into us or us into you," Machinist said to Hayden as though just recapitulating what we'd already agreed to, "and to achieve fifty-fifty positions. Your burn rate is running at—what? I would figure near a million a month. Whereas ours is much closer to breakeven. That means we'll have to complete the mezz round. Do we complete the round before or after a merger, I wonder?" he asked rhetorically.

"I have no definite feelings either way," Hayden said, appearing to accept Machinist's notion of a merged entity, "but I think I'd like you in before the round. We'd like to do the round at seventy-five million dollars, which does not seem to be an issue, and I think actually with Patricof participation, even if you came in at sixty-five million, we have a strong shot at doing the round at eighty to ninety million."

I was working, frankly, at about a 50 percent comprehension rate. In hindsight, though, I can offer the following explanation:

Machinist began with the fifty-fifty leap, wanting to see if he'd be shot down on that. Taking no fire, he went on to characterize Magellan as losing $12 million a year and ours as near to a break-even position. Never mind that we were losing less money than they were losing only because we had less money to lose. Fleetingly, that seemed like a virtue. Where he was going with that—and I guess would have kept on going until he was definitively shot down—is that Magellan should raise the money they needed and suffer the necessary dilution accordingly (i.e., they'd be selling part of their company), so when a merger occurred our company would have the full 50 percent and they'd have divided their 50 with other parties.

On his part, Hayden seemed to have one thing and one thing only on his mind, which was to b .ing in Patricof, a blue-chip venture fund, at a high valuation. If Patricof came in at $65 million, the financial community would accept that value and be ready to take the next step.

It was unlikely, I knew, that Patricof would go into an Internet company at anywhere near full value. First, Patricof did not make its money, nor its reputation as a firm of tough financiers (sons of bitches and proud of it), by putting money in at the top of a deal. Second, Machinist would have to convince Alan Patricof, as technologically suspicious and maladroit as your average sixty-something-year-old who was rich enough never to have touched an appliance, to suddenly get the cyber faith and passion. Still, Patricof owned a significant chunk of our company, much of it gained at a $2 million valuation. Depending on how little they could put in at $65 million and how surely a mezz round could be completed at something more, they might be in a position to realize a paper profit of what looked like something close to thirty times their money.

Machinist took notes with a fountain pen on a leather card holder with specially engraved card stock, which he scrutinized now for a moment. "If we led the mezz round,"—he pulled down on his cheeks—"we'd want to come in with a package of warrants giving us five percent at a strike price at the level of your last round. Where was that?"

"At twenty-seven million."

"This would be in the combined enterprise. And five percent of the to-tal raised for the mezz."

"Of course," Hayden said.

This meant that for inserting themselves at this juncture, the Patricof firm would receive, in addition to what it would receive from its owner-ship of our shares and for no cash outlay, 5 percent of the value of the combined companies over $27 million. At the Lehman valuation of $150 million, Patricof had just earned $6.15 million. If we did indeed double the value with a combination of the two companies, then Machinist had just earned $12.3 million. Oh yes, and plus 5 percent of the $7.5 million to be raised in the mezz round.

"It's Monday," Machinist said, looking at his watch. "Why don't we meet on Wednesday? At your office. Perhaps the principals should spend some time together before that."

"Why don't you come for dinner tomorrow?" Hayden said to me.

"Great," I said, pretending ease with the coast-to-coast time–space non-chalance. "You're in town or on the Peninsula?"

"We're actually in Sausalito. We're right on the water. It's fabulous. You'll love it."

"Cool." I smiled broadly, if dazedly, too. In the course of a few hours, a plan had been put in place to make me one of the richest men in the country, partner me with the children of Robert Maxwell, and fly me to dinner across the continent.

"We've just turned this pile-of-shit company of yours into one hundred and fifty million dollars," said Machinist after Hayden left. "I'm going down in banker history."

"Honestly, I am somewhat concerned about the Maxwells," I said.

"Trust me, we're going to get them out of this before we're finished. We're going to squeeze them out. They're gone."

"How is he going to get rid of them?" Alison asked when I came back from the meeting.

"We're going to squeeze them out."

"How?"

"The deal. In the deal."

"Every time you go over to Patricof, you come back in a—what do they put in the water there? They charge you for the water, by the way."

It was true that when you reconstructed the specifics of conversations with Machinist, you often could not find the bridges by which we'd crossed these large chasms to great fortune. It was also true that they charged client companies for the meals.

"It isn't Bob who has to work with these people. It's going to be you. It's not even that you don't know who they are. You know who they are. These are the Maxwells. The Maxwells! Hello?"

"I know that. But—"

"They have a company on the West Coast which loses a fortune. You have a company on the East Coast which loses a fortune. So bringing them together . . . does what again? Adds, for the hell of it, geographic complexity?"

"I don't think you understand the larger picture. What you have here, what we have the opportunity to bring together here, is a strategic vision. Obviously, these aren't mature companies. If they were, we wouldn't have this opportunity. But you've heard of being in the right time and the right place? I really think there's a chance that we can make two plus two equal five here. Really."

"You realize that because you're flying at such short notice that ticket is going to cost over eleven hundred dollars?"

"How small-time can you be?"

I checked into my usual hotel in San Francisco, an establishment catering to businessmen needing over-the-top pampering. My trips to the West Coast had become so frequent that the hotel had set me on a spiral of upgrades that had lately put me in a suite of rooms larger and certainly more lavish than my apartment in New York.

Regretfully, I asked to be downgraded this time. I thought that the Patricof boys, and Jon Rubin with his technology advisor, all soon to join me, might raise an eyebrow at my rock-star-like accommodations.

It was midnight, at least it was for me on New York time, before I met Hayden and party for dinner at a downtown restaurant.

Whereas in the rest of the country the Internet was still obtuse and odd, in San Francisco restaurants the murmur was a rich stew of words like "Java," "ubiquity," "search sentence," "economic model," "registered user," "banner ad." I wondered how many other mergers and alliances and consolidations were being planned in this restaurant this evening.

Our party included Hayden; his wife, Isabel Maxwell; the Magellan marketing VP, Cindy Martin, a young woman with a soft southern accent; the square-faced CFO, a fraternity type; and the chief technology officer, a small man who looked his part.

Isabel Maxwell sat at my right. At forty-five, she was an intelligent and somber-looking woman, plainly dressed, who seemed to me more like someone you might meet in an academic setting. There was something hair shirt about her. Maybe to her credit. She probably could have lived like exiled royalty, drifting through the world's pleasure spots, but here she was trying to build a business from ground zero like the rest of us, and working like a dog. Perhaps there had been some distance between father and children, or at least between father and daughters, to have created in them a technology-business work ethic.

But as soon as I turned to her, she asked, "Did you know my father?"

In a way, I was flattered to be included at the level of people who would have known Robert Maxwell. But when I realized I was struggling to have a respectful conversation about him, I wished she'd pretended to be just another Internet entrepreneur.

"He was a visionary," she said.

"Yes." I nodded.

"He knew what was happening with information."

"He did." My head wouldn't stop nodding.

"I wish you had known him."

"I really, really would have liked to have known him."

Perhaps she was making the best of it. I'm sure in therapy they would say she was avoiding denial. It was, however, slightly disconcerting to be reminded that it was they who were losing nearly a million dollars a month of someone else's money.

I turned to the others at the table. It was interesting to meet the competition. Through the modern miracle of mergers and acquisitions, parallel lives are revealed.

"What I'm really dying to know is how you did that AT&T deal," I said.

David Hayden looked across the table at the demure Cindy Martin, the marketing VP.

"It was Cindy's deal," he said.

"I don't know how you got those guys to make a decision. Unbelievable. They were like Soviet bureaucrats. Not even. Albanian bureaucrats."

It was an Internet industry subplot, how the "telcos" had failed to understand what was going on with the Internet.

Once, I had been driven out to the AT&T headquarters—the kind of structure that might be erected in an oil-rich one-party state—in Basking Ridge, New Jersey, to talk about the Internet. In a large linoleum Pentagon-style conference room, the AT&T Internet commissars struggled to explain the world's largest communication company's Internet strategy. By the end of the meeting, we were left with a nutty professor's blackboard covered in intricate formulations and Venn diagrams. Crazier still, they tried to implement this plan. The upshot was a series of expensive and hopeless initiatives, all of which would finally be abandoned in favor of a simple dial-up Internet service. One of the ideas was that AT&T would create the ultimate navigational system for the Net, which, they suggested, could be my *deus ex machina* to unbelievable fortune (that week's *deus ex machina,* anyway). "You can make a penny a day from each of our eighty million customers," said a generous AT&T executive. "If, *if,* you can create a product that can habituate the customer!"

"I can! I will! Yes!" I had said, rolling over in my mind this word: "habituate."

But then, suddenly, as we exchanged deal memos and contracts, the deal was pulled away, lost. Gone. Puff. Magellan, in a deal announced at a news conference held at Radio City Music Hall, had emerged the winner.

"You did an incredible job, getting those guys to do the deal. Really, wow!" I said to Cindy Martin.

"No," Hayden said softly, with a slightly embarrassed smile. "It was Cindy's deal at AT&T. Cindy was working in New Jersey. Cindy was at AT&T. We hired her after we did the deal."

Damn. There it was. Clearly, I hadn't done what you're supposed to do: embrace the executive on the other side, draw them in, make them part of your team. Surely, that's business. I was kicking myself. Obviously, I deserved to lose.

"Wow," I said.

Everyone laughed in a we're-on-the-same-team-now sort of way.

"Cindy," Hayden said, "is perhaps one of the most brilliant marketing executives in the Internet business. Really. She's one of our critical assets."

He gives credit, I thought. Good. I liked that.

In her Southern voice, breathy but firm, Cindy said, "I think it's incredibly exciting that discussions seem to be going so well. We are really about to put something together that is going to mark a fork in the road for this industry. Our deal will change everyone's thinking."

"The depth of our two organizations, together with the strategic support of Patricof, means that we become the team to beat," said Hayden proudly.

"It's probably too early," said Cindy, almost blushing, "but I'd like to offer a toast." She raised her glass. "To a very productive discussion tomorrow—"

"And a speedy one, too," Hayden said.

"Yes," I said, raising my glass, willing to accept the spirit.

"It is important," Hayden said, "that if we're going to do it, we do it. We don't want this to drag on and on."

The hotel limo took me the next morning over the Golden Gate Bridge into Marin County and down the hills into the fog of Sausalito. Surely, when you build in your mind the ultimate entrepreneurial fantasy, that relaxed and fulfilling and profitable business, you locate it here.

This was much better than the office parks of Silicon Valley (as a taste issue, Silicon Valley is not appreciably more with-it than New Jersey). You could look out over the water. You could hear the gulls. What more was required?

There was a white-shirt-sleeves-rolled-up meeting going on in the glass conference room off of the reception area when I arrived.

"Our CFO is going over the mezz round papers with Ameritech," Hayden said. "I wanted to show you around and get you going with a few people first before I go into the meeting."

That was the day. I would visit with the various executives in my position as the new . . . what? Boss. The new Boss. I would be trying to get a sense of what was amiss in the operation. I would be looking for telltale signs of . . . what? I thought, I have to adjust to this role . . .

Then at about 4:00, Jon Rubin and his technology advisor would arrive. Rubin would meet with Hayden, and the technology advisor would meet with Magellan's technology chief. Machinist and his factotum would arrive then for a dinner affair, a gala-ish gathering: dinner for twenty or so in the wine cellar of a celebrated San Francisco restaurant.

Certainly, the Maxwells knew how to do a deal.

The economic premise of Magellan's business was not terribly different from every other Internet business: Spend now for what will come in the future. The only difference was one of extreme. Magellan was losing money at a top-of-the-industry rate.

Magellan's staff was almost twice the size of ours. Their salaries were real moneymaking-business salaries. Indeed, the only eyebrow I had seen Bob Machinist raise so far in the deal was directed at the large outflow of cash to Hayden and the Maxwell sisters.

Otherwise, Machinist seemed to accept the economic premise. I was starting to appreciate that he liked the lever of the Magellan losses. To date, we had lost $3 million or so; Magellan had lost $10 million or thereabouts. So, we were buying our 50 percent for two-thirds less than Magellan was buying its 50 percent. That somehow seemed to make sense.

It was a marvelously well-heeled everything-right-with-the-world evening.

The ambiance and organization and attention to detail and, no doubt, the price tag of the evening were at quite a distance from our mutual hemorrhage of cash.

Machinist was in a good mood. Expansive. He was in a deal now with Peter Guber, the free-spending former chairman of Sony Pictures and legendary Hollywood dealmeister. In one of those investment banking all-in-the-family stories, it had been Jon Rubin's uncle, Mickey Schulhof, who, as the president of Sony America, had backed Peter Guber's wild excesses at Sony. Guber had been fired from Sony Pictures but, with the backing of Schulhof and the promise of a few hundred million more from Sony, had started a new company called Mandalay Pictures. Guber, in the spirit of the surge in cross-media deals, had recently brought in Machinist and the Patricof organization to help him buy a major book publishing company. Machinist, who had come to San Francisco fresh from doing Mandalay business, was already thinking maybe we wouldn't do an IPO after all, maybe our company merged with Magellan would make the perfect new media acquisition for Guber and Mandalay and Sony's ever-flowing torrent of overvalued investments.

Machinist was in a there's-no-way-to-lose mood.

The long, rustic-style table was set in a private room that doubled as the restaurant's wine cellar and evoked Tuscany, a favorite San Francisco theme. The various courses flowed with mock-Italian abundance.

There was no real business discussed, beyond gossiping back and forth about Internet companies and the investors who funded them. It was an evening for socializing, for cementing a compact, for hurriedly building a foundation of trust and bonhomie. We had all become friends, cohorts, partners. I was learning.

Machinist held court at one end of the table. His presence was large enough to hold the attention of at least half of the unwieldy group. It was a great performance. You felt, couldn't help feeling, that there was a leader at the table. And that the deal, this highly complex and fragile process, had a leader with the gifts and prowess and wisdom, even, to guide us to where we all wanted to go. You naturally yielded to him. You were pleased to yield. In fact, it was hard not to turn to jelly.

All this was working fine—we felt like a team, it felt like a done deal—until Christine Maxwell, the other Maxwell twin daughter and the real founder of the company, made her entrance halfway through the evening. She had flown in from France, coming to the restaurant directly from the airport. Here, I thought, was the genetic thing at work. She was much more commanding than her sister. Isabel Maxwell seemed fragile, thoughtful. Christine seemed alarmingly solid and beyond reproof. Matronly, but in the way of a royal. She went to the exact center of the table, the fulcrum spot, which at that point was occupied by Jon Rubin's technology advisor, and said to him, "It would be helpful if I could take that seat; perhaps you could find another."

Christine Maxwell addressed Machinist over the heads of everyone else. She questioned him now with hauteur and specificity as to the terms of the Patricof commitment to a Magellan deal. In so many words, she indicated she was still quite a ways from making up her mind about doing a deal with us and with Patricof.

"Christine," David Hayden said.

"I'm sorry, David," she said regally, "I think we should know—"

"Christine, why don't I fill you in later on where we are in the overall discussion."

"Of course, David. You must fill me in." But she turned back to Machinist and persisted in questioning him as though she were a prospective investor in the Patricof funds, rather than a potential investment of them.

There was a kind of mask that crept over Machinist's face that allowed him to remain unfailingly polite with her but at the same time expressed to his particular circle, in which I was included, that this woman was history.

The evening wore on, and on, past several less and less reasonable hours, with ever more food and drink until finally, blissfully, Christine Maxwell rose in a manner to indicate everyone else should rise, too, and said, "This has been an enjoyable evening. Thank you all for coming. I look forward to making progress on our discussions tomorrow."

▪▪▪

What I want to know is, How do these people, these business combatants, these financial warriors, come by the wherewithal, what with late nights, jet lag, and strange beds, to get up so cheerily the next morning?

There they were—Machinist, the factotum, the technology advisor— sitting by their luggage with their briefcases propped open and their cell phones working, in the lobby by 7:30 the next morning.

"Ready to get 'em?" the factotum asked, grinning.

I could barely even smile to this.

The technology advisor was in the lobby, too, but not Jon Rubin, who would—a message had been left—join us later. Maybe, I thought, this means that if you are really rich you can sleep in.

"I'm ready to stay if we have to," Machinist said. "But I want to check out. I want it to look like we have no intention of staying. I'd like to get the six o'clock flight. If we have to, we'll get the red-eye. And we want a deal by then."

"Oh, the red-eye," I said, exhausted at the thought.

Machinist gave instructions for the factotum to give instructions to get us seats on all flights to New York.

In the hotel limo we crossed the bridge and descended down through the fog into Sausalito again.

There was an hour of preliminaries—of securing the conference room, of phone calls that had to be made back to New York, of a tour of the premises for Machinist and the factotum, and of gathering most of the same people from the night before into a large conference room to begin the formal negotiation.

I liked David Hayden. I was responding well to his equanimity. I knew what it was like to be losing what I was losing every month, and he was losing much more than that and still breathing normally. What's more, I figured if the Maxwell family didn't make you hyperventilate, nothing much would. I could see him as someone steering a hard-to-manage ship, a captain just trying to stay faithful to his course.

Whereas, I was starting to feel that many other people were steering mine.

Magellan had two buildings near the water's edge. The second, across a small parking lot, seemed to house most of the company's technology systems and the large conference room where we would be meeting.

Machinist dawdled in the parking lot, conferring with the factotum. I went back out to see what was holding them.

"Always look at the parking lot," Machinist said, indicating a lineup of stellar automobiles—a family of Range Rovers and other upper-end vehicles.

The point eluded me.

"They're losing a million bucks a month with a fleet of luxury autos out back," Machinist said with a whip of venom. "So that's where we start to squeeze."

There were donut and bagel platters. There was a quieter Christine Maxwell, sidelined overnight it seemed, now busily working in her date book, as though to say she was not quite paying attention here. Machinist had his these-are-just-the-details face on. It was an I-am-bored expression together with a give-me-some-credit-for-showing-up look. Hayden was nervous. I was, too, although I recognized how little control I had over the direction and the outcome. I was just sitting at the gaming table.

"We're scheduled on the six o'clock," Machinist said. "So we should leave here by four? I think that will be enough time."

"Can you push that if you have to?" Hayden asked.

"We can do anything," Machinist said. "I'm not sure what we'd be able to accomplish, though, that we won't be able to accomplish by four."

"If we're going to do this, if we're going to do a deal, we'd like to do it, really move as quickly as possible," said Hayden, trying to put the pressure on a little.

Machinist blinked. "Yes."

"I've had a discussion with our board, and they have authorized me to move forward, hopefully toward a merger agreement with you," announced Hayden.

"We can stay if we have to," Machinist shrugged. "We can stay until next week if we have to. Whatever works. But I think we are relatively close to an agreement. Why don't I try to itemize the main issues?"

No one was grabbing at the food. I was debating whether to go for a bagel now or wait for a more opportune moment.

"We have an issue of governance," Machinist said, minimizing no doubt one of the most potent issues, namely, who would run the company, our side or theirs, me or Hayden?

"The point I would like to make—" Hayden began. You could tell that he had prepared for this, that it was certainly one of his biggest issues.

"I have a simple proposal," Machinist went on, holding the floor. "Neither of you wants to give this up. Neither of you should give it up. We have two organizations at disparate locales. We have a variety of different functions. I propose that you each serve as co-CEOs. Michael will be in New York, where he will run creative, marketing, and sales; Hayden will be based in California, where he will run finance, technology, and business development."

Hayden was caught off guard. This seemed to be both less and more than he had hoped. It gave us both another day.

"If you two guys want it, I would be willing to serve as the tiebreaker. We'll create an office of the chairman, made up of the three of us," Machinist affably proposed.

Nice work, I thought. We'd be in control. There was a delay before it dawned on me that, actually, Machinist would be in control.

Hayden was nodding. "Philosophically, I think I can get on board with this plan. And, obviously, we want the Patricof interest, if it's meaningful enough, to be suitably represented."

"On the other hand," Machinist said, "I don't have to do this. What we want is an efficient way to make a decision and a way that the Street will understand and buy into."

"Yes. I get that," Hayden said. "You and I should talk," he said to me.

"Can we get a recap on the status of the mezz round?" Machinist said.

Hayden turned to his CFO.

"Why don't you just run through it," the CFO said to Hayden. "You're probably the most up to date, I think."

Machinist's head bounced just slightly. "You're comfortable with the round so far?" Machinist asked the CFO.

"Ah, yes," he said.

"Why don't I just go through the players?" Hayden said. Perfunctorily he ran down a list of international communications companies, including GTE and Ameritech. He earmarked $5 million in hard commitments and $2.5 million in soft.

"Why isn't Lehman bridging this?" Machinist asked, almost with annoyance.

"That's a possibility—"

"If Lehman wants to do this deal, they're going to have to step up on this and handle the bridge," Machinist insisted.

"Well, if Patricof thinks it can encourage Lehman—"

"We do a lot of business with Lehman. This is a home run for Lehman with these two companies combined. There's no question that they'll have to do the bridge. When were you planning to close on the mezz round?" Machinist asked.

Hayden looked to the CFO.

The CFO shifted. "The next ten days," he said softly, sheepishly even. "We have operating issues," he added.

Machinist registered this. He did a thing with his lips, a fishlike thing. It was a kind of snatching the fact, like a fish grabbing a morsel in the water and then pulling it in and just hanging there, inert, passive.

Christine Maxwell, writing furiously in her book, suddenly said, "What about Patricof's investment? I'm sorry, but can we talk about that?"

Machinist's face became especially unreadable and expressionless. It didn't say in the least "No, I won't talk about it," but it certainly didn't say "I'm in the mood to talk about it," either. It was "See if you can make me. Go ahead. Try."

"Christine," Hayden said. "I think it makes more sense that Bob and I talk about the Patricof position later."

"You know the board's authorization of a merger agreement is contingent on Patricof's meaningful participation?" Christine Maxwell said in the manner of a parting shot.

"We are already, and plan to continue to be, a meaningful participant," Machinist replied. He stood up and excused himself.

It was quite a commanding bathroom exit, I thought.

***

I was trying to figure out where we were. It seemed like we were where we were supposed to be, or where Machinist wanted us to be. But at the same time, it felt that we were mostly in the same place.

You had to separate the *stated goal,* which was to join two organizations in order to make a more complete and valuable enterprise, from the *underlying goal,* which was to get control of this enterprise, from the *necessary goal,* which was to secure the capital to run our various businesses in whatever combination became necessary, and from the *business goal,* which was to accomplish as much of the above as possible with as little risk to our respective interests as possible.

Because Patricof clearly had its own interests, which were not necessarily mine, I could not be entirely sure how Machinist was strategically envisioning the play. But I guessed that if he could tie up a neat package here (neat enough for Lehman to get a hard-on for, as he would undoubtedly put it) then Lehman would have to put up the risk money, which would cover the operating capital needs, which would in turn motivate Lehman to complete a successful offering, which would provide Patricof with lots of millions for having put up nothing.

"Can we take a break?" Machinist asked, returning to the room.

I took this to mean that he wanted to solidify a gain or cement the status quo.

"I need a phone for a little while," he said.

The meeting splintered. An air of idleness settled over it. It was not unpleasant. It was quite relaxed.

Hayden caught me as I returned from the bathroom.

"Are you comfortable with a co-CEO arrangement?" he asked.

"I am," I said, as though I had given it substantial consideration. "I think Bob is right that there are so many different disciplines at this point that we can easily carve out the autonomy we need, and also, frankly, I think for the both of us the issue is the immediate goal. Let's get this company out. Let's do the IPO. Then we'll see how we want to play it."

I believed that was the correct answer.

"Bob is really something," Hayden said, not so much admiringly but as if he were trying to size up the beast.

"He really is something."

I was sitting and waiting. But the meeting wouldn't come back together again. The factotum sat in the corner on his cell phone. Rubin's technology advisor, who unexpectedly was wearing a tie rather than a T-shirt, had found a modem jack and opened his laptop. And the Magellan executives seemed to have drifted back to their real jobs.

I went out to try to find some meaningful-looking thing to do and found Hayden and Machinist together. I would like to have overheard them, if just for the sport of the thing. The game was a clear-cut one: Hayden wanted Machinist's money, and Machinist didn't want to give it, or even commit to giving it, until he absolutely had to, until all the risk factors could be assessed, until every last bit of leverage could be accrued—if then. I had no doubt who was winning this game. This was Machinist's real job, the real craft, art even: make people think you are ready and able to give them money, so ready and so able that they will reveal themselves totally, prostrate themselves completely, so that when you do give them the money—and of course by this time, knowing what you now know, you probably won't give the money—assuming that you do, you will give the money on absolutely the most favorable conditions imaginable.

Jon Rubin arrived, finally, and I brought him up to date.

"That's ridiculous," he said, about the dual CEO solution. "God, that Machinist."

I told him then about Machinist in the tiebreaker role.

Rubin let out an endearingly explosive laugh. His tense body suddenly loosened, almost dangerously. I thought that he was going to literally roll on the floor. "The amazing thing is that people take him seriously."

"Yes, yes," I laughed. "It is so amazing."

After my conversation with Rubin, I found a private corner and called Alison.

"I don't understand what that means, co-CEO," she said.

"It means—it means we see how things develop."

"It means," she said, "that Machinist is in control of your company."

"Yes and no. I think you have to look at a larger picture. The question is, What do we have to do at this juncture to get ourselves to the next juncture?"

"Do you have any idea of how to play this game?"

"I think I'm learning. I actually do."

Meanwhile, Hayden had been trying hard to shepherd people back to the conference table, but Machinist was immovable and impervious to suggestion.

The arrival of lunch delayed the meeting further.

"We should turn back to this, Bob, and look at the other issues," Hayden said, corralling us.

"I'm ready," I shrugged.

"Yes," Machinist said. He was carefully piling high an elaborate sandwich, studiously applying his mustard. "By the way, what kind of expansion room do you have here?"

Real estate was a favorite digression for businessmen, and Machinist handily pulled Hayden in. They got deep into renewal terms and options on additional square footage and the general price of office space up and down the West Coast.

Machinist did not want to continue the meeting. I was not sure why, particularly if he wanted to arrive at a general agreement before we left that evening. I feared that he had just lost focus, that he had had a burst of attention that had passed and that he was now mentally out of here. But I knew there might be a strategy, too. I was, in fact, very much looking forward to finding out what he might have up his sleeve.

It was Jon Rubin, sourly indicating that at least *his* time was valuable, who got the meeting going again.

"We wanted to discuss the mezz round," Hayden said, assuming that it was now his turn to lead, "and into what entity that comes in. I'm assuming that even if Lehman does the bridge, we will want to complete at least part of the round. Our board feels that it would not be appropriate for us to suffer the dilution on the round alone."

"If it's an issue of funding operating losses," Machinist said, "we ought to apportion the dilution *pro rata* rather than *pari passu*." He drew his lips together in his porcelain statuette pose.

"Bob," Hayden said, and already you could hear the note of frustration—that was a mistake, I realized, there was a lot of line to let out here before you pulled—"That doesn't begin to acknowledge the value of this round for what it does to the whole deal. This is not just about funding operating losses, this is about bringing in partners whose presence in the deal will increase the overall valuation and offering price. You have to understand how this industry works. It's all about how you get your credibility."

That was an interesting notion.

"We have to get credibility from a credible source," Hayden said.

"I accept that," Machinist said, seeming to accept not only the acquisition-of-credibility theory but Hayden's point about an even-steven dilution on the mezz round. "If we can do it at a valuation of one hundred and thirty million dollars on a combined basis, we'll share the dilution." I know that I felt for a moment at least that Bob Machinist was one of the most reasonable people I had ever met.

That valuation, I noted too, was at least three times more than we thought we were worth.

"I'm reasonably satisfied," Machinist said, putting the tips of his fingers together, "that we can do this deal from a corporate finance point of view. I want to have a conversation with Lehman. I'm trying to see them as early as tomorrow, by the way. I want to have an additional conversation with Cowen [an underwriter in the Patricof camp] because I can get an honest reading there and backstop the Lehman valuation. I should take a look at the operative private placement agreement for the mezz round. I'm somewhat concerned about how we do the merger and then do the round in your timetable." Had he, I wondered, just taken back what he had acceded to minutes before? "But there are other ways we can deal with that."

"We can do the merger concurrent with the mezz round," the factotum said. Judging by Machinist's sharp look, I guessed that the factotum shouldn't have spoken at this point.

"We can do it following, too," Machinist said, rolling with the miscue. "I don't see a problem."

I thought I got where he was going. He didn't want to merge until he knew the mezz round was done and the financing for the deal was in place. He was, of course, trying to structure a sure thing.

"I don't think it will be that difficult to amend the private placement," Hayden said.

"Let's do it this way," Machinist said. "Let's make sure Lehman is on board—and, again, we're not obliged to use Lehman, but if they're on board and up to speed, that will be a strong chit in our pocket. Let's get ducks in order on the mezz. Then, well, I think you guys,"—he indicated Hayden and me—"have to work out the operating details. You have to decide how you guys are going to work together, how the organizations are going to mesh, and what the going-forward business plan will entail. That's the big job now. The operating side is where you guys should be focused. You don't have a video conferencing system, do you?"

"Here?" Hayden seemed surprised. "No."

"We have to get the Lehman piece and the mezz round into place before we can start to structure. You guys"—again indicating Hayden and me, somewhat dismissively—"can start to work on operating issues, if you want. But right now I think the deal is better served if I'm pinning Lehman down. Can you guys"—he meant the Magellan guys—"get to Palo Alto? How far is Palo Alto from here?"

"We can get to Palo Alto," Hayden said, with just a slight note of exasperation that the conversation was moving in a new and seemingly far-flung direction.

"If you can get to the Patricof office in Palo Alto," Machinist said, with mounting enthusiasm, "we can get together tomorrow via video conference. Our system is high-end. It's ninety percent seamless. No delay. It's ISDN. Have you ever done a video conference?"

"On an older system," Hayden said, taking the bait.

"This is going to knock your socks off. You'll love it. You'll immediately want to get one."

"What is it, about a sixty-five-thousand-dollar unit?" Hayden said, demonstrating a grip on electronic products.

"Eighty," Machinist shrugged. "It will be a major time-saver. I know what I want to do," Machinist said, as though it had all just tumbled for him. "I want to get Lehman in place. I want you to be available to see them tomorrow," he said to me. "I'm going to try to see them first thing in the morning. We'll get together tomorrow afternoon via video conference. You want to have someone set that up with the Palo Alto office," he said to the factotum.

I had the sense that Machinist wanted Hayden to keep up with us, to be running after us, to be the one pursuing. Also, there was something about a string of meetings, of seeing how the nuances changed from meeting to meeting, where the emphasis fell, that, if you were attentive, gave you an advantage in a deal. But, equally, Machinist may just have been bored. Because clearly he was in motion. He wanted out of here.

He was standing.

"Fine," Hayden said. "Okay. So the agenda will be your conversation with Lehman, and then I would like to see if we can start to structure something. Can we do that?" He was trying to take back a little ground.

"Sure." Machinist spread his arms. "Do you want to have lawyers present? Great. Let's move this along. Absolutely." He was moving.

Still, it took us an hour or more to get out of there. Hayden kept trying to hold on, to be left with something firmer than a video conference opportunity. I felt, I think, what he felt. We'd entered into a flux state. We were agreeing but we weren't deciding, sort of. I was hopeful, of course, that Machinist had a whole different level of insight here, that when it came to the art of the deal, he'd be Picasso. Hayden insisted upon driving us to the airport. Jon Rubin was heading back to San Francisco, so it was Machinist, the factotum, and me with Hayden in the Range Rover. Machinist sat up front and held the floor through the 4:00 traffic by discoursing on the history of fine motor cars.

"I didn't want to push it anymore," Machinist said, as I sat between him and the factotum on the shoe shine dais at the United gate. The 6:00 flight had been delayed, of course.

"They're right there," Machinist purred. "They're ready to fall. Time is absolutely on our side. They're starting to panic. They can't hold out."

"How do you know?"

"How do I know?" He chuckled.

Then he said, coldly, "We're not merging with them anymore, we're taking them over."

The plane did not get off for several hours, so we rode east into the late night and early hours of tomorrow. I'd managed to negotiate an upgrade to a seat with Machinist and the factotum in the front of the plane.

"I'm going to make you a hundred million dollars." Machinist did not say this humorously. There was not much that was as serious as one hundred million dollars after all. "If I do this deal for you, I want you to do something for me."

"Sure," I said, with some feeling.

"I want you to give a building to the college." It was always a small shock to remember we had gone to college together. Machinist was now a member of the board of trustees. "I'm serious. Talk it over with Alison. But it will be something that you can do. We can call it the Wolff Center for New Media."

It's interesting how seamlessly you can move from being an ordinary middle-class working person to being a person with Medici levels of wealth. It doesn't feel like there's been an error; it feels, in fact, like there's some logic in the world. If you work hard, you will succeed. It was satisfying to find out this was true. And reassuring to learn that my feelings of generosity were real.

"It's really not important for me to have my name on a building," I said.

"You'll see how you feel when you write the check."

⬛⬛⬛

"We're not merging with them anymore, we're taking them over," I said to Alison, who woke up as I came into the bedroom sometime before dawn.

"Who?"

"We're taking Magellan over."

"With what?"

⬛⬛⬛

Almost as soon as I got into the office just after 10:30 Friday morning, Machinist was on the phone.

"I've just been with the Lehman guys," he said. "They're buying into this. They have a hard-on for an Internet play. They haven't had anything here. They've got to get something. It's very neat to them. They're coming in to see you after lunch. I want you to talk big picture. Content. Technology. You need to talk technology."

"Okay." I was excited. "So Lehman really thinks this combined company will be worth three hundred million dollars?"

"They'll say anything we want them to say to get the deal. Doesn't mean anything what they say."

I was caught up sharply by this. "I thought they were the—"

"They're just a placeholder for now. They haven't done an Internet deal. Why would we want them? But if we have them, we'll trade up. Or maybe we won't. If they do the bridge, maybe we'll go with them."

"What about the valuation?"

"Don't worry about that. There is no valuation. There's only orchestration."

Given that, as I was starting to understand, there were no givens, that each building block of this deal had countervailing forces that at any time could push it out of the edifice, I was at best a passive participant.

Still, I couldn't keep my mouth shut. I was being taken along; others would come along behind me. Within a short time, I could start to feel the rhythms of our office change as the word spread. There were many people here, people who had put their hearts into their jobs for a few years—or a few months—after college, who were going to wake up multimillionaires.

The Lehman guys who rushed over to our offices that afternoon, surprised me. They had rough edges. The Patricof people not only had a particular sense of dress ("Dress British, think Yiddish"—they loved to say that) but a sense of presentation. Patricof partners embodied the magic of finance. Their skills encompassed considering markets, creating businesses to fit those markets, attracting talent, providing strategic growth plans, identifying merger and acquisition targets, masterminding corporate finance strategies, and providing capital from their own funds or attracting capital from other investors.

The Lehman guys, it seemed, just sold stock. These were two senior executives who wanted to leave one impression: "If it can be sold, we can sell it."

"Do you think that a three-hundred-million-dollar valuation of a combined company is realistic?"

"No question," said the older one, spreading his hands.

"The Internet? Slam dunk," said the younger.

"Of course, you can never tell what the market is going to do," the older added. "But assuming there isn't a crash or technology doesn't go down the crapper or the government doesn't step in and regulate the shit out of the Internet, fuck yes. This is good stuff you got here. Very sexy."

"I'm hot," said the younger.

"And you've spent time with Magellan," I said, "so you're comfortable with the company?"

"Sure. Loses a goddamn fortune," he shook his head, not without some admiration, "but I guess all you guys do."

"We're working on that," I said with humility.

"The market," he shrugged, "doesn't seem to care how much you're losing. You have two or three quarters in which you can be pretty free and easy. After that, you'll get gutted like a fish."

"Schedule-wise, what do you see as the best time to do the offer?" I asked.

The older one looked at the younger one. The latter shrugged.

"So ASAP," the older said.

"Let's do it," the younger added.

In the main conference room at the Patricof offices Machinist was directing the efforts of two harried MIS types toward getting the video conference unit up and ready to send and receive for our 5:00 video conference. This was fun for him, you could tell. This held the meaning of life, such a gadget.

"The Lehman guys," I said, "seemed really enthusiastic."

"They're idiots," Machinist said, getting behind one of the monitors to make an adjustment.

"Can they do it? Can they really do this offering?" I asked, slightly concerned for a second.

"They can do it. Today, anybody can do it. Tomorrow?" He shrugged. "Let's not think about tomorrow."

An empty conference room in the Patricof offices in Palo Alto, California, popped into view. It looked to be in a C-Span sort of limbo; it was pre-air time, but through the awkwardness of modern technology we were seeing it anyway.

The room in Palo Alto was coming in on one large sixty-four-inch monitor; on the side-by-side matching monitor we, in this room, popped into view.

"How weird," I said.

"God, I love this," Machinist said.

Our lawyer arrived.

Alison was out of town, so she had sent in a colleague who, I think she hoped, could balance Machinist's fervor.

I was having more and more trouble reconciling the different world-views of my lawyer (and wife) and my banker. Alison had a rationalist's need to see the world with greater and greater degrees of specificity. There were Newtonian laws that she insisted on applying to most business analyses. Machinist, on the other, was more priest-like, or even shaman-like. He was all-knowing, all-controlling. He envisioned the larger picture, from whence details would flow, rather than the other way around. Indeed, he had never met a detail or encountered a number that could not be "massaged."

Gentlemanly, scholarly almost, Alison's colleague was a type of pre-1980s lawyer in New York; that is, a more remote figure, one who was objective and above the deal, a disinterested advisor rather than a hungry participant.

"I hope I can be of some assistance. Alison has filled me in on some of the details. I've read the draft of the S-1. Very promising," he said, and sat down to look quizzically at himself on the big video monitor. "Do we have a specific agenda for this . . . meeting?" he asked Machinist. "Or is it still exploratory?"

"This deal is happening," Machinist said. "We want to go forward with the intention to complete this merger. This meeting is just to divvy up the lawyering."

"I had not gotten from Alison the impression that the deal was that far along," he said with equanimity.

I think part of the Machinist method was to speed up when it was least expected and to slow down unaccountably just when you did have a head of steam on. It was hard to explain this to someone new.

Soundlessly, we watched David Hayden come into the Patricof Palo Alto conference room with his lawyer.

"David?" Machinist said to the television, which seemed no less strange than speaking to any television. "David Hayden?"

No response.

"David Hayden?"

Still no response, but a moment later a sound tunnel seemed to open into the room in Palo Alto and there was murmuring and breathing and the audible displacement of small objects.

"David Hayden? This is Bob Machinist in New York."

"Hello, Bob." Clear as a bell and properly cued.

"We see you and we hear you, David."

"I'm glad, Bob, we could help you amortize your equipment costs," David Hayden said dryly. He introduced his counsel.

I introduced ours.

Machinist was working the joystick, which offered a number of camera angles and a zoom.

"Both Michael and I separately met with Lehman today," Machinist said.

"I spoke to them," Hayden said. "They were very enthusiastic. They were on board before, but I think this deal is much more exciting to them."

"Yes. I think the appropriate time to have a discussion with them regarding their participation in the bridge is when we have the companies set for the merger."

"I agree," said Hayden, leaning forward slightly, as though at a congressional hearing.

"Fine. Let's move forward with documents and requisite due diligence as we finalize the business points. Attorneys should have an off-camera discussion about the division of the drafting responsibilities."

"Bob, on our side, we'd like to move this along. Can we meet on Monday? We'll come in with our team."

Machinist shrugged. It was hard to read. It certainly wasn't: Yes, definitely, let's get it done. It was more: It's your nickel. "We'll be here," he said.

"We'll be in on Sunday. Do we all want to get together for dinner?" So much of Hayden's business approach seemed to be centered around large dinners.

"All right." Machinist, I sensed, however, was noncommittal.

"Hello," our lawyer said, seeming to resist the transparency of the video connection. "I'm new to this discussion, so I just want to make sure I'm looking at the materials correctly. There's a draft of an S-1 that I've seen. Now there's an additional round of financing that's expected to close, I take it, before the S-1 is final. Am I understanding that correctly?"

Hayden and his attorney conferred, again congressional-hearing-like.

"Yes," Hayden's lawyer said.

"I see," our lawyer said. "It will have to close soon, then, this round?"

Hayden seemed to hurry in saying, "Bob and Michael are up to speed on the round. We've spent quite a bit of time on the status of the round with them."

"Do I have a copy of the private placement documents?"

"Yes, you should."

Our lawyer looked befuddled for a moment, and for a second I was annoyed with Alison for introducing someone into the discussions who was not up to speed.

"I've only seen . . . a draft . . . I think," he said falteringly.

"That's correct. There's only a draft," Hayden's lawyer said, as though pleased to be understood.

"It's ninety percent," Hayden said.

"So there isn't an offer out?" our lawyer clarified.

"No," Hayden's lawyer said openly (and guilelessly, I realized).

"These prospective investors haven't seen documents then?" Our lawyer prodded further.

"No," Hayden's lawyer said again.

"They're all up to date," Hayden said. "They'll be getting documents within a few days."

"Maybe another week," the lawyer said.

"All right," our lawyer said, "I just wanted to understand what I'm looking at."

There was a complex etiquette moment when the video conference finished. How much emphasis did we put on the new mezzanine documents' facts? Somebody, and I guessed it was logically Machinist, had overlooked a spot of softness in the melon. If Magellan's prospective investors didn't have documents yet, it meant that the round, in the best-case scenario, was weeks from closing and in the worst case was still in the hope-and-pray category.

To belabor the point, or even to bring it up now, seemed like pushing Machinist's face in it.

I didn't get to speak to him until the next afternoon. If he had had a moment of self-doubt, it had passed.

But it had altered reality slightly.

"What do you think? Did you expect this?"

"I expect everything. They're fucked up."

"But you think the deal is still doable?"

"Of course it's doable. We have to decide if we want to do it."

"Has that changed, our thinking?"

"Has it?"

"If Lehman thinks it can do an IPO for that much money—"

"We'll see." He seemed distracted.

"What about dinner tomorrow?"

"With Hayden and the Maxwells? I don't think so."

Something seemed to h .ve just dropped in my lap.

"I should call him," I said.

"You and Hayden should have dinner. Ask him what else he hasn't told us."

═◼═

"I don't know where the deal is," I said to Alison.

"It's the same place it's always been. There is no deal. At least there is no deal yet."

"We have a rationale for why there should be a deal. Now we have to massage the various pieces."

"I honestly think that's bullshit. The Maxwells have told Lehman they can put enough money in the bank to do an IPO. Then on the basis of Lehman's interest, they've brought us in, figuring that Patricof will solve the mezzanine round problem. What has to be massaged is a missing seven and a half million dollars," Alison said, firmly outlining the reality principle.

"So you really have doubts about their prospects for the mezz round?"

"Didn't you listen? They have no mezz round."

═◼═

It was hard for me to read Jon Rubin's tone when he called me at home late on Saturday. It clearly implied a failing on someone's part—Machinist or me, and certainly the Maxwells—but most of all a failure by someone other than him.

"The Magellan CFO," he said, "has applied for a job at First Virtual."

This was the other Internet company that Rubin had a big investment in.

This sounded bad, but I was not instantly sure how bad. "What do you think that means?"

"It means he doesn't think there's going to be a public offering of Magellan. Certainly, if the CFO leaves eight weeks before a planned offering, there isn't going to be one. I've put a call in to him."

"Will he talk to you?"

"Considering that he's the CFO of a company I'm trying to buy and that I've just discovered he's applied for a job as the CFO of a company I own, I don't think he has much of an alternative."

We had a mole. My first mole.

═◼═

It made sense to me that as we pushed, the weak parts of the structure or the proposition were going to start to fray. It seemed like something to expect. This was an industry, I thought everyone understood, of weak companies. How could they be strong? They were new companies, composed of people who had worked together a very short time, without a sufficient capital base and without a dependable business model. That was the page we were on.

⚏

I called Rubin several times the next day for an update, but he had heard nothing yet.

I stayed by the phone.

When he called, he was muted, dispassionate, as though there existed a mortal flaw at the heart of all business and to be a businessman, a real businessman, was to have gotten past that.

"According to the CFO, the company is in disarray. The Maxwell sisters are in a different reality. The CFO will only stay with the company if we complete a merger and step in to control and get rid of the Maxwells."

Rubin, Machinist, and I got on a conference together.

"But this doesn't change anything," I said. "Why should it?"

"Well, you would be merging with a company in a management crisis, in economic free-fall, three thousand miles away." Rubin clearly spaced each word.

"I'm not sure that that's anything other than what we knew before," I said. "Tell me if I'm wrong."

"Michael, when you have dinner with Hayden tonight," Machinist said, "you'll tell him that the Maxwells are out of the company. I want this to be understood before we go any further."

"It sounds like something we should handle as part of the overall negotiation and not make it punitive. Over dinner makes it a slap in the face, I think," I said.

Machinist made a sound that seemed to indicate a slap in the face was exactly what he wanted to give.

"I would like that issue to be addressed," Rubin said.

They wanted Hayden to suffer. All right, I could deliver the slap.

⚏

David Hayden was staying at the Athenaeum, among the most expensive hotels in New York, on Sixty-fourth Street off Park. We had dinner at the Park Avenue Cafe, just around the corner, a thoroughly genteel restaurant that was, coincidentally, in the Park Avenue building where Jon Rubin's parents maintained their Manhattan apartment.

It was a pleasant, almost soporific, dinner.

I said, almost casually, "There is a concern about Isabel and Christine's ongoing role."

"That won't be a problem," Hayden said. Everyone understands what happens in an ongoing situation."

Then I said, because it seemed to be the thing to say when you had a mole inside, "Is there anything you want to tell me before we go into what I hope will be the final deal meetings? Any surprises? Any skeletons in the closet? Anything we should put on the table?"

Pause. "No," he smiled and shook his head. "Not a thing."

That's what I would have said, too, I thought. I wonder if anyone really ever confessed.

It was a full house on Monday morning at the Patricof offices. It included the Patricof team: Machinist, factotum, factotum's factotum, factotum's factotum's factotum, and drop-ins by other Patricof partners. We were clearly the biggest thing going that day. There was Rubin's team, including the technology advisor and another business advisor, holding their cards closely. There was Alison, weighing everyone's motives and leaps of logic, accompanied by her colleague, with his affable skeptic's air. On the Magellan side, David Hayden maintained his calm and elegant exterior, his marketing director seemed crisp and clear-eyed, and his lawyer acted like he had a straightforward job to do; his CFO, however, seemed uncomfortable, pulling at a tight collar.

And there was me. I was curious and nervous; cold drops ran down my sides.

"I thought I might just take a second," David Hayden opened, "to try to refocus us all on what we're trying to do here. What the goals are and what the opportunities are. The way this business works, for those here who may be more new to it than others, is that it requires a large, upfront investment before anyone will see a significant payout. We've obviously made a large part of that investment—a larger investment for a larger return, we could argue, than you've made. I don't think, though, that any of us here think that's a useful direction to go, trying to gauge relative sunk value. The premise here is that by joining these two companies we produce a combined entity that can make an immediate and significant impact on the marketplace. Search engines are going to be at the center of this business. If you believe in this business, if you want to be in this business, then there's no better place to be than involved with a search engine, and no bigger opportunity than to become one of the leaders in this area."

Machinist was getting impatient, perhaps even indignant. "Okay," he said.

"No, Bob, really, I think it's important that we understand the business that we're operating in and the competition that we're up against," Hayden insisted.

Machinist's face became expressionless. He made a hand gesture that said "Go on," and seemed also to say "Hang yourself."

Hayden rambled. What he was trying to do was to explain a premise that everyone understood: you had to sink a significant sum to launch a product and build a brand. But it was a mistake to put it this way. In the end, there is not an acceptable rationale for how much money you're going to lose, only an acceptable rationale for how much you're going to make. Hayden had, understandably, become focused on his losses. They stared him, hungrily, in the face.

The sourness that had begun with our video conference and the doubts that had been raised about the status of the mezzanine financing, which had deepened with the CFO's back-fence conversation with Rubin, expanded. Hayden appeared to be saying: Let me lose money because I am so good at it.

If you stop selling the larger vision, the long-term fantasy, the grand strategy, and find yourself saying that others have to buy whatever it is you're selling because you have to eat, you've lost the sale.

Machinist interrupted Hayden quietly but firmly: "This is how I'd like to proceed: I'd like to finalize a memo of understanding for the merger agreement, and I'd like to set up procedures for producing a set of combined financials. With those documents in hand, I'd like to engage Lehman in a discussion with regard to the bridge financing." He folded his hands.

The meeting hung awkwardly for a second. Then Hayden said, "Bob, we want to finalize the memo of understanding, we think this is going to create a great company, we are all enthusiastic about the prospects, but what my board has asked me to do, and what they would like to do prior to finalizing the merger terms, is to come away with the specifics of the Patricof commitment to the deal. I was speaking to our board this morning about this. The board feels pretty strongly that that's the proper order we should be going in."

Machinist let a shroud descend over the long table. Then he said,

"That's not how we invest our money, David. I don't think you'll find any funds that would invest on the *quid pro quo* basis you're suggesting. Either the merger makes sense from an operations and market and personality standpoint or it doesn't. We believe it does. You seem to believe that, too. The way in which we finance this enterprise is, while a no less important issue, a separate one. I have expressed to you my belief that this is a business that I'm confident would be of considerable interest to Patricof, and with a merger agreement and combined financials I think Patricof can begin to consider whether this company is an appropriate place for its funds."

I was always amazed, and impressed, by how artfully and effortlessly he slipped out of giving the money that I would have sworn he'd offered.

"Bob," Hayden said, "that doesn't make a lot of sense from our point of view. From the beginning, I think I've said how much value the Patricof involvement lends to this deal."

"David, we're involved in this deal. We're as deeply involved with this company as we are with all the companies we represent and hold an interest in."

"Bob, come on."

Machinist remained unforthcoming and impassive.

"Bob, this is not what we discussed. I made it clear, from the beginning, that you would have to take a meaningful position. I understand your procedures, but I'm sure they can be expedited." His voice was hardening. His face was getting red. "Let's get real about this, okay? I can't fool around anymore with this. I have a payroll to meet next week."

Mistake. Big mistake. I knew it. It was the utterance that would change everything.

You can't say to investors, I have a problem, I have a big problem.

You can't say, I need your money to feed the mouths I have to feed. I need your money to pour down the maw.

You can't say, Hey, what did you think was going on? There's a fire burning like crazy that we have to keep throwing dollar bills on.

And that was, unmistakably, what Hayden was saying.

And while that was true of his business and of every other business in the new Internet industry and while everybody knew it was true—that is, that cash was just being consumed at a rate and with an illogic that no one could explain, much less justify—you must never, never admit it.

The facade of the business compact hangs on these premises: that value can be and must be measured dispassionately and that the purpose of business, and certainly the purpose of a businessman, is to maintain control, compartmentalize, deal, and always keep his cards judiciously close to his chest.

"I'm sure you'll find a way to meet your payroll, David," Bob Machinist said.

Hayden literally threw up his hands. They went back, involuntarily, spasmodically. "Then we have nothing to talk about," he said. "This deal is dead!" Under the even fluorescence, there was a separate light of emotion on him, hot and illuminating.

"I don't think the deal is dead, David," said Machinist, firmly but calmingly. "If you have a problem, I think we should look at it as partners. Why don't we all just take a break for a minute, and then we'll start again."

What happened after the break was something almost close to a show trial. Machinist had spoken to Hayden, man to man, during the break, and Hayden had returned, understanding, it seemed clear, that he had few options other than those that emerged from this meeting and that if he threw himself upon the mercy of the court and Bob Machinist, things would go much better for him.

The meeting went on for several hours, with all concerned held there by both fascination and embarrassment.

Piece by piece, excess by excess, expense account by expense account, Machinist deconstructed Hayden and the Magellan burn rate. He had a white board brought in and had Hayden, like a classroom punishment, list salaries and the value of perks and other bonus plans.

It was not without a sympathetic interest that I followed the intricacies and the rush of this river of cash.

When it was all spread out, after several more white boards had been brought in, Machinist outlined a solution for David Hayden. The Magellan company's excesses would be stripped away, including its Range Rovers, the Maxwell sisters, and legions of its employees, and it would hand us control in a merged entity and use the cash we had on hand to meet the short-term operating needs of the enterprise.

So that's how it's done, I thought. Not with a bang.

It was a chastened mood. The enthusiasm and exuberance were replaced by a hard reality of business: Where there is profit, there is loss.

The Maxwells, however, seemed to become more and more irked by the outcome. Kevin Maxwell, from points around the globe, began to call Machinist to replay the negotiation and to try to modify cause and effect.

Clearly, in the combination of circumstances, in the tumble of events, in the climate of confession, Machinist had become very comfortable with his contempt for these people and for their business.

"If this was a golden opportunity yesterday," I asked, "how did Magellan become an object of our pity today?"

There was no suitable answer here because practically nothing had changed. Magellan remained the same money-losing company (as did our company). The Internet remained the same barely born business.

What had changed was that one of the players had faltered—had stepped out of character and panicked—and had stopped playing the game.

For Machinist, the Magellan business became "a house of cards," a "shell game," a "fantasy land," a "reality problem."

"Yes, but . . ." I kept saying.

The problem, I understood, was not the reality but Magellan's inability to sustain the fantasy.

"Bad timing," Machinist said. "If Robertson Stephens hadn't bumped them in the winter . . ." he shrugged. "Magellan's business, after all, is no different than Excite, Yahoo, Infoseek, Lycos."

"If that's true," I said, "then why are we so cool about the deal now?"

Machinist seemed to genuinely consider this, to comfortably acknowledge that the logic had a flaw. "We're not dealing with hard assets," he said. "We're not dealing with ordinary balance sheets. We're not dealing with businesses that you can analyze in any conventional sense. This is a real-life drama. There really will be winners and losers. The winners will win because they have great luck and because they're . . . well, tough sons of bitches. They manage to smile when their competitors get a quivering lip. Hayden and the Maxwells couldn't hold it together. Then they got sloppy about it. Weak. Wet." This was clearly revolting to him.

<hr>

The market for technology stocks, and Internet issues especially, held in the air and then dropped dramatically, dizzyingly.

There would be no more search engines to go public. There would be few Internet companies at all to try to "get out" over the next year.

"The window has closed," Machinist said.

"What does that mean about Lehman?"

He thought my question was humorous, ironical, black. He laughed.

He stopped returning David Hayden's telephone calls. I made excuses for Machinist; then I stopped returning Hayden's calls, too.

The Maxwell sisters fired David Hayden. They briefly tried to do another deal, which failed. Then they hired David Hayden back again. In distressed circumstances, Hayden sold Magellan to Excite, the Kleiner Perkins company that had kept Magellan from going public in the winter.

Chapter Five

Internet Time

"There's a casting problem," Machinist said, searching for a new strategy and stroke of brilliance shortly after our prospective deal with Magellan collapsed. "Everybody's thinking—what's that guy's name . . . Netscape . . . super gentile?"

"Barksdale," Jon Rubin replied, naming the professional manager brought in to run Netscape, pursing his lip with just the slightest disapproval at Machinist's casualness toward the names and addresses of our industry.

"Who's our Barksdale?" Machinist asked. "I want a Jewish Barksdale."

"I have CEO resumes a pile deep," said Rubin, whose other cyber company, First Virtual, was trying to address its own casting problems.

"What I'm looking for—" Machinist paused to conjure. "We have Michael," he said, letting me slip quietly into the third person. "And he's our visionary," he said, using an affectionate term of deprecation in the technology business not unlike *writer* in Hollywood. "Now we need someone who can really sell the shit out of this. I don't want a dry eye in the house."

"We do need someone who's hot," said Rubin, warming to this approach, because even a rich man respects star quality (the only thing, perhaps, that he respects).

"We need somebody who's going to make you look good," said Machinist, sizing up my deficiencies.

"Let me restate that," Rubin said. "We can hire somebody who can increase the value of this company overnight, two or three times."

I felt a kind of sudden schism between loyalty to myself, and my company, and a willingness to sell myself out for two or three times more than I otherwise would have gotten.

"But who?" I asked.

Rubin, keeping track of these things, reeled off the names of industry personalities whom rumors had identified as possibly looking to move on.

No doubt because I was putting myself out of a job, I found that it was easy to quibble with each one.

"What about Judson?" said Machinist, pulling down on his jowls.

Rubin made a murmuring noise. "Perfect."

"Hmm," I said, grasping how the story would unfold. Bruce Judson was an Internet personality at Time Warner. He was a hero in *Ad Age* ("a marketers marketer!"). He was, arguably, one of the few people in the cyber business who had experience selling ads. What's more, lending the perfect sense of inevitability and partnership to our story, Judson was the author of the book we had published about marketing on the Internet. We could get a double bang for the money we'd already spent promoting him. I could see the press release:

PROMINENT TIME WARNER EXEC
JOINS WOLFF NEW MEDIA
Internet Marketer to Lead Content Company

"This will make a great press release," said Rubin.

"Except that he loves Time Warner. He loves a big firm. He won't do it," I said.

"You better get him to do it," said Machinist, with a measured snarl, his Suge Knight side emerging.

"Seriously, I know his wife, I know his mother—"

Women did not frighten Machinist. "Set up a dinner," he quickly replied.

Machinist, at a table at Bice, the popular Eurotrash restaurant, was a little more like Sidney Greenstreet in *Casablanca* than Suge Knight but to the same effect. He knew, and by his physical presence others knew, that in the·end all things would come to him.

I had the sense, too, of the illicit side of the casbah, of a kind of trade in human (or, in this case, executive) flesh. Professional managers were the letters of transit for the entrepreneur. If you had one, you could proceed.

Judson, in fact, was a wonderful choice. He knew the business as well as anyone. With only a little critical interpretation, you could say he was among the inventors of the business (its paternity would no doubt be as disputed as that of most inventions). At the very least, he would insist that he had sold some of the first ads on the Internet. Certainly, he was a promoter and a believer and, as many noted while taking a step back and out of the way of his whirling dervishness, a ball of energy. Additionally, I knew my job was safe, because Judson believed he could see the mountain top at Time Warner. He was blithely confident that Time Warner could be for the Internet what it was in cable and pay TV and music and movies and magazines. What's more, Jerry Levin, the Time Warner chairman and CEO, had made his bones at HBO with an assignment not that different from Judson's position in New Media. No doubt, Judson saw a direct line from the Internet to the top of Time Warner, one of those forgivable leaps of the imagination.

Judson, who bore something of a resemblance to Dennis Day, the Irish tenor and Jack Benny sidekick, squirmed throughout the dinner. He squirmed not only because he knew I must be holding my breath (if he said yes, my company would be saved; by the same token, I would be out of a job) but because he had no idea what he should do. His role at Time Warner was no different in substance, responsibility, or workload than that of entrepreneurs who had paper fortunes worth tens of millions, but at Time Warner, he was a salary man. Still, he had built a career at a mighty organization. He had personal, if not financial, equity. Captains of industry took his calls. He had an old-fashioned secretary, too—a nurturing presence making appointments, serving coffee. You don't see that much anymore.

No, he was not going to leave Time Warner.

Machinist showed a brief flicker of impatience. "No doubt, you have a variety of opportunities at Time Warner. Only you can judge their value. What we are proposing, however, is that you come along on the ride we're going to take this company on. I have worked with a wide range of companies in their various stages of growth. I know what a company is positioned to do and how far it is capable of going. We will do what is necessary to take this company the distance and turn it into a home run. This company has our total support and commitment. Everyone at this table, and the managers perhaps most of all, will realize significant personal wealth within what I will tell you is an extremely narrow window of opportunity."

In very precise strokes, Machinist outlined a package of salary, bonuses, and incentives for Judson that would have made an athlete happy.

Machinist expected further negotiation (in fact, he would have contempt for anything else). Judson, instead, showed the agony of indecision.

"In the end," Machinist said spreading his hands. "There's only one is-sue. How big are your balls?"

(While I once thought those were fighting words, in business this seemed to pass as a perfectly reasonable question.)

"I may not, you know, have the balls," Judson said plaintively as I walked with him up a sultry Madison Avenue after dinner. Options were killing him. He was clearly torn between the possibilities of substantial personal wealth and great corporate power. As he openly struggled with the choice, it occurred to me, with some surprise, that he honestly be-lieved these were the options. He didn't regard either as lottery-like. Each, to him, seemed a kind of ineluctable business outcome. My own pessimism suddenly seemed like a tragic flaw, businesswise. Success was surely possible, but it was, I suspected, random; business was, to me, a matter of closing your eyes and making the jump.

Although I was, once again, charged up by Machinist's invocation of my imminent personal wealth (not riches but *wealth,* such an enveloping word), I was fairly sure by now that Machinist would say anything. He spoke in modular units; nearly verbatim paragraphs recurred in disparate conversations. The buttons he pushed were all buttons he had pushed be-fore. Salesmanship, of course, was all about immediate goals. The fact that those goals might have to be contradicted ten minutes after the sale closed was another set of issues.

Knowing that Machinist could forget my name at any time, I was reluc-tant to encourage Judson too much. "I think you should think about it. There's a lot of upside. Of course, upsides always have downsides," I said.

On the other hand, I didn't have huge faith that Time Warner would turn out to be any more reliable.

It was a world of precarious propositions.

"Are you really comfortable with what's going on at Pathfinder?"

"Why? What do you hear?" Judson snapped to attention.

"I don't know any more than you do."

"Like, what do you know?" Judson, like everyone at Time Warner, was aware that gossip flows from the company at a marvelous and uninter-rupted rate. "Just 'the black hole'?" said Judson, echoing the words that Time's CEO Don Logan had affixed to Time's electronic ventures. "We have a redesign coming up. The redesign will do it! It's good! It's good. It's very good."

I sighed. "Do you think Microsoft is just going to shit all over every-body?"

"In a *Business Week* article someone from Microsoft gave an unnamed New Media executive at Time Warner the credit for convincing them the

Web was the future. Me. Me. That was me!" He shrugged. "We'll have to see how much Microsoft likes selling ads. You know, it's different from selling software."

This seemed like one of those strikingly obvious truisms that ought to smack Gates alongside the head. Except that maybe in the end the Internet would not be about selling ads. Maybe that was Time Warner's mistake.

"You and I go way back together in this business," I said, wearily.

"We do."

We were the Lincoln brigade, the Stevenson volunteers, present at the creation. We felt good about this. But a little sheepish, too. It was not an industry where experience necessarily paid off.

≡≡≡

I have taken an unscientific poll of Internet hands old enough to remember the early days of the Internet (i.e., before 1994). The question I asked was, If you could pick one event that got the business started, that precipitated the onslaught, what would it be? Remember, prior to 1994 there were still no Internet businesses. There were no Internet executives. There were no Internet entrepreneurs. There were intellectual propositions, an open architecture network. And there were, certainly, intellectual poseurs—avatars of a new way of thinking, communicating, procreating, and so on. But there was no business.

Nominations for the event that might be considered the Internet equivalent of the assassination of the Archduke Ferdinand, included the following:

1. The debut of Mosaic, the first piece of software that allowed you to see images on the World Wide Web.

2. The sudden increase in modem speeds and the drop in prices, quickly bringing the Internet to a one-hundred-dollar 14.4 standard.

3. The National Science Foundation deregulation decision allowing commercial traffic on the network.

4. The Murdoch organization's purchase of Delphi, the online service that first offered national Internet access, a purchase that suddenly called the media business's attention to the network. It even seemed to many people that Murdoch had bought the Internet (Murdoch's lurch into the business turned out to be more absurd than visionary—a kind of "let's buy it because we can afford it" business plan—and presaged Delphi's long and costly collapse through the creation of IGuide and the Murdoch organization's ill-fated partnership with MCI).

There was even a vote for the green card lawyers, Cantor and Sie-gel, the infamous duo whose junk mail advertisements to Internet newsgroups—spam!—to promote their services as immigration lawyers prompted the wrath of the Internet community, a response that in turn focused attention on the Internet as a potential advertising medium.

My vote was for Time Warner. Suddenly, quixotically, in 1994, Time Warner turned some of its best minds and brightest lights to the Net, an event that, in addition to sucking me into the vacuum of that organ-ization's limited knowledge, more than anything else proclaimed the Internet media—with the potential for advertising, personalities, enter-tainment, OJ! The big boys were ready to play. The game had suddenly gotten interesting.

Well after even normal Manhattan work hours, one evening in early 1994, I picked up a ringing phone in our office, not half a block from Time's, to hear a large, embracing, overpowering voice from inside Time Warner:

"Is this Michael Wolff? The Michael Wolff who knows more about the Internet than anyone in New York? This is Larry Kirshbaum. I want to know everything you know. When can I come over?"

Everybody knew Kirshbaum. *The Celestine Prophecy, Bridges of Madi-son County,* the Madonna sex book, and the *Gone With the Wind* se-quel—all were born in Time Warner's book division out of Kirshbaum's overbrimming enthusiasms and phenomenally accurate commercial in-stincts.

"You're so brilliant. You're so fabulous," announced Kirshbaum the next day, rushing to embrace every Internet accessory in my office (my mo-dem, my *Wired* magazine, my T-shirt collection, my conference badges). "You understand. You get it! I love you! We have to work together! We're going to do incredible things. What can we do? How do you want to do it? Whatever you want. Whatever! We'll merge! Time Wolff!" he crowed, his face in mine, one hand grasping one of mine, his other hand rubbing my back. A large man with a Lyndon Johnson physicality (reaching, clasping, hugging, rubbing), a watermelon-shaped head, and eyes with an unnat-ural power surge, it was hard not to get excited by what excited Larry Kirshbaum.

"In five years there won't be any books or magazines or newspapers. It'll be all Net! We're ready. Come over. Let's do this! Let's just do it! We've got to do it!"

It was two hours of pitched and manic enthusiasm. I came to understand that I had somehow become (at least in Kirshbaum's mind) the Dalai Lama of New Media, and that, according to Kirshbaum, the world as we knew it, and my life as I had known it, were about to change.

What the hell.

I had a whirlwind of Kirshbaum and Time Warner over the next few weeks. I found myself marveling at the speed and efficiency and decision-making process of today's synergistic megacorporations. I was beginning to believe that Kirshbaum and I were destined to turn Time Warner into the world's greatest Internet company overnight.

Then, on a rainy afternoon, as I considered the shape and the direction of Time Wolff and waited for yet another executive from Time Warner to arrive, my revelry was interrupted by a smallish, soaking-wet man who seemed to have somehow gotten by our usually vigilant receptionist. As it happened, he was the executive I was waiting for.

"Bruce Judson, general manager, Time New Media," he said, putting out his hand and pulling up a chair to my desk. He had the sense of purpose and entitlement and yet unassuming air of an IRS auditor.

He was really wet.

"I have your book," he said, holding up a dripping copy of *NetGuide*. "I can't tell you exactly what we're planning," he said in a lowered voice. "We'll need you to sign a nondisclosure first, but it's big. We want you to come over and be our consultant."

"Yes," I said. "Kirshbaum has told me all about everything. I'm up to speed."

Judson looked momentarily saddened. "It's all been moved from Larry. We're centralizing all Internet initiatives. We're creating a committee to study what Time Warner should do. Larry is of course a very important voice at Time Warner, but he's not going to be directly involved."

"I'm a little confused."

Judson seemed genuinely contrite. "I know."

I saw political reality setting in. Kirshbaum, who had made a play to go beyond books—a profitable but not glamorous commodity at TW—to the new electronic media, had been brought up short (it was not *that* easy to escape from books). It also seemed that in my first Time Warner political battle, I was a survivor.

"The New Media group has been asked to report to the CEO on the company's Internet options."

"Poor Larry," I said.

"Oh, he's a team player." This would have seemed coldly corporate to me, perhaps the ultimate corporate put-down, were it not for Judson's own boyish enthusiasm. He was really very excited about the Internet.

"The committee is me; Curt Viebranz, the executive vice president for New Media, who's my boss; and Walter Isaacson, the editor of New Media," he said, as though outlining the prom committee.

"I know Walter," I said, tensing.

Walter was undoubtedly the most successful journalist of my generation. Everyone else I knew at Time in our age group looked so much like water carriers next to Walter. Not only had Walter Isaacson been recognized as a sure shot to the supreme editor's chair for all of Time and the heir to Henry Grunwald, Time's last true editorial pope, but he had written (when? at what time of day? with what energy?) two big books about American diplomacy. The first, with Evan Thomas, was *The Wise Men*. The second, written alone, was a nine-hundred-page biography of Henry Kissinger; it was the definitive work on the Kissinger career.

There was no faulting Walter's journalistic talents, so his contemporaries were reduced to something that sounded pretty clearly like sour grapes. I knew an old friend of Walter's who claimed that he dropped her shortly after her father, a member of a high-brow club, recommended Walter to the club's membership committee. I knew a writer who seethed at Walter's prominence on the celebrity-filled Hamptons softball team and couldn't say enough about the paucity of Walter's athletic talents. I myself was prone to pointing out that on the many times we had met after the first time (when he had complimented me on a book I'd just written), he never failed to greet me as though for the first time ("Glad to meet you. I'm Walter Isaacson").

Every doubt I'd ever had about my own career choices and progress resurfaced when I considered Walter's success. I was suddenly filled with self-loathing that I would be working with Walter as an Internet person (even as the Dalai Lama of New Media) instead of as a real journalist.

"I don't know him that well," I told Judson, lest Walter not remember me again. "We've just met a few times."

"But you know what it means that Walter is involved in this?"

"I think I do."

You could say that one of the most significant players in the world's most significant media enterprise had turned his attention to the Internet, which might well mean that the Internet had arrived; it was going to be as big as television, after all. This was no longer the world of geeky boys and messianics and computer magazines. It was Time Warner, which knew a thing or two about inventing media, about marrying technology to ideas and entertainment and commerce.

Still.

It *was* a bit of a surprise to find Walter Isaacson here. Walter's was an old-fashioned career: its models were old-fashioned (the journalist as intellectual), its principles were old-fashioned (loyalty to a corporation—he'd worked for the same company since college!). So far, the Internet had attracted people who were pretty nearly the exact opposite of Walter. These tended to be people—like Wired's Louis Rossetto, for instance—not all that grounded in success and not all that directed in their careers. A certain philistinism seemed to be a help, too. You had to allow for the possibility that the Internet would do weird things to reading, writing, even—egad—editing. Hell, to the whole information structure as we know it.

One Internet manifesto, propounded (oddly by the mega-pulp author Michael Crichton) in Wired, argued that traditional news organizations were falling way behind the information curve because the Internet gave readers immediate access to primary sources—the same sources that, for instance, *Time's* reporters were using. What's more, it argued, we all had our special interests—sports or business or health or books or politics—which we'd soon be able to follow to our heart's content online. We'd soon see—as anyone who has ever had firsthand knowledge of an event covered in newspapers and newsmagazines has seen—how news organizations misunderstand the issues, mangle the facts, and generally get it, by a goodly measure, wrong. Such a newfound empowerment and perspective would quickly undermine what credibility these news organizations had left.

This quickly became the ever-rising mantra on the Net. The way we receive news and information was going to be fundamentally changed. The information end user (i.e., reader) would take control of the experience and the process. The middle men (editors, reporters) and the publications they worked for (*Time,* for sure) were on their way to the ash heap.

It was hard not to be infected by this anarchic possibility. For one thing, it was at least a little bit true. For another, you could quickly get a little giddy starting to reimagine the whole structure and basis of the information flow. And, of course, who wouldn't want to deliver a smarting blow to Time and a tweak to Walter?

At Time, Walter was the editor of New Media. While that title sounded suspiciously vacant, it put him at number three on the masthead for all of Time, Inc. It was a position without real portfolio, set up so that Walter could do his thing—surprise everyone, find opportunities, expand. Almost every media organization had someone devoted to new media. (New media was supposed to include games like Nintendo, interactive TV, and

CD-ROM. In any event, it was certainly not supposed to replace old media. Nor was it supposed to have anything to do with the software business, which was not media at all.) But they were auxiliary types, without real authority. They weren't princes of the company, like Walter.

"This is big," Judson said, lowering his voice. "This is so big! Jerry Levin has taken a personal interest in what we're doing. He's going to be paying close attention to what we recommend. And we don't know a thing about this, so we're depending entirely on you!"

While I had offered plenty of people plenty of advice, I had never truly been a consultant before. Consultants appear frequently in the technology business, because the business involves a constant turnover of skill sets and knowledge bases. The technology business is, in effect, the business of acquiring new knowledge. Of the many ways that process can be accomplished, hiring consultants is one of the cheapest ("Maybe you can spend a couple of weeks with us and do a brain dump"). It is, however, often a pretty vague proposition. I would imagine that most consultants are secretly startled that they have ever been hired and, in their heart of hearts, profoundly question the value of the knowledge they have to impart. No one more so than I.

The Online Steering Committee, of which I was now a member, met on the thirty-fourth floor of the Time Life Building. In all large corporations there is a holy area. The thirty-fourth floor of Time is among the holiest in New York. It is the Manhattan office of my imagination. Think of movies of the '40s. Secretaries in tight-waisted suits. Hauteur. Formality. Henry Luce.

The meeting was in the office of the president for Multimedia, Curt Viebranz, and by protocol, Judson told me, would always be in his office when he attended, because in the corporate hierarchy Viebranz, nominally outranked Isaacson, whose office was also on this hallowed floor.

There can't be that much real estate left like this in corporate America. Viebranz had a three-office suite. The anterior office was for the secretary/personal assistant. The next room (as large as the largest room in my house) contained, with room to spare, a desk and a conference table and an intimate seating area with couch and easy chairs for five or six; this seemed to be where the work of the world was done. The ultimate room was the private chamber (twice the size of the largest room in my house), and this seemed to be where the executive retreated from the hubbub and distractions of the world.

A rising star at TW, Viebranz, in his late forties, with blond-gray hair and fine suits and carefully contrasting shirts, had come from more than a decade at HBO and then a stint running Time Life Books in Europe. One of the surprising things to me about my interlude in the business world was how few people appeared true to type. In general, I could find little apparent reason why a given person was doing what he was doing. Matching success and failure with education or looks or temperament was a toss-up. Aristocracy, meritocracy, old boys—such order, at least in the business circles in which I'd been moving, seemed to have been thrown to the wind. But Viebranz fit perfectly. He was male, Anglo-Saxon, and precise and athletic in appearance; he had both clear leadership qualities and a short attention span. He had a whip of interest that would strike quick and efficiently and then be gone. He was, in style, an inquisitor (different from being inquisitive) in pursuit of the weakness in the argument, presentation, or thought: "Why?" "Is that right? I don't remember it that way." "Can you present that again?"

The contrast between Viebranz and Judson, his lieutenant, seemed extreme, at first. Viebranz was seamless whereas Judson was ragged with anxieties and details and options and countervailing forces and a million considerations—and, invariably, a suit that was too big for him. But after a while this seemed classic, too. The general officer remained above the fray, a beacon of objectivity, while the field officer mastered the logistics of the battle (and in the end was the only guy who knew what was going on). Judson, actually, was both field officer and warrant officer, always running off to secure supplies.

While Viebranz was the formal business head and Judson the designated detail man, it was clearly Isaacson's show.

It was amazing how unprepossessing Walter was. I tended to forget this between encounters, because people talked about him with such awe. I knew more than a few women from his class at Harvard who, once on, couldn't get off the subject of Walter; they carried wounds from his lack of interest. Up close, though, the fair-haired college boy was now short and stout in a worn-too-many-times suit, his blond hair faded and limp, an odd remnant appearing, even, not necessarily to be his own.

But when he sat down at the piano . . .

By now I've been in a thousand meetings that have had as their agenda what to do with the Internet—what it's best suited for, how consumers will be willing to use it, what functions are needed to enhance it, and how in the world you make money from it. Each of these questions is helped by a synthesis of past, present, and future trends in media, technology, commerce, advertising, and finance. But while all these industries converge in cyberspace, few people can bring all these disciplines together. West Coast people tend to be ignorant of everything save technology, New York media people have virtually a learning disability when it comes to technology, and finance people don't know enough about anything except finance. And that's only on the most general level: when you break these groups down to geeks (and you can break geeks down to UNIX geeks, Mac geeks, Microsoft geeks, game geeks, and so on), content people, venture players, investment bankers, advertisers, and agency people, the chances of bringing all the various aspects of the business (aka "the moving parts") together grow ever slimmer.

But Walter Isaacson was the Toscanini of convergence. It was really something to listen to him. Extemporaneously, he could represent wildly diverse interests. He could hold a truly global battlefield in his head. His diorama of the conflicts and potential alliances of technology and media and marketing was breathtaking in its detail and in its vision. Walter, I found myself hard pressed to admit, was the only person who understood it all.

It wasn't for nothing that after his Kissinger biography Walter had plunged into the life of Benjamin Franklin, one of the few truly Renaissance men in American history, an opportunist in the humanities as well as the sciences.

Walter was used to navigating between competing interests. He came from the church side of Time's famous church and state division (i.e., editorial affairs separated from business interests), and while having clearly achieved a cardinal's status, he was at ease with all the personalities from state and was comfortable with their issues—advertising and circulation issues, share price, personnel, real estate even. What's more, at the same time he was a *Time* editor and a Time executive, he was also a writer, and somehow had managed to take the conflicts there—conflicts of sensibility and of hours in a day—and manage them. By all accounts, what motivated this remarkable talent for convergence and synergy and political acumen was the most competitive nature of our generation; he needed to achieve not just in one way but in all ways. "Walter has turned overachieving into a force of nature," jealously explained one of his Harvard classmates. "He will learn everything you know, befriend everyone you know, and get your job done better and faster than you ever could. Or he'll kill you."

Walter and the New Media group were waist deep in something called the Full Service Network, then being tested in Orlando, Florida. This was Time Warner's literal version of the information superhighway. Using the television set, augmented by a cablelike box, ordinary consumers would, in theory, be able to access movies of their choice, video games, shopping services, various print publications, and customized news programs.

"Our new electronic superhighway will change the way people use television," Time Warner chairman Jerry Levin said when the service was announced in January 1993. "By having the consumer access unlimited services, the Full Service Network will render irrelevant the notion of sequential channels on a TV set."

Within Time Warner throughout 1993, people would say, "We're building the information superhighway in Orlando," and they would mean it. It was not for them a metaphor. They thought they were building it, the actual information superhighway thing.

While the Full Service Network was Time Warner's big interactive enchilada, the new media group had also inherited *Time's* relationship with America Online. By early 1994, AOL had begun to pose a bit of a conundrum.

"We're actually getting screwed," said Judson. Annoyingly, AOL was becoming what the Full Service Network was supposed to be—and it was doing it on Time Warner's dollar. AOL had been a computer bulletin board service that specialized in member chat groups and offered a smorgasbord of mostly unbranded, and in some cases homespun, information (legal information for laypeople, career help for job seekers, directories of country inns—anything it could get cheaply and without extended negotiations). In late 1993, AOL began trying to recruit national information brands. *Time* became one of its first major deals—and in many ways the engine of AOL's growth. The idea was that *Time* would "publish" on AOL every week; that is, it would offer certain interactive events with its editors and writers, and it would make available to AOL's subscribers a searchable archive of *Time's* articles. Then, too, the idea would provide AOL with free or low-cost advertising space in *Time*. In return, *Time* could look forward to a small percentage of AOL's hourly connection fees.

By 1994, FSN, having been taken through its paces in four thousand households in Orlando, looked a lot like a dud (technology problems, consumer resistance, bad press)—and a supremely embarrassing one at that—and AOL, partly on the basis of its relationship with *Time*, looked like a rising star. What's more, it was becoming evident that modem-to-modem communication (what AOL was based on) could offer—and might do it cheaper, faster, and better—the kind of mixed bag of information, entertainment, and services that FSN was promising.

In the first year of their relationship, Time's share of AOL's proceeds would amount to little more than five hundred thousand dollars. AOL, on the other hand, had realized tens of millions of dollars in new subscriptions from the ads it had placed at no cost in *Time* and from the appreciated share price that came from its association with the magazine. *Time,* it would seem, had actually screwed itself.

There were obvious options for Time, Inc.: negotiate a new deal with AOL, buy AOL, start an online service, or buy a competing service—CompuServe or Prodigy.

Hence, a committee was formed: the Online Steering Committee.

"But it's not just online. It's the Internet, too. It's the World Wide Web," Judson told me in a stage whisper. "We believe in the World Wide Web. Walter believes in the World Wide Web. It's so incredible."

"Have you seen it? Have you played with it?" I asked.

"I've never really 'surfed,'" he noted, making quotation marks in the air. "But I've seen it. I've looked at it."

America Online had clearly aroused Walter's competitive instincts. AOL was playing Time, Inc. for a fool (interestingly, Walter believed in Time earnestly and passionately—it was hard to tell if this was a virtue or a flaw). It was making money from *Time* without fairly dividing the spoils. It further annoyed Walter that AOL seemed to think that just because it had the technology to deliver information to the American people, it could be a news and information organization, too, no big deal. And it annoyed him because, in the end, AOL users didn't seem to be all that interested in reading *Time* online. What AOL users wanted to do was chat and chat and chat! ("What are you wearing?" was not a question you necessarily wanted to ask a *Time* editor.)

Walter's one, seemingly formative, experience with AOL had come on Christmas Eve in 1993. He had sat down at his home computer and found lonely people online, strangers who wanted to chat with other strangers on Christmas Eve.

"I was disturbed," he said. "I was quite disturbed."

Walter believed, however, in all the virtues of online communication: its speed, its interactivity, its changeability, and the promise of customization. *Time's* area on AOL offered users the weekly magazine sooner than you could get it in print form; it offered users the chance to chat one-on-one and exchange e-mail with *Time's* editors; and Walter could easily envision it changing as regularly as television and being tailored to each user's interests.

But, in truth, AOL users were more interested in chatting with each other (chatting with strangers! chatting, most often, about sex!) than they were in chatting with *Time* editors or in catching up on current events.

Walter blamed it on the fundamentals. This was AOL's audience, the lonely people he had met on Christmas Eve, and not *Time's* natural audience. What's more, the packaging, the presentation, the look and feel, were AOL's. Time, Inc. was severely handicapped—not to mention foolish, in giving AOL all that free advertising and getting little in return.

Time began a negotiation with AOL to try to improve the deal. But Walter wasn't particularly optimistic; he knew that AOL users weren't signing on to AOL to read *Time*. "You won't win at the negotiating table what you can't win on the battlefield," the writer of two books about diplomacy acknowledged.

Anyway, where Walter was really heading was the Internet.

The Web—or the software that allowed viewers to see graphics and programmers to create structured layouts—had debuted in spring 1993 at Internet World (what was then a ragtag group of tables in a small corner of Manhattan's Javits Center is now a three-times-a-year multitiered extravaganza of million-dollar convention booths). By early 1994 there were still only a handful of Web sites, mostly one-page jobs with straightforward hypertext links. Envisioning the Web as a breakthrough multimedia publishing platform was the working of a very academic mind. Walter, while having had very little firsthand exposure to the Web, had done the reading.

For Walter, the Web, or at least the theoretical Web, was Time's opportunity to go back into the publishing business, to do what it did best: present and package information, rather than just supply and license it to an online service. Walter got the theory of the medium quicker than anyone I had seen grapple with it before. At that moment in time, most conversations about the medium never got too far beyond trying to explain where this stuff existed and how it just hung there and who was in control and who owned it.

To me, it was wonderful, revolutionary even, that a major media company would embrace the view of the Web as a profoundly important new publishing tool, but also odd. In the online services, you had a functional, understandable business model. People paid to get access to the information and entertainment that was being provided. The Web, so far, had no economic model. It was not yet clear how many people would ever be able to reach the Web. Even among the rarefied group that had access to the Internet, most had text-based access available over a telephone line; giving them the ability to use a graphical browser, that is, to *see* the Web, was not, as programmers say, trivial ("That's trivial." "That's *not* trivial").

All other major media and software companies who had the foresight to be involved in online delivery—Ziff-Davis, Apple, AT&T, and Microsoft, for instance—were thinking about closed online services rather than the

Internet. (Each of those efforts—Ziff's Interchange, which was sold to AT&T; Apple's eWorld; the first several versions of Microsoft's MSN; and the AT&T-backed Europe Online—would die agonizing but quick deaths.)

Nor were the existing online services giving much thought to the Internet in early 1994, except to dismiss it. AOL executives had a litany of objections that ranged from technology incompatibilities to pornography issues to a competitive analysis (information was available for free on the Internet whereas on AOL it cost money, so why should AOL encourage people to use the Internet?). Duh. Executives at GEnie, G.E.'s online service destined for oblivion, maintained that because GEnie used excess time on G.E.'s mainframes and because G.E. serviced the Defense Department with some of these same computers, giving GEnie subscribers access to the Internet would pose a national security risk. (They said this with a straight face; they actually seemed to believe this.) In a fabled meeting with CompuServe executives out at CompuServe's vast complex of aging technology in Columbus, Ohio, the Time Warner delegation was told that CompuServe would never expose its subscribers to the lethal computer viruses that thrived and multiplied on the Internet. Walter grew more and more insistent, telling this gathering of network specialists and technology executives why the Internet was inevitable, why online services as we knew them could not survive, and why the business model for conveying information was inalterably changing. When the CompuServe executives showed little interest in accepting Walter's view of online communications, he declared Time's participation in the meeting over and, Timers in tow, stormed out. ("You must remember," he told associates back in New York, "when you storm out of a meeting in Columbus, Ohio, you won't be able to find a cab.")

It is surely worth noting again that Walter himself had virtually no first-hand knowledge about the Internet, about the experience of using it, about the technology it required, about what Internet users were looking for or thinking about (part of my job was to brain-dump this knowledge from me to him). Still, he was right and CompuServe was wrong. Sort of. (In April 1995, as it finally followed Walter's advice, CompuServe would plunk down $100 million to buy Spry Communications, an Internet access and browser company, in one of the many deals it would make, transforming itself from the most profitable company in the online access and information business to a has-been enterprise).

Virtually every element of Walter's argument for the Web contained greater and lesser untested assumptions. The largest of these, and perhaps the most unchallenged, was surely that the Web could be an efficient and compelling advertising medium. The significance of this argument was that it provided a way to make money from the Internet in its free form and it justified Time's presence, even auguring for its dominance, in the medium. If advertising needed to be sold, who better to sell it than Time?

On the thirty-fourth floor of the Time Life Building, the Online Steering Committee met each week in a purposeful fashion that resembled a trial, and maybe even a court martial. Isaacson was prosecutor and, representing an authoritarian state, virtually all-powerful. Judson served as both clerk to the court and an assistant in the prosecutor's office. Viebranz was judge and jury. It was left to me, oddly, to be the hapless defense attorney representing the online services. This was a good example of the dexterity with which Walter could work a meeting. How was it that I had come to argue for the online services? I had spent the past year saying to anyone who would listen, "Hey, you've got to see the Internet!" Hell, I was the only person in the room who had ever been on the Internet.

One of the ways Isaacson took control of a meeting was to be on his feet when everyone else was sitting, and he now paced restlessly, his shirt pulling from his pants, his arms held tight across his chest (he was a sloppier version of William F. Buckley), waiting to pounce, as you hit the period or paused too long at a comma in your sentence, or to dash to diagram a concept on the white board. "The Web puts us back into the driver's seat. We can control our content. We can target our audience. We can use our resources to reach that audience. We can sell that audience."

This seemed like a grand and wonderful notion to me, but it also seemed highly theoretical. There were no real examples of a magazine making the transition to the Web. It was still amateurs and academics out there.

"Okay, but why do you think that people are going to come to *Time* when it's on the Web? These are young men. This isn't *Time*'s audience," I said, trying to be a responsible consultant.

"Not now!" shouted Judson. "Not now! But tomorrow, the next day. You're the one who says this is going to be a mass medium. Like TV!"

"But I don't really believe that!" I said with my best Cheshire smile.

"What was that?" Viebranz said, not smiling.

"I'm just trying to say that while this certainly may be a mass medium, right now it's pretty focused. You're going to go out there with *Time* magazine when what people really want is sex, drugs, and technology. You have to see what's out there. It's strange. It's very peculiar. It's not like what you've seen before."

"Early adopters," said Viebranz.

"It's changing very quickly," said Walter.

"You've got to see it," I said, meekly insisting. "The voyeurs. Alt.sex.voyeurs. You can find out what room to request in a hotel for the best view."

"Really?" Viebranz said.

I was annoying Walter.

Out in San Francisco, *Wired* magazine was laying the groundwork for a Web presence of its own. While Wired's vision was transcendent—it believed it was truly inventing a new medium and through that medium a new way of life—its efforts were more like Time's than not.

Both Time and Wired, separated by coasts and sensibility but united as print publishers, shared two assumptions. They both wanted to stay out of the business of providing people with connections to the Internet, and they both believed they could create a revenue stream selling advertising on the Web.

As they each in turn expressed it, the goal was to be CNN (creating shows for the cable system) rather than TCI (wiring the nation's homes).

Eschewing the business of Internet access was both visionary and, I couldn't help thinking, arrogant. Neither Walter Isaacson nor Louis Rossetto wanted to be involved in an aspect of the business, of the medium, that seemed lesser, and certainly dirtier (technology was, in the end, to both Walter and Louis, just nuts and bolts) than creating content. Each saw himself positioned beyond delivery, saw himself in an almost utopian context where he could deliver a message unfettered by the chief bugaboo in the media business—distribution. Indeed, Time would almost disdainfully turn aside the chance to be one of Netscape's early backers.

"Content," Louis had said (with a growing hauteur) as we sat in a noodle restaurant in Times Square in the spring of 1994, "is king."

"Content," Walter said as he stood at the head of the long table in Curt Viebranz's conference room, "is king."

Which brought both Louis and Walter, at nearly the same time, to begin to believe that the Web could be an advertising medium. This is an important and not necessarily inevitable moment. Almost right up until Wired made this dialectical breakthrough—that users prefer to accept advertising rather than pay for the cost of content and that the Web is a part of the Net where advertising will be acceptable—most people who knew anything at all about the medium would have considered advertising on the Internet an unlikely outcome.

"We don't want to do anything to offend the community, of course," said Judson.

I had, myself, been on the receiving end of the opprobrium of the Internet "community"—that population of science and computer students and professionals and Johnny-come-lately geeks who'd been using the network, largely undisturbed, over the past ten years. We'd posted, at least half innocently, a series of messages to a variety of newsgroups about one of the books we'd written and published about the Net. For instance, to the newsgroup alt.spankers, we wrote, "We have described this group in our new book *NetChat* in the following way: 'If spankers had their own nation, alt.spankers would be its congress. . . .'" Within hours these postings, construed as thinly veiled advertisements, unleashed an attack upon our motives that included a vigilante with the *nom de guerre* Cancelmoose deleting all our messages on more than a hundred newsgroups, a torrent of hate e-mail messages that shut down our mail server, a place on an official-seeming Internet blacklist, two columns of censure in the *Wall Street Journal*, a general threat that we would be forever associated with the hated green card lawyers, and, indeed, a rather virulent attack by Louis himself. "The Net," he wrote in an e-mail, "is a community, it has standards, and it has the right to enforce them. . . . What you did was a more sophisticated variation on what Cantor & Siegal did, and I think you got what you deserved." All of which caused young people in our office to publicly confess in various online forums to their association with us.

But *Wired*'s stature in the Internet community, and *Time*'s stature in the advertising community nearly overnight made advertising part of everyone's plans for the Web.

("What's your business model?" "Oh, advertising.")

Why not? The Web had the *feel* of radio and television and cable broadcasting. Certainly the Web seemed to mirror the competing interests and the lack of clear business models of early broadcasting.

Even "dial-twisting," the practice in the early days of radio of sampling and seeking, was regarded at both Time and Wired as the equivalent of Web surfing. And the assumption was that on the Web, as happened in radio by the 1940s, users would settle into specific habits and favor specific content selections. In other words, the Web would become a predictable world for advertisers—and there is no more important virtue for an advertiser than predictability.

Oddly, I don't remember anyone asking, "What if the Web doesn't become a mass medium?" Or "What if people use it differently from television or radio?" Or "What if advertising doesn't deliver an economical return?" Or "What really is it that makes media, as we know it?" The shared faith that the medium would outlast its own infancy allowed everyone to overlook, or avoid, the most taxing, and interesting, questions.

There was a kind of tutorial going on among the editorial select at Time Warner. Walter was the master. He in turn had sought out almost anyone with an Internet expertise that came to his attention. "We did a Barry Diller," said Judson, meaning that, like Diller, who after he left Fox went on a literal and emotional journey talking to experts in new technologies (from which experience he decided to buy QVC), Isaacson and Judson sought out the experts in the new medium. The Internet savants of the moment included people like Brewster Kahle at Wais Inc., an informational retrieval company; Spry's David Poole, creator of Internet-In-a-Box; and the McGill University team that invented Archie, the search protocol. The fact that each of these technologies and approaches to the Internet would be moribund within the year is, well, Internet irony.

Walter went out to Wired to visit with Andrew Anker, who was leading HotWired, Wired's Web effort. "Walter acted somewhat like an anthropologist or biologist," recalled a HotWired staffer. "Lots of poking and prodding and dissecting of the subject under study. Made some people here feel like lab animals."

Walter returned from his journey of technological discovery to mobilize 1271 Sixth Avenue, Time's headquarters. Overnight "digital" and "cyberspace" became part of the Time lexicon. *Time* ran a series of cover stories about the new digital generation. (It recalled *Time*'s embrace, in 1967 or so, of the counterculture.) Elite editors from across Time, Inc.'s titles were assigned to the Online Content Committee, which in turn reported to the Online Steering Committee. There was a cascade of memos: how *Entertainment Weekly* would go online, a structure for *Sports Illustrated* online, thoughts for a health and fitness node ("node" was a Time word that, fortunately, did not catch on in cyberspace) . . . kids . . . games . . . shopping!

Once the decision had been made at Time to focus on the Web rather than on one or another of the online services—the magazine would still maintain a presence on AOL and CompuServe (the online services thought so little of the Internet that the exclusivity clause in their agreements with various Time, Inc. magazines specifically allowed Internet use)—my job became to explain the technology of the Internet to Time

Warner and to warn, like a forlorn prophet, that you had to create for the
medium and not just slap a magazine online.

For the former, since Internet technology was serious Greek to me, I
had to call up Weird Stan, my friend the data visionary (decamped to
Plum Island, Massachusetts), to get a little lowdown before each meeting
of the Steering Committee.

For the latter, it was easy. I wrote my memos:

"I think we have to face head-on the perhaps uncomfortable circumstance that this audience which has not bought Time, Inc.'s products on
the literal newsstand may not want them on an electronic newsstand either."

And:

"The online medium is not only an information tool but a communications tool as well. To date, its driving engine has been the explosion in e-
mail use and in chat. In terms of system appeal, content may well take a
back seat to . . . functionality. We have to be able to say our service not
only has the following content but does the following things."

I argued passionately: "People don't want to read newsmagazines anymore. They want an application that will read a newsmagazine for them.
If we think television took its toll on reading, trust me, you haven't seen
anything yet. We're looking at this as an information medium. But in a
profound way, this medium is going to represent the death of information
presented in an appealing and literate way." Take that, Walter.

"It's extraordinary. You can say anything," I said to Alison.

"Of course, you're a consultant."

"But while everyone is very respectful of my opinion, they don't particularly listen to me."

"*Hello?*"

"It's interesting but frustrating."

"You don't have to be a consultant. You can do what they're doing just as
well as they're doing it. It's the Web. That's the point you're always making."

"But do I really believe it?"

Actually, this was, at that moment, a sentiment—that the Web was
Gutenberg redux, a democratization of media—that many people in different spheres of interest were starting to take seriously.

Unfortunately, never having created a Web whathaveyou, indeed, there
never having been a successful Web thing (there were no words, really, to
describe what a Web presentation was or what it was supposed to do;
"site," to designate a place, "product" because that was the word used in
the software business, later "channel" in a desperate attempt to recall

television, but never a word to express what we wanted this whathaveyou to do or to be), I could hardly say that I knew how to do it.

Which leads me back to wondering, at this late date, Why did Time Warner become the first major organization, among the first organizations of any kind, to plunge headlong into this medium?

Why did Time Warner choose to start and operate a business based on a technology it had no firsthand knowledge of? What made it assume that its talents were relevant to this technology? Why did Time Warner, with little to prove and everything to lose, want so desperately to be first?

The reason that was often given, and one that seems honest enough, was that Time Warner was doing this to learn. "Technology is destiny," Walter said. While clearly not really believing this, he nevertheless believed that technology was a big factor and could be an interesting advantage for those who knew a thing or two about it.

But the more conventional approach to learning about technology— making an investment in a company on the front lines of this technical development—Time Warner rejected, forgoing its opportunity to be an early investor in nearly all of the initial, and wildly successful, public offerings. Instead of losing $50 to $100 million of its own (and, no doubt many would argue, learning too little too late), it could have turned some relatively modest seed capital into a billion dollars of market value and a position of high influence within Silicon Valley. (In Time Warner's defense, all of these companies were seeking investments at valuations that seemed absurd, at least until the public started buying; then those early valuations seemed like giveaways.)

It was certainly interesting to see a large company plunge so precipitously into a business it knew nothing about. The word must have spread quickly up and down the Silicon Valley peninsula that there was a new dumbest in the business, because a whole series of executives and salesman arrived on Time's doorstep to pitch technologies that would shortly be headed to the ash heap.

Conference rooms filled up with highly intelligent, well-educated, nicely suited-up Time editors and executives who listened intently and gullibly to presentations from networking companies and search engine companies and hosting facilities.

Granted, it was impressive how quickly and comfortably Time men picked up the technology terms ("html," "routers," "frame relay") and lingo ("drill down," "achieve ubiquity"). And disconcerting, because I had seen them go from zero familiarity to conversational expertise in a matter of weeks; it was a Ponzi scheme built on talking the talk.

Even with my scant knowledge, I knew that a mess of plans were being made on the basis of assumptions about technology that were comically haphazard. It was often a cascade of misunderstandings or knowledge synapses: a wonderful, patrician, 1950s-style *Time* editor having a weighty discussion with the salesman from WAIS, the search software company, and throughout the discussion helplessly confusing the client–server relationship; a determined Isaacson acolyte insisting to a programmer that while something may not be possible now, it would surely be possible in the next twelve months or so ("Wouldn't it?"). They treated technology like a service arm of what they were trying to do. Technologists were vendors; they were like printers. Their attitude toward them was, "We don't have to understand what you do, we just have to understand what you provide and how we work with you." I was worried enough to recruit Weird Stan to come with me to a meeting, a gentlemanly conclave of *Time* editors respectfully giving their attention to a West Coast salesman. Weird Stan's few exchanges with the salesman seemed, well, weirdly inappropriate at the meeting, as though two doctors had suddenly started to operate in the middle of the country club.

Afterwards, Weird Stan took a highly censorious position: "These guys are really fucked."

But technology alone was not going to stop them. Large organizations are used to being dependent on a technology structure that they don't understand and that predictably malfunctions. This dependence is annoying, even frightening, but tolerable because these organizations are not, fundamentally, in the technology business. Likewise, Time Warner did not see itself, even a small part of itself, as going into the technology business. No one characterized Pathfinder as a software product. What would be the point of that? Isaacson, Judson, and everyone else at Time Warner would have openly admitted they knew nothing about technology. Nor did they particularly want to. After all, Content was King. What Walter & Company were going to deliver was a whole new way to access the mother lode of content that Time was producing every day. Who wouldn't want that?

In the fall of 1994, Curt Viebranz announced he was leaving the New Media group for one of the senior slots at HBO. This seemed right. Of all the people involved in the launch of Pathfinder, he seemed the least ready to don T-shirt and cap. He never really talked the talk. His departure left Isaacson and Judson indisputably in charge. Isaacson, in fact, would hold both the church and state positions at Time New Media.

Pathfinder launched in October 1994. It was unveiled at the Time

Warner annual meeting by Jerry Levin and Walter (Judson wasn't there, but his mother, a TW shareholder, was in the audience). Levin pronounced it a natural evolution of Time Warner's plans to be the leader in interactive media. Overnight, Pathfinder became the most popular site on the Web. It had a real audience. It was selling real advertising. Everything about it was real. It was professional, businesslike, managed. It had real executives, it had a growing staff (soon to reach one hundred people), it had professionally written content. It had a sales force! And it had promotion. It had *Time* behind it! It had users. Traffic!

There was an astounding (and, as it turned out, astoundingly brief) moment when it appeared that Time's bet would pay off massively, that Time would tame and own the Internet. This period, the first part of 1995, may have been the most purely optimistic moment in the development of the Internet business. Whatever you were doing, you couldn't do it fast enough. Interest seemed geometric. Every day offered a doubling effect—sites doubled, e-mail doubled, traffic doubled, friends-who-didn't-want-to-hear-about-the-techy-thing-you-were-doing-but-were-now-saying-hey-can-you-show-me doubled.

Judson flowered.

His *raison d'être* was target marketing. At Time, he had gained minor renown for his role in creating the "selective bind-in." (As a magazine headed down the bindery line, it suddenly got your name on it in a customized ink-jet spray and a special ad earmarked just for you—or, in reality, your zip code.) There was no higher calling for a marketer than to create an efficient one-on-one relationship with the consumer. Out of one hundred prospects, one buys. If, however, by using special knowledge about these prospects you can increase that ratio to two or three buyers per hundred prospects, than you've potentially changed the economic basis of your business.

What Judson understood and, quite likely, understood before any other professional marketer in New York, the capital of professional marketers, was that the Internet, with its communication and data properties, would help define the universe of a product's buyers and therefore vastly increase the probability that a likely buyer would buy in some unimagined way.

In a nutshell, this was the fear—the veritable apocalypse—foreseen by the early Internet community.

The devil, though, comes in many guises. There was the Web—which, to true Internet hands living in the world of telnet protocols, s-key encrypted passwords, and ftp sites, was a vulgarity ("Why do you find pictures necessary?" Weird Stan kept asking me) and easily shrugged off as irrelevant to the real Net. And then there was Bruce Judson himself. He was so boyish and enthusiastic and eager to please and likable (in his too-big suits, he seemed a kind of vaudevillian tramp on Sixth Avenue) that, well, what the hell, sure, go ahead, if Bruce wants to do a little marketing.

Within a few months, Judson goes from being an executive without a computer on his desk to being an Ivy league (Dartmouth and Yale Law School) Ziegfeld for the Internet. There's not a conference he doesn't speak at. Not a technology executive he doesn't know. Not a marketing or technology reporter he doesn't harangue. Not a marketing group he doesn't preach to: Interactivity is the future; strange and wonderful new capabilities and economies are coming to the marketing business. What's more, his sheer manic energy, a geeky kind of energy, him sweeping along in his flapping suits . . . talking . . . talking . . . so excited he can't keep from interrupting you . . . "WHAT? WHAT?" he shouts in your face . . . are just perfect for this incredible thing that's happening, exploding.

For Walter, Content is King.

For Judson, marketing is, well, democracy.

It's 800-numbers, it's catalogues, it's one-on-one.

With this perception—seeing the Web as some kind of direct marketing solution, a medium that can cut the cost of a response—the scramble began. Suddenly there was a sense of what people were doing here, of what the pot of gold was going to be, of how the geeks would be moved out and America moved in.

Judson, representing Time, perhaps the most respected media company in the advertising business—followed close behind by *Wired,* the new hot magazine (there is little the ad industry likes better than a "hot book") representing the digital generation (there is nothing the ad business likes better than the word "generation")—told the marketing community that a kind of direct-response heaven on earth was close at hand.

The potential here was boggling lots of minds. Every consumer, in theory, could become a distinct entity in cyberspace. "Clickstream" began to be the metaphor. We would be able to follow a consumer's every click of the mouse! We, as marketers, would have that information! This was holy grail stuff! The rah rah was a little like what the advertising business must have felt after the war, with the coming of television.

Suddenly, you would have been hard-pressed to find anybody but some old fools who didn't think the future of marketing was in interactive media.

Big brand names flowed into cyberspace—AT&T, MCI, Ford, Club Med, Chrysler . . .

What's more, for a lovely moment, Time Warner pretty much controlled 100 percent of cyber advertising budgets.

By spring 1995, certain analysts on the Street were ascribing an independent valuation to Pathfinder, which had yet to earn a real dime of revenue, of $300 to $500 million. And as a stand-alone business, Judson said, spinning it out, the market would give it a premium value as a pure play (that is, as a business not compromised by any influence or strain beyond the Internet) of possibly a billion dollars.

"*Spin,*" I said, "is the word." But he wasn't listening to me.

Oddly, I became the voice of moderation and concern.

Success in advertising is built on two fairly immutable factors: (1) the number of people the advertising medium can expose to the advertisement and (2) the propensity of those people who are exposed to the advertisement to act upon it (to take up "the call to action"). Without reasonable measurements, it was of course impossible to say how many people were exposed to an ad on the Internet—or even how many people were on the Internet. By early 1995, though, a numbers game had begun in earnest, with Internet promoters (including myself) accepting and passing along the exaggerations of other promoters (the *Wall Street Journal* turned claims we made up on the spot—absolute, if well-intentioned, fabrications—into very authoritative-looking charts). The gap between the claims and the reality were easily as high as forty to one. That is, the commonly ascribed number of people with "access to the Internet" was forty million, while the real number of people who could access the Web was probably no greater than one million, and perhaps half that. The second element of a successful advertising business—the propensity of those seeing the ad to act (i.e., to buy)—was sorely compromised by the lack of actual consumers in the group of users. It would be reasonable to argue that in 1995, there were very few, if any, innocent consumers online. More likely, most people using the Net were people who thought that maybe *they* could get rich from the Net.

Interestingly, claims versus reality did not lead to a crushing credibility gap. This was partly because the world of the Net was expanding so quickly—today's lie so often became tomorrow's fact—and partly because the people who would have most questioned the medium's credibility couldn't use the medium and so acquiesced to what they were told about it and partly because there was this belief that no matter what problems and issues arose, technology would offer better and better solutions.

"The Internet is the single most important development in communications in this century. It not only combines radio, television, and telephone but dwarfs them and has begun the process of making them obsolete. The

Internet is changing our lives, and we can look forward to it changing our economy," I said with great rectitude, addressing an Internet conference in early 1995.

Why did I say this other than the fact that I could get away with saying it? Not that it wasn't possibly true. But it was true like astrology. New technologies *are* advances over old technologies. Our habits and behavior change in response to those advances, which, in many instances, change the economic focus of the time. What was wrong was not the sentiments expressed, but the attitude—a revivalist certainty that caused people to be reborn in cyberspace.

Still. On the one hand there was the juggernaut of momentum (a band-wagon which anyone could get onto without regard to skills, experience, and personal hygiene) and on the other hand these fearful balance sheets.

The people at Time especially—and Judson particularly—knew the economics of businesses that sold advertising. And they knew that for the foreseeable future, if ever, advertising as the sole source of revenue could not support online content. Simple.

"Mostly," said Judson, "the people who think they can build advertising-supported businesses have never sold advertising before."

The solution? Simple, too: as it does with the more than fifty million magazines it produces every month, Time would not only sell advertising on the Web but charge for content, too. Without that assumption it is un-likely that Time Warner would have agreed to launch a business that, sup-ported by advertising alone, had no chance of ever achieving profitability.

The assumption of subscription income was not unfounded. AOL and CompuServe and Prodigy, after all, charged users for their content. On-line service bills for active users could average as much as fifty, sixty, sev-enty dollars per month. Time was talking about magazine subscription rates, a few dollars a month. Who wouldn't pay a few dollars a month for the mother lode of Time's content?

The Pathfinder plan called for limited charges to begin in early 1995. There had been initial resistance to even free registration, however, and this first deadline was allowed to pass (other efforts to register users, no-tably at HotWired, petered out, too). September '95 was the next goal.

This is where a little chaos theory sets in. The chaos breeds two impor-tant outcomes:

1. In its rudimentary form (and all sites were rudimentary in 1995), it is so cheap to produce and mount a Web site, and so easy to do, that a once-barren landscape becomes Los Angeles overnight. Time's Pathfinder, which is now running at the staffing size of a weekly magazine—and pay-ing Time Warner salary and benefits—finds itself competing with thou-

sands of self-created and self-funded Web producers everywhere and finds that users are at least as interested in, and certainly more charmed by, these amateur sites.

2. Because no enterprise has found the formula to create a profitable business, this failure, oddly, inspires a host of others to try. The thinking (my own included) goes something like, Hell, if that's success, you can't fail. Indeed, the worst that will happen is that I won't do it any better than Time Warner does. A further mutation of this thinking went something like: A company with the opposite attributes of Time Warner would succeed, i.e., a start-up company without experience, capital, or business know-how to hold it back. The "logic" then almost becomes "Time Warner can't do it; therefore, I can." Between Pathfinder's launch in October '94 and September '95, a new generation of companies is born to compete with Time on the Internet, including Yahoo, Excite, Infoseek, and CNet.

Having to fight for audience share, Time allows the September '95 subscription deadline at Pathfinder to pass. This means that for its first twelve months of operation, running at an annual cost of more than $10 million, but less, I am told (perhaps not so reliably), than $20 million, Pathfinder will have revenues of $2 million. In 1996, it will look to achieve total revenues of $4 million, with its costs exceeding $20 million. With no plan for how to charge its users, Pathfinder is now formally a business without a viable business plan. This becomes clear to greater and greater levels of senior managers throughout Time Warner.

▬▬▬

I pick up a rumor in early 1996, filtered through the West Coast, that I immediately report to Judson.

"I hear Walter is leaving," I call Judson and say.

"Not possible. Where did you hear that?"

"Middlingly reliable source," I say.

Judson calls me back at the end of the day: "I just spoke to Walter and he categorically—cat-e-gor-i-cal-ly—denies that he is leaving."

"Well," I say, "if it's a categorical denial."

Judson ruefully compliments me on my sources when some time later the announcement is made that Walter will leave Pathfinder to become the managing editor of *Time*. Paul Sagan, who started NY1, the all-news channel in New York, and is often described as Walter's consigliere, will take over at Pathfinder.

The most sophisticated analysis says that Time Warner management has gotten Walter out of harm's way. You don't want to waste one of your key stars on a vehicle which, it's clear to accountants, can't succeed. (This could be overanalyzed, of course. It's just as logical to assume that the *Time* job opened up and, of course, Walter had to take it. Perhaps.)

What if Time's interest and belief in the Internet is waning? What does that mean?

Well, cyber mania quickly turns this into good news:

In the death star battle between the East Coast (content) and the West Coast (technology) for the soul of the Internet, the East Coast's most significant planet is imperiled. Time Warner, the King of Content, has failed to make it on the Web. That means the technology players are ascendant.

It does not, in fact, mean the technology players are making more money, or losing less money, than Time. It does mean, however, that their money is different from Time's money. West Coast capital is a technology play. Technology investors can rationalize losses in a way that Time Warner's investors can't. Technology money follows different assumptions than content money. Technology money believes that for a more or less extended period a lot of different entities and approaches duke it out for market share, which leads to market dominance. The dominant player then provides a historic return on investment to its investors (there are often positive outcomes for the losers, too, as the industry and products consolidate). Content money is of an altogether different mind-set and experience. Content, by its nature, doesn't usually dominate a market: Stephen King, no matter how successful, won't force all other fiction writers off the shelves (exceptions to this include local newspapers with monopoly positions, which have higher profit margins than even the software business). Content is also a business that tends to be driven by hits instead of by market share dominance. With content, what you see is what you get. The weekend grosses or the response rate on a mailing or the advances at Barnes & Noble or the position on the *Billboard* charts usually don't lie.

While the Internet on the Time Warner balance sheet looks only like a black hole, at Microsoft, which will lose significantly more on the Internet than Time Warner, such losses appear to be the key to the future. Go figure.

═╍═

Walter's departure takes place, relatively speaking, still in the nineteenth century of the Internet. The Internet is still a business that has the feel of, well, businesses as we're used to them. You build a staff. You build a customer base. You invest against a more or less predictable outcome. If you do your job well, *you* do well.

But it begins to be clear by the start of 1996, with the growth of the Web sweeping away all prior assumptions, that something different is happening. Anyone who has lived through twelve months of the business is beginning to understand that it's not an industry based on a developmental model (i.e., we will get better and better at our job) but an industry based on radical obsolescence—what you are doing now will be meaningless tomorrow.

We begin 1993 thinking the information superhighway will be based on set-top boxes and services accessed through the television. The year isn't finished before it's clear that the interactive future will be spearheaded by the online services, suddenly growing at a fantastic clip. Then, by the spring of 1994 the Web is clearly coming. It's not even referred to much as the Web but as Mosaic, the free, University-supported Web browser that makes the Web visible. Paid online services are, therefore, doomed. Then Mosaic, by the end of the year, gurgles and dies. In the course of several months, Netscape, an improved version of Mosaic with a for-profit software business model, transmogrifies from a start-up company with zero market share to the Model-T of the industry with a near-total market share (i.e., it "achieves ubiquity"). The effect of this is that overnight a widely dispersed, anarchic, unregulated, come-as-you-may audience is now owned by a single company. In some measure, Netscape challenges the original premises that had drawn Walter Isaacson to the medium in the first place—free distribution. It's now no longer a medium without the cost of distribution. The distribution bugaboo is as big as ever, and suddenly there's a monopoly player. Netscape has become the Web's exclusive distributor. The mere fact that when Web surfers open the Netscape Web browser, they open to Netscape's home page means that Netscape holds the power to anoint the next Web successes—and this does not include Pathfinder.

Each of these chapters in the development of the industry, little more than a year old, come to be regarded as something blithely, even affectionately, referred to as a "paradigm shift." In other words, it is not that every few months there's an upgrade or natural growth and progress but that there's an event or altered state that requires you to rethink every assumption about the business—from who pays whom, to if people will pay at all, to the tools that will be used and the language that will be spoken, to the accepted morality, to the fundamental system of organization and governance ("We must keep rethinking our rethinking"). Each of these developments impacts the interactive business in about the same way the atomic bomb affected warfare.

There is the odd time–space synapse whereby if you haven't spoken to someone in a few months, you start to think of them, based on your last conversation, as a dinosaur.

The notion of "Internet time" gets invented to excuse the laggards. After all, who could keep up? "The industry reinvents itself every three or four months," sighed Judson.

Around the time of Walter's departure, they start to say at Time Warner, echoing a favorite Silicon Valley taunt, "If you eat lunch, you *are* lunch."

But, actually, they do eat long, mannerly Manhattan lunches at Time Warner. The software business basis of round-the-clock workers, of an industry built on twenty-four-year-olds without families at home needing attention, of hermetic environments, of a team psychology, of companies directed forward by a weird, cultish rah-rah marketing, is hardly Time Warner.

In fact, what happens at Pathfinder is the exact opposite of the carnivorous, guerrilla, chameleon, reinvent-yourself-every-day approach.

Time and Pathfinder display, well, just about the worst thing you could display in the technology business: ambivalence.

In part it's personality. Paul Sagan, running the show after Walter, is a laconic, bemused, remote leader, perhaps most successful at avoiding phone calls. Don Logan, who runs the Time side of Time Warner and reports to Jerry Levin, and bears responsibility for Pathfinder, is a gruff mid-fifties magazine executive out of Alabama (he ran a company that Time bought called Southern Progress). In a moment of incomprehension and frustration, Logan characterizes Time's interactive ventures to a *New York Times* reporter as a "black hole," thereby sending something less than a rah-rah signal.

And then there is Norm Pearlstine.

Pearlstine joins Time in early 1995, the first outsider to run the church side. Pearlstine is a glamorous and flashy figure—he led the *Wall Street Journal* during the 1980s and managed to give money and business a dramatic persona. Remember how boring business used to be? Pearlstine filled his *Wall Street Journal* with larger-than-life figures and great morality tales. Plus, Pearlstine had married Nancy Friday, famous for her sex fantasy books. Then, too, he was an advocate of technology. When he left the *Journal,* he started a company, called Friday Holdings and backed by Barry Diller, Paramount, and Texas investor Richard Rainwater, to invest in new information technologies. But Pearlstine is also a strangely brooding figure, marked more by doubt and ambivalence than by the certainty and optimism and devil-may-care that glamour usually requires.

It is perhaps his ambivalence most of all that comes to overshadow Pathfinder and Time Warner's plans for the Internet.

When he speaks at the industry conference in Laguna Beach about

Time Warner's interactive future and the threat of Microsoft and the integrity of journalism, he fails to mention Pathfinder even once, sending murmurs through the room.

As other cyber companies make alliances, change their business models, turn from technology companies to content companies and back again, Time and Pathfinder, well, do nothing. In its single largest initiative, a personalized news service, in late 1996, Time Warner goes into partnership with CompuServe; the latter will sell this news service to its users (this is a kind of backdoor way for Time to sell information and secure subscription income). It is, however, a clear dumber dumbest transaction; CompuServe is even more clueless than Time in its understanding of where the industry is heading.

Pathfinder's editor, Jim Kinsella, who is ousted in late '96 in a battle with Judson, is not replaced for several months. Sagan announces his intention to leave "to spend time with his family," and it takes Pearlstine six months to fill Sagan's job. Half of the job is given to Dan Okrent, a longtime Time editor—clearly a vote for Time values over cyberspace ambitions.

Judson wages an all-out campaign for the other half of the job, but Pearlstine fails to make a choice.

In some sense, it is only Judson who is playing the cyber game, who has truly embraced the model of instant strategies and daylong alliances and aggressive publicity (shouting often characterizes a wild marketplace). In fact, he is becoming increasingly annoying to people at Time.

I run into Paul Sagan on the red-eye from San Francisco back to New York. Sagan, a tall, slightly wasted-looking man, has almost a Lincolnesque appearance of humor and homeliness.

"He's very energetic," Sagan says about Judson.

I don't want to hear more. I don't want him to tell me that Pearlstine isn't going to give Judson the job. If I know that Judson isn't going to get the job at Time, I might use that information to get him to run my company.

* * *

The rat-a-tat-tat of cell phone calls from Machinist and Rubin unnerves me. They want to know Judson's answer. For them, a yes from Judson— "I'm ready to join the team"—would be money in the bank. Value would be increased by their casting choice. Judson is bankable.

But the issue is also, Can *I* deliver? It's a performance test. Can *I* make it happen? Because if you can't make it happen, if you can't figure out what it takes, short of indictment, to make it happen, well, then maybe you're not where our money belongs.

I have known, however, all along that I'm going to fail at landing Judson—making him our Barksdale. Either because I don't want to give up my starring role or because I don't want to be responsible for Judson leaving Time for another uncertain world or because I don't want to *make* it happen but, rather, want it to take a natural course.

My ambivalence is perhaps not that different from Pearlstine's and Sagan's and Time's. I'm tired of Internet time. I just want to hang out for a while and see what develops.

Although I know what Judson's answer will be, I'm grateful that I have nothing official to tell Machinist and Rubin. Not officially having bad news isn't bad news. Even Internet time seems to stop, or appreciably slow down, when you're waiting for the other shoe to drop.

"You know," Alison says, "you could really convince him if you wanted to."

"Are you saying—"

"I'm not saying you don't want to convince him. I'm just noticing that you seem just to be letting fate take its course."

"There's no reason for me not to convince him. He stands just as great a chance of losing his job with us as he does with Time Warner. He has a better chance, I think, of keeping his job with us."

"Well, you have to do what you think is right."

"Or, I guess I should say, *we* have a better chance with him of not losing our jobs."

"Will this really get Machinist and Rubin excited again?"

"For about another ten minutes."

"Then what's the point?"

"This is the Internet; a lot can happen in ten minutes."

Then I get the call from Judson. "I want to come over and talk to you," he says.

Well, this is certainly the gentlemanly way.

"I can't do it," he says, arriving in my office.

"I know."

"Do you want me to go through my thinking?"

"No. I think I know it pretty well. Do you want me to make a last pitch? We can revisit the compensation discussion, too."

"No. The money is fine. That's not the issue. I just have to go with where I think my shot is."

"Of course." I tried to rally but, again, ambivalently. "This is my prediction: You may not come to work for us, but you won't end up working for Pathfinder, either."

He wasn't about to disagree.

One of the fascinating things about this business, and one of the things that makes it almost impossible to predict, is that virtually any prediction you make is bound to come true.

Chapter Six

Something for Nothing

"You better be prepared to get skinned," said the factotum, subdued and businesslike on the cell phone (he on his, me on mine).

"Excuse me?"

"You're out of cash. Unless you have someone else who wants to value you, you're at the mercy of the newest money."

"I thought we had a deal with Jon." I tried to remember the exact phrasing of his offer to invest another half million dollars.

"Apparently we don't. I don't. Have you spoken to him?"

"No, but—what does Bob say?" I was taking a break from a sales meeting where I was trying to rally the troops to go into the retail wars and sell our books about the Internet (now increasing at the rate of a new title every twenty days) to the nation's bookstores. The sales meeting was not going as well as I had hoped. These fifty normal working stiffs had only the haziest notions of the what and where and why of the Internet. It was, I knew, imperative that I make them believe! The primacy of salesmen— the fact that nothing happens without salesmen who are willing to sell your product—is something else they don't tell you about in college.

"Bob isn't going to say anything different. This is a banking situation. Unless there's another option, Rubin's new money will dictate the terms."

"But why? He's never indicated he was unhappy. Why would he want to screw me?"

"Well—"

"Just because he can?"

"He's not going to want to pay more than he has to pay, obviously."

"Which means?"

"You're probably going to get squeezed."

"Badly?" I swallowed.

"Until he thinks you'll pop."

"I'm going to call Bob."

"You can always call Bob, of course."

I was confident that Machinist carried something in his back pocket, that "financial engineering" was as much a matter of personality as it was a matter of balance sheet. I called the Patricof office, but Machinist had just left for a rafting trip in France, bonding with the bankers in his Paris office.

I called Alison, who was annoyed by my panic.

"What do they mean you're going to get squeezed?"

"Well, it means . . . I don't know. I guess it means—"

"That we're not in as good a position as we otherwise might be. But does it mean anything more than that?"

"Not necessarily," I admitted.

"Okay, so we don't know what's going to happen. That's what you're telling me."

"Right."

"But you think we should assume the worst, although we don't know what the worst is?"

"Do you want to call the Patricof people?"

I had a clear picture of her sour expression. She found the factotum's inarticulateness, his inability or refusal to entertain an emotional nuance, more frustrating than I did.

"I think I know what we have to do," I said. "I don't think we have an option—"

"We haven't begun to consider what the options are," she interrupted.

"I'm going to call our friends on Long Island."

Silence. Then: "You would do that?"

"I think it's time. I do."

The issues of raising money are broad at first: Is there anyone who will give you anything? And then increasingly complex and subtle: Among the field of bad and worse alternatives, whom will you choose? Or, more accurately, in front of which unhappy alternative will you get on your knees?

I flew into La Guardia and headed out to Long Island for an impromptu meeting with CMP Media, a $500 million-a-year company that, with Ziff-Davis and IDG, dominates the most lucrative area of the publishing industry today—computer magazines.

CMP, whose headquarters housed a couple of thousand people, was in the bedroom community of Manhasset, at a purposeful distance from the glamour-pusses of Manhattan. CMP, which held the distinction of being the largest private company on Long Island (although it, too, would go public before this story is through), got started in the early 1970s and came to specialize in magazines for the travel business—free magazines for travel agents with advertisements from resorts, hotels, and airlines. By the late 1980s, by creating more free magazines, this time with ads for computer hardware and peripherals, the company became another of those improbable and outsized technology industry successes—more improbable, because it was not the success of young techno-geeks, but the success of an elderly Long Island couple, Gerry and Lilo Leeds.

The magazine business has always maintained a hierarchy between consumer magazines, which emphasize editorial content, and trade magazines, which emphasize advertising matter. Successful (or prideful) journalists made their living from the former and dreaded a descent into the latter (you might have to go to work for *Lab Rat* magazine!). Almost no one I know in the mainstream publishing business ever gave a serious professional thought to trade magazines. Computer magazines changed that.

As a young lawyer, Alison was approached in the early 1980s by a company called Ziff-Davis, which, I was of the vague impression, published comic books or off-brand men's magazines (*Gent,* "Home of the D Cup," perhaps). It turned out to publish a stable of magazines for the travel and aviation industries and other magazines for hobbyists and sporting enthusiasts. Against my strong advice—what would we say to our friends?—Alison went to work for Ziff-Davis and promptly helped it go on a buying spree of magazines about personal computers, including *PC Magazine,* bought for pocket change and now among the world's most profitable magazines. (Alison sent in the Pinkertons to eject the existing staff, which then went on to start *PC World* for IDG, one of Ziff's main competitors.)

In 1984 Ziff sold its hobby and trade magazines for almost a billion dollars and ten years later sold its computer magazine properties for nearly $2 billion, making Bill Ziff the most successful man in the publishing business (and putting him among the top billionaires in the technology industry). These sales undermined many of the comfortable snobberies of the magazine business: that fashion, style, and attitude equal money and prestige.

The Ziff formula was to create magazines specifically designed for buyers of particular products. Under this formula, the ads were often more interesting than the editorial matter. With the introduction of the PC in the early 1980s, you had an industry that needed to find a way to reach beyond the small circle of corporate buyers authorized to make big-ticket computer purchases to a new and vastly expanded customer base able to make the decision to spend a few thousand dollars on a PC and printer. The computer magazine was born and became the most successful area of the publishing industry, the main way that the computer industry communicated with its customers.

But by 1994, particularly after the Ziff sale (Bill Ziff was legendary for selling at the top of a market), there was a sense among the three largest computer magazine publishers that the industry was in the throes of a powerful change, that growth in the office market had plateaued, and that the future was with the home user, with families, with women even. CMP launched *Windows* for the consumer market and followed it with *HomePC*. Ziff partnered with Disney on *FamilyPC* (the clonelike nature of computer magazine titles suggests their market share focus, reminiscent, in fact, of girlie magazines—*Leg Scene, Leg Action, Leg World;* when it comes to sex and computers, men buy the category, not the magazine). IDG went after the consumer with its Dummies book series.

While each of these companies had a pronounced aversion to consumer publishing—from the high-maintenance writers you had to deal with, to the press attention you had to endure, to the lower profit margins you had to accept—they also, of course, had a hankering to make it big, truly big. Why not? They were in the computer business. And not just Bill Ziff big (although this was important because they were all keenly competitive with one another. It was not enough to make money; it had to be money that Bill Ziff would otherwise have made), but so big that they could transform their businesses from parochial precincts to household brands. That was the American way (and, perhaps more importantly, the Microsoft way).

Of all the success models in the publishing business—Luce, Murdoch, Newhouse, Wenner, Hefner, Ziff—the most successful was Walter Annenberg, who created *TV Guide* and accomplished the most elusive goal in the publishing industry: a successful mass market magazine. Indeed, *TV Guide* became the most successful magazine of all time!

The Internet was technology in a box through which would flow a cascade of services, entertainment, and information. That this experience would have little to do with television was tomorrow's realization and angst. For now, in early '94, the simple concept of a magazine that saw this new medium as being in need of a programming guide passed for genius. Mine, as it happened.

We had moved out of our downtown space and into uptown offices at Fiftieth Street and Broadway, a formidable media address variously called the Hachette Building or Paramount Plaza (it housed Paramount, Showtime, NBC, MTV, Macmillan, and Hachette Magazines, which published scores of magazines, including JFK Jr.'s *George*), where Alison had a client with vast expanse willing to sublet us some space.

Our elevator rides were filled with MTV gossip and whispers of Kennedy sightings.

The setting was of great help as I tried to convince people that the Internet was, well, media—something not otherwise self-evident.

It is important to remember that a really cool site on the Internet circa 1994 was one with a lot of documents or programs to download.

Internet users, working in ASCII text and UNIX commands, were really very modest in their claims about the medium. The grandest metaphors had to do with community, with town meetings and bulletin boards. No one was saying that the Internet had anything to do with TV or entertainment. (Even if you could, why would you want to turn this into a medium that mimicked television? We already had television.)

The notion that the Net was developing into some kind of organized carrier of entertainment, information, and service programming was, at best, a rhetorical excess. At worst, it was a delusion, but it was an important one because it could be communicated to people who had not been on the Internet. People could easily imagine a hopped-up, heated, tactile, multitasked, controllable version of what they already knew, which was television.

The guide we envisioned—*NetGuide*—completed that metaphor, linking the Internet not only to television but to *TV Guide*.

It was, therefore, extremely important, as we set out to convince the media community of the coming age of the Internet, that we discourage these people from actually wanting to see the Internet. We invented many diversionary tactics, including almost entirely made-up samples of what the Internet might look like one day, or what we thought people wanted it to look like.

Soon, however, after our book *NetGuide* rose to the best-seller lists, Alberto Vitale, the much-feared chairman of Random House, the book's publisher, began to ask probing questions about the Internet, which were referred to me. After many efforts to delay or cancel an inevitable demonstration, or to bring him to our office for a phony one ("Mr. Vitale will want the demonstration at Random House"), I was cornered. We had a new intern, a prep-school runaway whom we were housing in my mother-in-law's apartment because of his UNIX talents, whom we sent over to connect Random House to the Internet. With Random House's top brass shivering in a cold computer room (apparently, still under the impression they had to refrigerate these machines), we projected the Internet onto a movie-size screen ("Mr. Vitale doesn't like to look at computer screens"), where it took a torrent of abuse under Vitale's scrutiny.

"Let me see something. I don't see anything. Is this what I'm going to see? Go to something else. How long will this take? What am I waiting for? How long has this been going on already? You must be joking. Who will have the time for this?"

He wasn't wrong. What he was seeing was not the experience so many people were starting to fantasize about. He was seeing, well, the real thing—text. A grubby kind of government-document-looking thing.

The power and attraction of the Net required a fairly wild leap of the imagination.

And yet the phone calls poured into our office, and the books flew off the bookstore shelves. You could feel the desire. There were Americans out there, American men in love with technology, down in their finished basements, booting up, seeing something in the green screens of cyber-space.

In early 1994, as *NetGuide* rose, unexpectedly, up the best-seller lists, we quickly assembled a plan to turn *NetGuide* into a magazine and online service. Why not? *TV Guide. NetGuide.* Get it? Wow. We proposed, in our plan, to get the magazine off the ground for a half million dollars. We sent out our plan haphazardly—to *TV Guide;* to Time, Inc.; to the computer magazine publishers, Ziff, CMP, and IDG; and to *Rolling Stone*—curious to see who, if anyone, would respond.

CMP's penultimate executives were in our offices within twenty-four hours of receiving the plan. CMP was psychologically a long way from Manhattan and the culture of consumer publishing. Coming into the city from Long Island was not an easy trip for them. It was a journey fraught with calls from secretaries to check on the location of nearby parking garages and calls from car phones to report progress through traffic. The executives were more than an hour late, sweating and anxious by the time they arrived.

Almost immediately, I had the sense—a sense that I would have throughout my sojourn in cyberspace—that there was a gulf between what I did and what the people on the other side of the table did, between what I understood and what they understood. (It was a culture clash, in part, between Manhattan and the rest of the country—a growing problem for me because the technology business is in the rest of the country—but also, I snobbishly sensed, between people in the product business and people in the idea business, between people who sold units or data and people who sold point of view.) I don't doubt that within seconds we knew we were incompatible. At the same time, we had what they wanted, and I found myself enjoying the tyranny of the marketplace, sitting back and re-laxing—and judging. I have touted enough projects and pipe dreams—good ideas and horrible ideas—to have spent a lot of time searching for that moment when a buyer's needs and urgencies are greater than my own. The Internet offered me a vivid demonstration of such an appetite.

Ken Cron, about forty, I guessed, a plump pixie with tie askew and shirt gaping at the buttons, was CMP's chief operating officer, but he seemed more clearly practiced as a salesman than as an executive. He drew his chair close to my desk in some weird combination of conspiracy, ingratia-tion, and intimacy, and I soon learned that he had spent his whole career with CMP, had seen it grow from a fledgling company to an important fix-ture in the technology business, and that while not a member of "the fam-ily" (i.e., the Leeds family, the billionaire owners), he himself, he would have me know, had a vision for where the company was going (and was taking home a seven-figure salary to prove it). CMP was going to be a force in bringing computers into every single American home. Comput-ers, he confided to me, were on their way into every *room* in every Amer-ican home! His number two was a lumbering bear in his mid-fifties with the euphonious name of Drake Lundell and an Ed McMahon avuncular-ity. He seemed more a toastmaster than, as Cron described him, the "cre-ative genius" of the company.

They were a great audience. They had never seen the Internet but were convinced of its charms. Because they published magazines about com-puters, they, unlike executives in more mainstream media companies, were predisposed to the virtues and the inevitability of digital technology. Still, they did not personally use nor did they have any special abilities for technology. They had no real experience, in other words, to get in the way of their enthusiasm. They were at that point in time, for instance, and for several years to come, unable to receive e-mail successfully. But no mat-ter. We were all very self-congratulatory that we all had the foresight to understand that this new medium would be the next television.

"We saw your proposal yesterday morning, didn't we, Drake?"

"We did."

"And, well, open kimono here, Mike . . . or Michael?"

"Michael."

"We've been thinking about something very similar."

"Great minds," said Lundell, "think alike."

"Of course, we never put it together with such flare. Right, Drake?"

"You gave it a lot of flair. It was super."

"We were at a company retreat. Right, Drake?" Cron then lowered his voice: "We were trying to figure, you know, what's the next big thing? We had just launched our *Windows* title. And we beat everybody on that. Everybody got caught with their pants down. Ziff. IDG. *Windows* is the fastest-growing title in the category. So we're sitting around thinking about what's next, and one of the things we came up with was online. We thought online. Not yet. But it was going to come. You have to think like this. You have to think, 'What's next?' You have to think about what's next before everyone else thinks what's next."

"But not too much before," said Drake.

"Not too much before," grinned Cron. "So we started to think about everybody who's getting online. Prodigy. CompuServe. America Online. Internet. It's big. It's going to be very big."

"What about *Wired?*" I asked, wondering how the year-old magazine had affected their worldview.

"Pretty wacky," said Lundell.

"It's not competition for us," said Cron dismissively. "They just got money from somebody, didn't they?"

"Condé Nast," I said, but Condé Nast did not prompt any apparent respect or even, necessarily, recognition.

"Yeah, they're in real bad shape," said Cron.

Wired was some way-extreme techno rock and CMP clearly saw itself as top forty.

They handled the book version of *NetGuide* with both interest and uncertainty. "Where will you sell this?" asked Cron. "Where will people buy it?"

"In bookstores," I said, unclear what they were getting at.

"So . . . like . . . Howard Stern's book?"

As sons of Long Island, I supposed this wasn't an entirely illogical association. But I suddenly had the feeling that they could not have readily named another book.

"Let me tell you a little about how CMP works," said Cron. "When we decide to do something, it's a total commitment. It's 200 percent. We want to be first, and we will spend more money than the next guy could ever dream of spending in order to be first."

This is the credo of the software business. It's a marketing credo. The Microsoft credo.

"Actually," I said, "I wonder if that's necessary here. I think that we have an opportunity to create a magazine that can speak to this new—"

"But what happens when Ziff gets into the business," said Cron rather frantically, "or IDG or . . . even Microsoft? Drake?"

"There's a lot of synergies here." The Drakester bobbed his head.

"This is what I'd like to do, Mike. Let's have you out to CMP. Let's have you take a look at us. Open kimono. Meet the Leeds family. Give you a sense of how we do business."

"I'd be willing to do that."

"How 'bout tomorrow?"

"Tomorrow?"

Undoubtedly, this was the moment when I should have demurred. I should have pulled back because these two seemed like Stan and Ollie to me, or Vladimir and Estragon, and I should have been looking for better partners. But the truth is that it was 1994 and the Internet was not something whose inevitability could be taken for granted. Reasonable people looking at the Internet that winter might not have seen it as the television business, they might have seen it as the library business. Now *there* was a glamorous concept: not *TV Guide* but *Library Journal*.

"They want to do this," I said, immediately calling Alison.

"They do?" She seemed suspicious.

"I'm going out there tomorrow."

"Who exactly do they think you are?" She asked, in a tone that was not entirely flattering.

"I'm not sure they can place us. They clearly don't know from books. And they don't seem to have a good sense of the media community. I think they think we're the smart people and the hip people, which they basically have contempt for, and that they're the practical people." I shrugged.

"Do you think that's a basis for doing business?"

With more than a little incredulity (both CMP and the Internet seemed like odd occurrences in my normal life), I made my first trip out to CMP. Its headquarters, just off the Long Island Expressway, was one of those low, sprawling mirrored-glass office buildings that suggest from the outside little about what goes on inside. This exterior facelessness complemented the company's resolute lack of identity and a decor that was closer to a driver's ed school than to a media or technology company. Its walls were filled with framed awards and honoraria; the covers of CMP's lineup of publications, including *VAR News* and *Computer Reseller News,* and handmade birth announcements and other motivational posters and art-work.

My visit to CMP was at a "State" level. I was whisked immediately into a conference room which, while it could have nicely accommodated to-day's instruction on parallel parking, served as the executive war room, with overhead projectors and white boards.

There the bantamweight Cron, in an open-necked shirt, and the bearish Lundell, in a bulky sweater, were joined by a classically colorless CFO and the heir to all this, Michael Leeds, son of the founders, a slight and sulky man in his early forties with a remarkably full and lustrous pompadour (the heft of the hair made him seem all the slighter).

Leeds, who had grown up on Long Island, not ten minutes from where he now worked, was worth, quite possibly, a billion dollars.

Ten or twenty years from now, I thought to myself, computers will not make ordinary schmoes fabulously rich anymore. But one of the wonders and inequities of America is that if you inadvertently grasp the idea of the moment a moment before . . . well, good for you. I didn't yet dare say, "Good for me"—but I was starting to think it.

"Have you been given a copy of the CMP principles?" asked Leeds.

"We'll give you a copy to take with you," said Cron, trying to hurry the conversation off this point, I thought.

"Actually, I noticed them on the wall," I said ("Be a great company to do business with," etc.).

"You can ask anyone," said Leeds. "We adhere to these principles strictly."

"It's not just bull," said Cron.

"I think you'll always find that in dealing with us we'll go out of our way to do the right thing," said Leeds.

I nodded.

"Ken and Drake have been telling me about your idea," began Leeds.

"It's really a variation on an idea we've been talking about," said Cron.

"Why don't you tell me why you think it has a chance to be successful," Leeds said in a slightly aggressive manner.

"Have you taken a look at the materials we prepared?" I asked.

"I'd like to hear it in your own words."

"Those are, actually, my words. But . . . I think the opportunity we have—at the end of the day there aren't that many good ideas—but there's one and it's called *TV Guide.* And if you can find that model again, that is, to look ahead and to see what the whole country is going to be doing and to create a guide for how to do it, well—"

"I haven't been on Internet yet," said Leeds. "I'm going to be trying it soon."

"Hey," Cron said, either naively or with interesting calculation, "why don't we go to Mike's office and have him give us a demo?"

"In the City?" Leeds's eyes narrowed.

"It's really not necessary to come in, if you don't want to," I said with a sinking sensation that the jig would be up if we had to mount a demonstration (I thought of the painful experience at Random House).

"I've had it described to me. I can envision it."

"I think we should see it," prodded Cron.

"Sure," said Leeds. "We'll definitely want to take a look." But he clearly had little interest in looking at it, or in making the drive into Manhattan. "It's *TV Guide* for the Internet." Leeds had already convinced himself. "Everybody's gonna need something like that. It's gotta be coming. It's gotta be."

"It's a great idea," said Cron.

"Great minds think alike," said Lundell.

"We gotta do this," said Cron. "It's gonna be great."

The world seemed to be dividing cleanly between those who had no interest in the Internet, saw no logic or sexiness in it, and those who were just dying to believe in it.

"What do you want?" Leeds asked. But that question made him impatient. "Let me tell you how I see this," he said. "It's 1967. Mossad has just picked up rumors that Egypt is planning a first strike. Israel's response is unequivocal, overwhelming, decisive. That's the way I want to get into online." Anger flowed off of him.

"There's a lot of synergy here," said Cron, diving in. "We have a lot of leverage in the market, and you have a really well developed concept. I think we want to take the next step. We ought to decide if there's something we want to do together or not. If not, nothing lost. You'll do your magazine, and we'll do ours."

A hollow threat? I thought. That must mean something.

Leeds took me on a perfunctory tour of the CMP executive office area. He was an uncomfortable person. His facial expression moved from pained smile to a brooding scowl. People stiffened when he passed. Then, in a gesture whose significance I did not immediately understand, he brought us into a room where some desultory festivities were in progress around two miniature, carefully preserved elderly people.

"You're going to meet Gerry and Lilo, the founders," whispered Lundell excitedly.

And on the first date, I thought.

"Mom. Dad. This is Michael Wolff. He's working in online. Like Prodigy. We're talking to him about a concept."

I smiled. "It's a very exciting concept."

"Speak louder," said Leeds.

▄▄▄

They wanted to see something.

An ever-growing CMP delegation arrives in our office the next day with the same flurry of parking questions and apologies about the traffic. The delegation includes an executive assigned to the project and another new business development person and a chief technology officer, plus Cron, Lundell, the CFO, and Leeds.

The top executives—indeed, the whole top management layer—of one of the fastest-growing information companies in the nation gather around our Macintosh and scrutinize our hundred-dollar FileMaker Pro database (as rudimentary a program as you could pull off the shelf), into which we had haphazardly recorded a few thousand newsgroups, gopher addresses, ftp, and telnet sites. And they are dumbstruck. Notionally, they seem to believe that we have somehow blocked out the parameters of the Internet, that we have captured the Internet and bottled it. And they want it.

It is a condition I have come to recognize. If you have the money, if you are a buyer, then you want to own something. The fact that the Internet is not ownable is an annoyance that few buyers are willing to accept. They know there must be something they can buy. In the age of the Internet, many Brooklyn Bridges will be sold.

"What about sailing? Can you show me something about sailing?" says the Drakester.

"What about Porches?" Says one of the execs excitedly.

"What about skiing?" says Leeds.

Skiing it is, as we pray that we had entered something—anything!—about skiing into the database. Bingo. The newsgroup rec.sport.skiing pops up, which has everyone awestruck.

In part, this is charming. It is a wonder-of-technology tableau. Men at play. What they are seeing for the first time is the stark wonder of the medium, that anyone can access information about anything. On the other hand, it is unnerving. The Internet is as new to the technology industry as it is to the rest of the world.

Over the next week, CMP sends to our office the range and breadth of its brain power: its technical teams, its marketers, its outside consultants.

Then one fine day, Alison and I, with a $125-per-hour car (leather-upholstered Fleetwood) and driver, set out for the glass headquarters on Long Island to talk a deal.

I knew I was going to get rich.

I was not sure, though, what I was going to get rich for. Would I get rich for being a visionary? Or would I get rich for being a charlatan?

I was, alternately, giddy and embarrassed.

A life of fairly conventional ethics and ambitions had not prepared me for this.

Fuck 'em.

Our proposal was reasonable and straightforward: we were looking for partners to provide the capital to develop a magazine about the online world. We saw this magazine as having both a print and an electronic side, it should be represented on the literal as well as the virtual newsstand. I was not, in fact, thinking I could become Annenberg with this notion—hardly. I thought that the audience for this magazine was mostly made up of young men who were pioneering a fairly exclusive world of their own idiosyncratic design and that the magazine should be much less *TV Guide* and much more about a world that few people had access to—noir, sexy, new . . .

What CMP had in mind, on the other hand, was a magazine that would make the Internet safe for families. Indeed, they had no idea that it might not be the safest place for the whole family. Through the morning, I hinted and prodded at this cultural dissonance. It was hard, though, to communicate this divergence without insults. It is hard to tell people who are not sexy that they are not.

"It's a mass medium. Everybody will have Internet. Everybody will have to have Internet . . . like television. The magazine, *NetGuide* magazine, has got to have wide appeal," said Leeds, the believer.

"Yes and no," I counseled. "There's still a lot of subtleties to the medium."

"Netiquette," said Lundell. "That's kind of good online manners. People on the Net have made it up."

"Well, that's a good article!" said Leeds.

"I'm not sure you want to create a magazine about the Net for people who don't use the Net."

"But they will," Leeds said, sold.

"There's an interesting thing that happens with the Net. As soon as people start to use it, they become experts. So I don't think you want a magazine that isn't, well, cool."

"They all say 'cool' on the Net," said Lundell.

"You guys, for instance," I said playfully, "are not cool."

No one smiled.

I hurried on: "One of the virtues of working with us and of letting us create this magazine is that we have, I think, a feeling for this community, this sensibility." I was trying to find nonfighting words to tell them they were ploddingly square, dull, uncool.

"The essence," I said, "of a magazine like this is to get inside, not to be looking in from the outside."

"They hate you," Alison analyzed during a break in the meeting, after our steam-tray lunch.

"Why would they hate me?" For a second, I was honestly taken aback.

"You keep implying that the Internet is only for a certain kind of person, and not them."

"Well—"

"This is not high school. This is business."

"Fine. What do you want to do? I don't even know why we're here then? Why don't they just kick us out?" I asked petulantly.

"They think you know the secret of cyberspace."

"Then why don't they listen to me?"

"They don't want to listen. They want you to just tell them the secret, and they'll pay you."

"All right, let's just tell them the secret and go home. Let's sell them the Internet," I said getting up to leave.

I got one of Alison's baleful looks.

They filed back in. They were no longer salesmen. Now they were businessmen, deal-makers, gatekeepers of the family's fortune.

"I'm assuming that we should get to some ideas about the structure of a relationship," said Alison in her best practical approach.

There was a collective hesitation on their part, a mutual clearing of the throat; they meant to present a corporate consensus.

"What would you sell everything for?" said the CFO, clearly the appointed spokesperson.

"What is everything?" Alison asked deliberately but with some interest, as though this were fundamentally a philosophic question.

"The relevant assets, to be defined," said CMP's lawyer.

Alison was measured in her response. "This comes as somewhat of a surprise. And, honestly, I don't know if such a possibility might or might not exist. As you know, we came here looking for a partner. But to the degree that we can separate out certain relevant assets, essentially the intellectual property related to this concept, which might include database assets, trade and service marks, goodwill, and other concept materials, I suppose it might be possible for us to value that defined asset pool."

What she had just described, what she had just drawn a cordon around, was, as far as I could tell, absolutely nothing. There were, really, no assets. Unless they thought we could sell them the Internet. In some way, that *is* what they thought. We would sell them the right to start a magazine about the Internet, which right they obviously had before we walked in. We would sell them, Alison seemed to be saying, some outdated site lists.

It was very hard to know how to respond. It was scary almost—lest the moment go away, lest the moment be real. We had gotten the wrong change, a twenty instead of a one. Should we confess?

"Would you care to value that?" the CFO prodded.

I felt the pressure of Alison's shoe on mine.

"I don't frankly know if there is even a number at which we'd consider a sale. Even assuming there is, I'm not sure it's appropriate at this point to cast this discussion in those terms. We are looking for a situation that will allow the natural appreciation of value. I would doubt that you would be interested in fully valuing our concept-related assets at this point," she said.

"Well, try us?" pursued the CFO.

Again I felt Alison's shoe.

"Listen, if you have something in mind, let us know," he continued.

"Hey, this is just getting everything out on the table," said Cron. "Is there a number that you'd take?"

"Sure!" I blurted out. "Ten million." The stab of Alison's heel was instant and sharp.

The CMP side countered with sober looks.

"It would be my recommendation," said Alison, "that we adjourn to consider this. I think you should think about whether an outright sale of assets is the only way in which you're interested in proceeding. And I would advise that you consider this carefully, because it may well not be an option from our point of view. Likewise, we will do some serious soul searching and some careful numbers crunching."

"Why would you have said that?" Alison walked swiftly through the parking lot to the Fleetwood.

"Ten million? I'll do it!"

"You said ten million as clearly an exaggeration. That's your outside—and obviously a wild exaggeration at that. So what's really your number? That's what they're thinking. Considerably less than that."

"But what are we selling them?"

"The name. They think it's *TV Guide*. They do. They think it's the same thing."

"They don't really think that?"

"They do. They really think that by owning the name they will own the product."

For a second, I waffled. "Maybe they're right."

"Oh yeah. For sure. *TV Guide. NetGuide.* Quick, go tell Mom, *NetGuide* is here."

"All right. All right."

"And the database," she considered. "I think they want the database."

"The database?"

"Yes," she said with more confidence.

"What? That? Are you crazy? You think just because you call it a database it's worth something? In my day we used to call it notes."

"I think that they think it's worth quite a bit."

It was an oft-stated conceit or threat of large capital-plentiful businesses that they could afford to make mistakes, that, in fact, the process of doing something right was as much the process of doing something wrong. No industry seemed more to take this to heart than the software industry. The very notion of upgraded software had created a profitable business structure for trial and error. If you could confidently enough maintain the position that all mistakes, like all technology, were transitional, then the consumer (in a remarkable number of instances, it had been proven) was perfectly willing to go along.

What we were seeing, too, and getting ready to become a part of, was an entrepreneurial business structure designed to service this willingness for making big boners, this appetite for failure. The combination of salesmanship and technology was a sure recipe, if not for disaster, then certainly for a good con.

"They know nothing about any of this. And you know next to nothing," Alison said, struggling hard with the absence of reason. "It does appear, however, that we can sell them the next to nothing we know for a lot of money."

It paid, of course, to be married to a lawyer versed in the new alchemy of intellectual property.

Alison began the nimble and painstaking process of constructing a legal reality for assets that did not, in conventional reality, exist. What is the Internet? How do we define it? How do we describe it? How do we contain it? Those were the business and legal issues. It was also a rather complex philosophic issue (how can you tell the dancer from the dance? If a tree falls in cyberspace . . .) that reflected profound discomfort with the notion of form and its substance and property and ownership. Who owns the air-waves? was a popular question of the 1950s. That question has various legal, logistical, and philosophic answers. The question of who owns the Net is not reasonably addressable from any of those points of view. It is more akin to who owns the body politic, who owns the atmosphere, who owns the excitement of the city.

Technology companies need to own something in a way that media companies do not (not that media companies wouldn't like to, but their arrogance is of a different order). Even as technology companies have moved from hardware and code out to the much more loosey-goosey world of well-turned phrase and singular point of view, they've sought to colonize and govern. The industry is, for instance, paranoically obsessed with confidentiality and nondisclosure agreements. At Starwave, the Seattle-based Internet content company started by Microsoft cofounder Paul Allen, the guest name tag that you sign and affix to your lapel during your stay is also a broad confidentiality agreement and assignment of rights to what you've thought and discussed during your visit. From the technology-world point of view, the babble of the media world, the idea community, with its gossip and exchange of ideas in public places (i.e., restaurants rather than office cafeterias), is undisciplined, indulgent, and even self-destructive.

If technology companies owned the newspapers (and, not impossibly, one day they will—although I wouldn't bet on this outcome), they would not be entirely happy until they owned the town, or at least the shopping areas. It is not at all a secret that the competition among technology companies on the Internet is to own the network itself. It is perhaps the natural insecurities of most nascent industries—railroads, movies, oil, long before software—that make them monopolistic.

At any rate, like any self-respecting technology company, CMP needed to come away from their relationship with us owning something. It was not enough to share, partner, discuss, relate, enjoy one another's company, learn from, license. They had to own. So one of the largest technology publishing companies in the country, with the aid of White & Case, one of the largest law firms in the nation, was about to pay me a wonderful seven-figure sum (a movie-deal number), and in return I was going to give them, well, nothing.

I genuinely believe they thought that they were buying the Internet from us, that our FileMaker Pro database was in some way a treasure map, that if you had that, it was like having bought the experience of navigating the jungle without having to endure the bugs. Without the experience of the medium, it was almost impossible to fathom that the known world of cyberspace at that moment would be wholly remade the next moment. As for the simplistically magical name, which had begun in our office as somewhat of a joke—an exaggeration, certainly—it seemed a cruel irony that *Net* would become among the most generic prefixes of all time.

In fact, as we came to the final hours of making a deal with CMP, it turned out that the name was not ours to sell, that a consultant in Massachusetts was happily doing business at the address netguide.com. We quickly (with the mock innocence of this game: "This will be a hardship, but I guess I might be able to give you a little something for what didn't cost you anything") paid a few thousand, against our imminent fortune, for the address.

"This is not a normal situation," Alison said of the CMP deal with an almost reverse paranoia. (Because they were acceding so much to us, were we therefore acceding even more to them?) We had been left alone in one of the many paneled conference rooms at White & Case, sandwiches and coffee thermoses on the sideboard, the thousands (literally) of document pages on the long conference table. "We're going to leave here with everything we had when we came in."

"Plus a check."

"Yes, plus a check. This is so bizarre."

"You're getting me worried."

She considered. "We're selling them an off-the-shelf database containing information that they have, in theory, inspected. In fact, they've had a whole payroll of experts to inspect it. The fact that this information is or will soon be entirely out of date is not our responsibility. We're selling them a name that may soon be functionally generic, and, at the same time, we're preserving our right, obviously with their agreement, to go on using the name anyway. What's more, it appears that we have the right to use online anything they develop. In addition, we can compete with them in any way we like. We can, if we want, use all the money they're paying us to compete with them."

Our unease was mounting.

"But these are good lawyers at White & Case," Alison said, clearly rationalizing.

"What's so good about them?"

"They're doing a deal which is a straightforward transfer of intellectual property, which would work if we were talking about anything but the Internet. It just doesn't work here. Things change too quickly. Stuff can be replicated so easily. The business model is so . . . well, there is no business model. There's going to be a zillion deals like this," she said.

"Just think," I said, warming to the moment, "how many stupid people there are in this world who we can take advantage of."

"But they don't stay stupid."

That was hard to believe, however, as they filed back into the room.

They certainly seemed delighted with the results of their deal.

"We enjoyed doing business with you," Michael Leeds said. "I hope you agree that we follow our principles. If you ever need anything—anything—we want you to come to us. We'd love to do business with you again."

I confess to enjoying a brief moment of omnipotence. It felt like God had given me one. For free.

Now, here I was, two years later, back at the driver's ed headquarters.

I felt somewhat like Cool Hand Luke, briefly free of his bonds and now recaptured and waiting for the reprisals of the guards. Michael Leeds was the sadistic warden. Cron and Lundell were the trusties, shuffling and glum.

In the year and a half or so since our deal, CMP had spent as much as any company in cyberspace, with as little to show for it. They had spent a reported $15 million to $20 million on *NetGuide* magazine and had failed to catch anybody's imagination; they had lost as much as $10 million more trying to build a bridge from print to online. (What's more, we had competed with them every step of the way: our books had competed with their magazine and our Web products had competed with their online guide.)

In the course of its oh-so-brief life, the Net had become as vast as, well, nearly life itself. The two years had been like one of those fast-action movies in which all of human history is expressed in a minute of film. The Net was exaggerated and comical like that. To reflect that experience in a monthly magazine you had to offer Web sites. The problem was that these Web sites—and there were thousands upon thousands of them . . . hundreds of thousands . . . millions!—were not at all the point of the experience. Content was not the thrill. Content served as the signs on the highway or perhaps the view or the rest stops, whereas the experience of driving was altogether something else. The thrill was action, motion, control, freedom at the wheel.

"We're not a hype company, and it's all hype," said Cron, resigned.

"It really helps to have an attitude," said Lundell.

"Together we could have been Yahoo," said Cron.

"I'm not sure Yahoo is Yahoo," I said. "I'm not sure anyone has found the secret yet."

They seemed to perk up at this.

"To my mind, you have an unstable audience without learned behavior or ingrained habits. It's like someone dropped down in the middle of New York City," I said. "Or in the middle of Moscow. Straight from Dubuque. Nobody knows what they're supposed to do, how they're supposed to act. So it's not so easy to fit them into a commercial model."

"When we did the deal with you, we really didn't know what we were doing," said Cron.

Everything about them looked beleaguered. "Well, who did?" I shrugged. "Who could have predicted any of this? Our deal became absurd the moment after we signed it. It didn't—it couldn't—anticipate a whole sweeping evolutionary continuum. You know what I'm saying? How could we have predicted human beings, speech, civilization, culture, technology, the whole goddamn twentieth century. You know?" They looked at me hoping, it seemed, that I would have some answer, but beyond that they were still confused. "And the interesting thing is that the game hasn't even begun. This is warm-up. Nobody who is here today will be here in the same form tomorrow. Everybody will evolve into something, some form, that meets a whole new set of demands. It is, I'm serious, the first day of the rest of our lives." I really thought I could just whip them into shelling out another cyber-size sum.

"Mike is right," Cron said to Lundell.

"How honestly can I speak?"

"Open kimono."

"If we got together on this," I said, lowering my voice and peddling harder, "it could be an incredibly powerful combination. Just think about this. What you have and we don't have. What we have and you don't have. Putting that together. It boggles my mind. Let's think about this. Just for a moment. Okay. Putting your Internet assets together with our Internet assets. We would instantly create—instantly—the greatest Internet information company on earth! No question. Pure play. Then we roll it out to the public. Conservatively, what do you think? I'd say, conservatively, three hundred million dollars in a downmarket. And easily, on a better day, six hundred million." It was as though Machinist and the bankers had taken possession of me. I was their medium. I felt, suddenly, that my real interest in this whole business was the verbal excess, the total ridiculousness in which perfectly reasonable people would become complicit.

"Not impossible by any means," Cron said.

"I'll put it on the line," I said. "We've had a great year. Nothing in my life has ever prepared me for what I've experienced over the last twelve months. You remember that handful of people in our office? Now I look out the door—seventy! Cyberspace is a wonderful world! But, of course, I don't have to tell you, expansion is costly. We all know that. I have a group of investors who are very supportive. I couldn't have better partners. They're not only first-rate guys—true professionals—but they bring such experience, such real savviness. Invaluable, truly invaluable. At the same time, of course, I can't expect them to finance us at the level that this industry is burning cash. We are looking for a second-stage strategy now. Clearly, you are, too. I think the time is now for us to look at our common goals and natural synergies."

Cron and Lundell looked at each other. It wasn't hard to imagine that they were looking as much as I was for salvation. Inside CMP, I'm sure, Cron and Lundell were being blamed for the curse of the Internet. Indeed, there had been a whole generation of executives wiped out at CMP over its ever-deepening Internet hole.

"There is an interest on the part of the family in taking advantage of the public market," said Cron carefully.

For a second, I thought this was curious. If you had a successful privately owned company, why in the world would you ever want to be a public company? Except to make a fast buck, of course. If everyone else was turning dross into gold, come on!

It certainly had been a surprise to them, I imagined, that start-up companies, with no background, experience, or goodwill in the technology business, suddenly had all this money from the public markets to compete with a solidly profitable, responsibly run, good old-fashioned half-billion-dollar-a-year company like CMP.

"Together we can raise the money to go to war!" I exulted.

Lundell looked down.

"Michael Leeds hates you," Cron said heavily.

"What?"

"He blames you."

From Cron's defeated look, it seemed evident that I really had left a blood score in cyberspace. "He feels you took advantage of him."

"How could I have taken advantage of him?" I gamely tried to play the innocent.

It seemed futile, though, to protest. Everyone knew that I had taken advantage of him.

It was almost a commonplace now that all cyber transactions were a case of someone taking advantage of someone else. Clearly, if you buy something sight unseen, untried, untested, unknown, the chances are good that you'll get screwed. Many people were even ready to admit this was part of the game—no hard feelings, sucker. Still, I would not want to explain such a thing to my parents if they owned the company.

"Michael Leeds doesn't believe there is any business to do on the Internet," Cron said wearily. "He sees having to be on the Net as a necessary evil." Cron shrugged.

"What about Israel?" I said. "The '67 war? The first strike?"

Neither Cron nor Lundell were in the mood, though, to recall past enthusiasms.

The first dozen or two times when you get turned down, even when you're ready to beg for the money, it's a crushing blow. After that, you start to realize that somewhere out there is a bunch of money that wants what you want but doesn't know as much as you. Finding it is the job. Michael Leeds, unfortunately, in his short education in cyberspace had learned some bitter lessons.

On my way back into the city, I returned the factotum's call.

"How did your meeting go?" he asked.

"I think we have something. It was very positive."

"Everybody is waiting to hear. What should I tell Jon and Bob?"

"Well, I'm going to want to work this through a little longer. But I definitely think CMP is interested."

Chapter Seven

A Working Relationship

It works this way: Money comes into an entrepreneurial company in what's called a preferred position. The entrepreneur and employees and other founders receive common stock. The money—the professional money, the venture capital—receives preferred shares. These preferred shares have a lot going for them. They get their money back first, plus a rate of return (100 percent is not out of line), before anyone else sees a dime. Take an investment of $3 million. Sell the company twelve months later for $6 million. Preferred shareholders take all. In addition, the preferred shareholders often have a veto over raising new money. In other words, if you need more they can give it to you—on their terms.

So the cardinal rule for an entrepreneur with preferred shareholders is never to raise money when you *need* to raise money; instead, raise it when you can be choosy, blasé, nose in the air.

We knew that we would run out of cash early in the fall of 1996. Our plan, after all, was to spend as fast as we could. To buy into the market. To purchase "mind share." We're coming! Nothing can stop us! Believe it!

What we didn't know was that the Wired IPO would fail and that the market for Internet stocks would turn down. And that our principal new Web product would fall behind schedule. Of course, we should've known, should've assumed, should've, should've, should've. But you want to wait to see what the market is going to do before you make your plans, and you want to wait for the product prototype to be done before you're out with the round. And, of course, bankers go on vacation (or on rafting trips), so you have to wait another week or two or three before the revisions on the private placement documents get turned around. The industry moves at Internet time, but the world moves at normal, maddening, sclerotic real time.

Two days before the end of the month, we received from Jon Rubin's attorney (indeed, Jon Rubin's father's attorney, Jesse Meer) the paperwork that would provide us with the funding we needed to meet the next payroll.

Instead of an additional $500,000 to be supplied on relatively the same terms as the initial investment, as I could have sworn we had agreed, it was in fact $150,000, supplied in such a way as to give Jon Rubin and his family control of our company.

There is that watershed moment, part illumination and part sinking sensation, when you suddenly realize what game you have been playing.

In a controlled monotone, Alison recited the various draconian provisions of the agreement:

We would lose our seats on the board.

We would have no say in any sale or disposition of the company.

Jon Rubin would step into the company as chairman.

His technology advisor (the nature of whose influence over Rubin was endlessly debated), who had sat in our office, sphinxlike, all these many months, would join the board and effectively exercise day-to-day operational authority.

As Alison and I considered the end of the world, new desks were being brought into the office for the new employees who continued to arrive on an almost daily basis.

"There's so much anger here," Alison said, holding her hands to her face in a Munch-scream pose and applying something less than a legal analysis. "I think it's Jesse. Really, he's in control."

Rubin seemed as connected to his lawyer as I was to mine. You could not be sure to whom you were talking, whose ideas were really being proposed, and who really, in the end, had the final say-so.

Certainly, at first glance, Jesse Meer was an odd soul mate for his fashionable, technology-minded client. Early on, in an interesting bit of byplay, Rubin had said he was going to be represented by Wilson Sonsini, the hottest Silicon Valley law firm. Instead, Jesse showed up. He made it clear that he represented not just Jon but Jon's father, too, and that neither he nor Jon's father was at all enamored with my deal.

Jesse was from Brooklyn. He had a trodden face and wore artless suits. He reminded me of some of my uncles (and not the more successful members of the family). My impulse was to reach out, to bond with Jesse rather than his slicker client. But the least challenge to his authority just got you this inexplicable, sudden, and, it appeared, uncontrollable rage. Jesse's face came barreling into yours, you glimpsed teeth frothy with spit, and you caught the full force of some really scary threats—what he would do to you if such and such happened, what the consequences would be if you even thought in such and such a fashion—and always a little reminder of whom you were dealing with in case you had forgotten ("You better find out who you're dealing with").

His firm, on West Forty-fifth Street, handled garment industry clients, like Rubin's father. This was a tough-guy firm. It specialized in intractable situations: "get what you can," end-of-the-day meltdown situations.

"I'm reluctant to get involved with them." Alison had said when we first contemplated a deal with Rubin in early 1996. "In an ideal world, I'd walk away from this deal because they're here."

At the time, I barely registered her concern. I wanted the money. It was not an ideal world.

"He has aggressive lawyers," I had said. "But Jon seems all right, really. They're the lawyers. What can you do?"

Lawyers seemed like in-laws. While you might not be able to avoid them, you didn't have to sleep with them.

"There are four possibilities," Alison said now, deliberately, handling the papers as though she were a pathologist holding tissue samples. "This is a spasm of anger on Jesse's part, and Jon hasn't even seen these documents yet."

"Is that the most optimistic?"

"Or this is part of a strategy to force the common shareholders out, and realize some plan beneficial to the preferred holders."

"That sounds like the worst case."

"Or this is the first shot in a negotiation, a garment-business style negotiation."

"All right."

"Or Jon's father is calling the shots. And he's saying as much fuck-you to Jon as he is to us."

Just then, Ann—our children's English nanny, whom we had turned into our office receptionist and who would not be paid in two days' time if we didn't solve our present problems—put her head in to say, "Mr. Machinist's office."

"Mr. *Volff*," Machinist said on the speaker phone with strident jocularity in his hale and hearty alumni voice. "*Ve've* stubbed our toe." He liked to pretend he was some sort of German-Jewish eminence.

"You have these papers then?"

"No one ever said it was easy being an entrepreneur," he trilled.

Alison pushed the mute button on our end of the speaker phone. "He's going to throw you over."

"How are we going to respond?" I asked Machinist.

"How are *you* going to respond? You have counsel present?"

"Yes, I'm here, Bob." Alison leaned into the speaker.

"Listen, Bob," I said, reasonably, even affably, chalking this all up to a procedural snafu, just a bit of a misunderstanding or maybe a little jockeying for position. "What I would like you to do is to try to convey to Jon that he's overreached in a serious way. I think you should tell him that Patricof will pull out of the deal if he persists in this grab."

Alison frowned; my naïveté was unbecoming.

"I don't think we're in a position financially or ethically to do that," Machinist said with some formality.

Alison reached over and muted the phone again. "You got it, right? They've just given notice that they're not on our side anymore."

"Hey, there's no way I'm going to sign this deal. I mean I hope you know that, guys."

Silence. They were muting their side.

"Listen," Machinist said, cutting back in, "we all want the same thing. We all want to protect our investments."

"Bob, we're looking at losing all of our protections, every last one!"

Alison gave me a signal to get a grip; now, she indicated, was not the time to let it blow.

"Well, I would say that you have to look at the realities of securing the cash resources to allow you to arrange the further financing of this company."

"Bob," I said evenly (I hoped), "under these terms I'll resign."

"I wouldn't say that," he said with a kind of forced and practiced calm, as though I were out on a ledge. "If I were you, I would not threaten to resign. No doubt, the options become significantly different if we determine that this company has a loose cannon for a CEO."

"I'm a pissed-off CEO."

"If you're going to act against your economic interests, I think it's reasonable to consider you a loose cannon. I want you to consider your options very carefully. I want you to consult your counsel and decide what you think is important, what you want to go to the mat for. Then we will come up with a reasonable response. I don't think anybody disagrees that this is an aggressive document."

"Jon Rubin for you," said Ann, just as Machinist was hanging up.

"Take it," Alison said. "But don't tell him I'm listening. Can you do it? Are you okay?"

I wasn't bleeding. "I think so."

"Tell him you haven't read the papers through yet."

I pushed the speaker. "Hello?"

"Michael? Jon."

"How are you? Where are you?"

"I'm on my way to the airport."

"Are you heading to L.A. or coming to New York?" I pursued, envying and trying to imagine the freedom of his mobility.

"I'm coming to New York."

"Are you heading to the office or to your apartment?" I asked, as if I could solve all of our problems with unending itinerary talk. He had recently bought what sounded like a baronial apartment on Gramercy Park (he had described to me the wood wainscotting throughout the apartment in loving and monotonous detail).

"I'll be home. Michael, you're going to get papers from Jesse regarding the loan you need—"

"Yes, I've gotten them," I said as though without any concern at all. "I'm just starting to look at them. Thanks for getting them up. I'll try to look at them tonight."

"What I want you to understand," he said sternly, "is that these documents outline the only deal I'm in a position to offer you. This is not a proposal. This is not the beginning of a negotiation. This is not open to discussion."

"Jon—"

"Michael, I want you to understand where we are," he said deliberately. "Where *you* are. You've run out of money. You've fucked up."

"Jon—"

"I want you to go over this with Alison, if you feel that's necessary. And then I want this to be signed by the time I get to your office tomorrow."

Alison made a draw-it-out, get-more-time signal, as though directing a live talk show.

"Jon—"

"I just want to make sure you understand this."

"First of all, Jon, as I think I mentioned to you," I said, taking a little umbrage while I wildly grasped in thin air for a delaying ploy, "Alison's father"—I made this up on the spot—"is having open heart surgery tomorrow morning, and I, frankly, don't know if I'm going to be able to get her to look at this."

"Michael, you may have to call another lawyer then. I'm very sorry about Alison's father."

"I'll be honest, Jon. I don't know what's in these papers, although, of course, I know the deal that we've been discussing, but I'm a little concerned about what seems to be an abrupt adversarial turn in our relationship."

"Michael. I didn't call to discuss our relationship. Whether our relationship is good or bad is not relevant now. I'm in a business situation that I did not and do not want to be in. I am not a credit card. I am not a bank. I am not a member of your family. You should have understood that before you ran out of money." He was giving muffled directions to his driver.

"Let me look at the papers, Jon. I'll let you know what I think."

"Michael, I need you to understand that what you think is not of any consequence to what is going to happen. You should know that, and I hope you can appreciate it."

I was calm and collected—feeling some new reserves of strength, in fact—but, I noticed after I hung up, bathed in sweat.

"Nice touch, open heart surgery," Alison said glumly.

We were on the brink of disaster, just as we stood on the brink of success.

We had rolled out our new and improved state-of-the-art Web "product" just a few weeks before.

It was the culmination of nearly two years' and more than six million dollars' worth of shifts and turns and reversals in the industry.

It was based on a hard-fought analysis, involving many Internet generations and business lives, of how the Internet would organize itself and grow and envelop the mass of consumers.

I was wrong in my analysis only about half of the time.

For a long while I had believed that connectivity—that is, where your modem dialed to get you onto the Internet—would be the central organizing principle. If you owned the server, you owned the audience. Therefore, obviously, if you wanted to be somebody in this business, you better start an ISP.

Connectivity, I had presumed through 1994 and early 1995, would be organized at a local level because the consumer would only be willing to make a local call and because the price of entry into the connectivity business was reasonable for small operators at a local level. This would give way, I logically imagined, to a form of regionalization: if you were operating in Manhattan's 212 area code, it was easy enough to put a POP (point of presence) in North Jersey's 201 area code and in Long Island's 516 area code. After a while, of course, we would see a rapid form of consolidation. Major players would begin to emerge—nationals and regionals.

It would be, I had thought, a service game. Value added. Consumers would choose a provider of Internet service on the basis of the ease and reliability of its connection to the Net, the availability and affability of its service personnel, and on the other ways the ISP could add value—exclusive arrangements with particular content providers, friendly and compelling guides, contests no doubt, and a range of other helpful features and come-on gimmicks.

I wasn't really wrong about this. My screwup came in thinking that this would take ten years to unfold, whereas in actuality it took just about twelve months.

My notion had been that we would offer connectivity in the New York area—a flagship locale if there ever was one—and develop programming ("content") that, in what seemed like a perfectly tried-and-true television model, we would syndicate (that is to say, rent) to other ISP systems, most of which would be run by techies without the skills or interests to develop content of their own.

Rich from our CMP deal and with remarkable optimism and innocence, we set about building an ISP in the fall of 1994. If I had once questioned why Time Warner would so blithely plunge into a technology it knew nothing about, I never once paused to ask myself, as technically disinclined as the next fellow, what *I* had in mind. The motivation, I now think, was that seeing the future with what appeared to be greater and greater clarity, I just had to go there; anything else seemed like rank cowardice. To be told that you don't have the wherewithal or talent or temperament to deal with the mechanical world is not something that an ambitious American, accustomed to a lifetime of transparent technologies (after all, I can work a computer, and my wife and children can certainly program a VCR, even if I can't), would willingly accept.

Weird Stan said he could build me an Internet provider system. He wasn't happy about it. Nor did he believe that the average American belonged on the Internet. But, technically, he could do it. If that's what I wanted.

Determined that our system would be as technically proficient and as physically stable as possible (when West Coast companies go public, they have to disclose that they sit on top of geological fault lines that could destroy their infrastructure at any moment), we established our servers, after long negotiations, in a secure communications facility run by one of the hottest fiber-optic telephone companies in the country, on top of the

New York Stock Exchange overlooking Wall Street in downtown Manhattan. It had the perfect ring to me. I could hear the old radio announcers: "Coming to you from our transmitters atop the Empire State Building . . ." Now it would be "From our servers at the New York Stock Exchange . . ."

Anyone who has ever conducted a business that is even remotely dependent on a telecommunications company, a long-distance carrier, or one of the RBOCs (*Are-boks*, like Reeboks—Regional Bell Operating Companies) has stories of pain and frustration mounting to murderous rage rivaled only by, well, one's own family. There's no way out of the dysfunction.

The slick, humming, clean, climate-controlled, fire-proofed wonder-of-modern-technology "facility" we had rented at ground zero of efficient, triumphant capitalism turned out, in fact, to be a dusty, hot, garbage-strewn, just slightly oversize closet, with a cage surrounding our servers. The "support personnel," were off-the-waterfront guys blowing smoke (literal and otherwise) all over our Sun stations and Cisco routers.

For four months Weird Stan sat in the "cage," tinkering, storming, cursing, belittling, and then finally producing a system that could do, well, a lot—but not everything. Like bill our customers. It couldn't exactly tell us how much people owed. But that was okay. As long as we had something. It was okay because the opening of the system was six months overdue and for the last four months our six employees had been fielding calls from people who wanted to sign up for the expansive free offers (15 HOURS FREE!) we were advertising in *Wired* and in a variety of computer magazines.

Robert, our office assistant, whom we had hired out of a Long Island delicatessen (The Deli Button) because his mother had gotten me on the phone ("He just needs a chance"), had developed a whole new sense of corporate inefficiency and remoteness, which he communicated to our prospective customers. "Yes, I understand your frustration. I'll pass that upstairs. The final date hasn't come down to us yet. No, no, I'm not privy to that information." There was no upstairs. Robert sat directly outside my office, staring in at me all day, waiting for word that we would actually begin to offer Internet service.

In my short, unhappy life in the service business, I quickly came to hate customers.

The personal neediness, the demanding nature, the vast stupidity, and the predictable obnoxiousness of the American consumer were only part of the problem. The other downside of the service business was that none of this technology worked. At that time, the process of getting an ordinary human being connected to the Internet was so fraught with misunderstanding, breakdown, and sudden death that I find it painful to contemplate that this wilderness crossing, as fearful and as heroic as if it were made in a Conestoga wagon, will soon be forgotten as the Internet becomes merely another plug-and-play appliance.

Our tech support was Otis, a three-hundred-pound somnambulist who spoke at a ten-word-a-minute rate; Benoît, a twenty-four-year-old ninety-eight-pound self-styled digital intellectual with an ardent belief in the Internet and distinctive body odor; David, a Jewish nationalist in matted beard and sandals; and the other David, the one who was living on my mother-in-law's sofa, a runaway from the Choate School. It was a sitcom without a laugh track, burning my money at a 24-7 rate of inexperience and incompetence (on the part of both provider and user).

As fast as I thought it, the industry went from start-up to consolidation. Jim Gleick, a journalist colleague whose phlegmatic ambivalence and lack of interest in business made me look like Donald Trump, had developed a New York–based ISP system called Pipeline that, relatively speaking, was easy to use. It worked, sort of. And in less than a year managed to attract ten thousand customers or so. We had talked about joining forces, about working together ("Why should we both be hassling with this technical stuff? Why don't we just make one system?"), but Weird Stan would have none of it. "He's fucked. He's not Web compatible. He's gone." Weird Stan's assessment turned out to be largely true, but before Gleick got buried by the Web, almost the second before, he sold Pipeline and its ten thousand customers to PSI, a company buying systems around the country, for a reported $25 million. Ah, so.

My thinking was still (is still) this: if you don't have a real relationship with your audience, like somebody actually buying your book or your magazine or paying to sit down and watch your movie, then what you are doing is a lot more like street theater—mimes and jugglers and whatnot—than it is like the publishing or the entertainment business. That's why connectivity seemed important to me; it was an actual relationship rather than just a virtual one.

Still, I couldn't stand the hassle. The relationship with the consumer was too codependent. It was a mess of inadequacies; nothing was straightforward. Even the payment thing. We were each trying to hoodwink the other: I'll sign you up, hoping you'll forget about having signed up and racking up charges (aka "the health club model": you pay for it, but we count on you not using it). And on the other side: "Hey, I'll take your free time, then someone else's, then someone else's again. Then I'll come back to you, and if you do manage to charge me, I'll just complain to the credit card company, which knows that you're screwing somebody over, even if it isn't me, so I'll get the benefit of the doubt and Amex will void the charge."

Enough.

The other part of my analysis, that we could extend our content to other systems, was being hit by another market development. Contrary to the belief that Content is King, content was losing value every day. Content was just an ordinary schmo. There was a glut. Nobody had to pay for content, or license Content. Nobody had to hire writers and producers. Nobody could compete by offering content. Content was pure common denominator. All content was available to everybody through all systems.

Still, stubbornly, I couldn't keep myself from believing that if you had content that was smarter, funnier, and just plain easier to understand than the next guy's, cyberspace would eventually beat a path to your door. Free content was fine and the Web was charming, but you weren't going to get clean sentences or good jokes without paying for them. I was sure.

And I knew the competition. And they didn't know anything about writing a clear sentence or a strong headline or telling a funny joke. They really were nerds.

We were talking to the kids from Architext (later called Excite). Nice kids. They had a search program, which they would demonstrate for you until you begged for mercy. They had Kleiner money. We had numerous discussions about combining forces. They would supply the technology, we would supply the content.

If we didn't want to do it with them, they threatened in an entirely non-threatening manner, they'd do it themselves.

"We feel we can do, you know, content," said their marketing vice president. "Like, the guy we've hired. He was the editor of the *New York Herald Tribune*."

"Excuse me?"

"Ah . . . he's . . . yeah, I think he's the top editor."

"You do know, don't you, that the *New York Herald Tribune* has been out of business for thirty years?"

"Ah, no. I didn't know that. Hmm."

"You should maybe check his references—or his age."

Well, yes. That was the moment, or at any rate one in a series of confirming moments, when I decided to go for broke.

By taking investors, getting involved with Patricof and Rubin, I decided, we'd be able to take a set of New York skills—how to convey information in an efficient and appealing manner—and compete with the software companies, which were at the forefront of colonizing cyberspace but had no narrative skills and little sense of style and charm.

Of course, we had to solve our technical problems, Sisyphian in nature, too. In New York, as technologically backward as a European city, finding people who understood and who kept up with the nuances of network technology was not terribly likely. The Internet industry was dependent on a knowledge base possessed by no more than a few hundred people. That base now had to be turned into an intelligence pool that could service the fastest-growing industry in the nation. You had to find someone who knew someone who knew someone who had been at the Media Lab at MIT or Livermore or Cern.

Ah, the techies. The developers. The programmers. The project coordinators. The sys admins. The Webmasters. Who are they? Where do they come from?

Partly the answer is that they are nobody and come from nowhere. They are twenty-five or twenty-six or twenty-seven. Rubin's technology advisor, for instance, had gone to film school; the technology advisor's lieutenant had answered mail for the Clinton–Gore campaign in '92. Techies are quite often unusually smart, cleverly adept, and unnaturally dogged. But they are unformed. They should be in graduate school. Or interns. Instead, by default, they become the brains of the operation. With technology people you have dorm clothing and dorm living and eating, the junk food and dirty T-shirts, but then you also have a quality of earnestness and a tendency to take oneself so very seriously, which results in, among other things, a type of literalness and stultifying sentence structure, as well as meetings and hierarchies and team spirit that have a political youth camp quality.

Communication was clearly the problem. Like all technology people, ours told us they could do whatever we wanted done. Occasionally, they would say some problem was "not trivial," but they never said "impossible," never "not within my talents," never "not this century," never "not worth the time and effort." Literally, whatever we asked for could in fact be done, given the right circumstances. Unfortunately, whether it could be done on our budget and on our timetable was not what we had asked.

"You don't understand," I said to the technology advisor. "When I say something has to be finished, it has to be finished."

"Nothing," he replied quietly, beatifically, "is ever finished."

Still, we made it. Our grand Web site launched. Not on time. Not in another month, as promised. Not even the week after that. Not on the never-ending succession of new lines in the sand that were crossed so many times that the whole notion of credibility—them for the job completion, me for my threats—had long since been eroded and jettisoned.

Still, it launched. Not entirely finished, of course. Personalization features did not really personalize much at all. The World's Greatest Content Management System was a tad bit slow. The Most Advanced Database System Operating on the Web was a little too complex for everyday use. But we'd clean that up in version 1.1.

In fact, it was beautifully wrought. Your Personal Net it was called. YPN. It was certainly among the grander, if not most grandiose, Web sites of the moment. There was nothing on the Web that began to resemble the kind of coherent editorial vision that we had created. Designing a Web site has more in common with designing an airport terminal than it does with, for instance, creating a magazine. It is all about ingress and egress, about routing and traffic flow, about efficiency and convenience. Ours was clearly not a product created just by software kids but a product built by people who knew a thing or two about how people read and why. It was far ahead of everything else in the medium because it was proposing to tell its users just what this new medium was good for. What it would do for them. How it would save them time and save them money. It was a kind of city magazine. The Web was an undifferentiated urban sprawl; we proposed to differentiate, to offer judgments, to civilize, to make sense. We weren't offering a software solution, we were offering a relationship with our readers. Your interests are our interests, we were saying; we know you don't want to have to trudge through all this data and technology. Enter *Paris* in a search engine and get back six hundred thousand matches; while that might impress someone who was in love with computers, we figured it would only irritate someone who was going to Paris. We were proposing a solution. We were proposing to have actual normal people—intelligent, too—help you get this thing to work.

It crossed my mind, as I thought about Rubin and his ultimatum and his efforts to seize control of the company, that this was the perfect time, with the work done, the system built, the product brought to market, to squeeze out the founders (i.e., me). It was, potentially, a brilliant business move.

But at the same time that I was full of pride for what we had created, and possessed by a bit of paranoia that agents were plotting to take it from me, I was also uncomfortably aware that we might have given birth to a big beached whale.

The fundamental assumption of what we had created was that people needed and wanted a planned environment, a proscenium, a formal sentence structure.

Secretly, I thought I could be out of touch. People, perhaps, aren't waiting to be spoken to anymore. They want to hold their own conversations.

On the other hand, who knew? What existed today would not exist to-morrow. It was an extraordinary existential business environment. The real job was just to keep the cash coming while you shifted with the paradigm.

═══

"We need to meet the payroll," Alison said at breakfast. She had been up all night and was surrounded by legal pads and Post-it notes. "And we need to deal with Jon's demands. So our first challenge is to try to separate those two things. Because we'll lose the company if we meet the payroll by meeting Jon's demands."

I was glum, defeated, exhausted by a sleepless night, a huddled figure at the breakfast table.

"Will he risk missing a payroll," she said, hyper with scenarios, "and risk the possibility that missing payroll will have an immediate effect on the value of the company?" She continued to analyze, maniacally.

"He's wondering, of course, if we'll risk that."

"His risk is greater," she stubbornly surmised. "He has an IPO coming up. He's trying to get this First Virtual thing off the ground. He's not going to want a big public mess with us." She paced. "We need to get that money into the bank today. Obviously. But how can he expect you to sign this if your lawyer's father—your lawyer and your *wife's* father, for God's sake," she said dramatically, as though it were true "is having open heart surgery? How could he?"

"Maybe. Maybe I can pull it off." I nodded, thinking of how to play the sympathy card. I actually thought I could do it. Maybe. "But if push comes to shove, I mean, if we can't get him to wire the money without signing this, do we sign?"

"I don't know."

By 10:00 Jon Rubin was making his politician's sweep through the crowds in our office. He'd surprise the junior staff with a word and sometimes a touch (he was a back rubber), have a stilted conversation with several Mac crunchers who had been at Brown when he was at Brown (they, however, were formatting Quark pages while he was investing millions), ominously huddle with the new EVP, and spend twenty minutes behind closed doors with the technology advisor before finally making it to my office.

I had arranged to have Ann ring my phone as soon as Rubin shut my door. The phone now rang on cue, and I motioned Rubin to stay—we were partners; I had no secrets from him—as I conducted my "conversation."

"How long has he been in now?" I asked in a subdued tone.
Pause.
"What did the doctor say if it went beyond four hours?"
Pause.
"What kind of brain damage?" I asked, my voice rising in alarm.
Pause.
"Listen, calm down. Let's just wait." Pause. "I know." Pause. "We can't make any decisions until we've spoken to the doctor and options have been laid out." Pause. "Just stop it. Take it easy." Pause. "I know. Listen, Jon is here. Let me talk to him. I'll get over there right away."

I turned to Rubin: "They think my father-in-law has had a stroke. Jon, I'm really sorry. I have to get over there. Listen. I don't know what to say. Shit. We need to get that money into the bank today. Alison has some minor comments on the agreement, but obviously we're going to do what we have to do. You know that. I cannot get her to talk to you or to Jesse today. It's just not going to happen. But I think it's crazy for us to miss payroll. We'll have seriously compromised ourselves. Obviously, it's your decision. But I would ask you to make this money available today. And I'll give you my word that we will do what we have to do in terms of this agreement. I'm really sorry. I just—I really have to go. This is one of those times. To say the least."

I regretted the satisfaction I was taking in his cornered look, because I knew my advantage would be awfully short-lived. And yet a reprieve of any duration feels very good. Happiness is just the remission of pain.

"Michael?"

"Yes?"

"All right. I will do this. On one condition."

"Of course. Anything."

"There won't be any misunderstanding. We understand each other. This is it."

I nodded solemnly.

How many fairly grievous lies had I told? How many moral lapses had I committed? How many ethical breaches had I fallen into? My rationale would surely be that I had been brought to the document, pen in hand, at virtual gunpoint. Whatever I had said, whatever promises I had made or representations I had fudged, were coerced. So fuck it. In addition, like many another financial conniver, I was in a short-term mode. With just a little more time, I thought, I could make things right. I could pull it off. Just one more day. True, I was about to forever alienate our main investor. That could not be good. On the other hand, it could not be helped. And now I had a month to get rid of him.

⌐▄⌐

I played telephone cat and mouse all weekend, using my children as perfect buffers. You could not leave a threatening message with a child (on a machine you can do all sorts of threatening), and if you couldn't make the threat, you couldn't act on it, either. On Monday the message being given out was that I was spending the day in the hospital and was unreachable (no cell phones in hospitals).

On Tuesday I was set to appear at a gathering of venture firms; media, communication, and technology companies; and other investors at a hotel in midtown Manhattan. It was a financial beauty contest. Promising companies, such as ours, were invited to make presentations to the investment community. There was a rabble in the halls, then fifty-minute periods, then the bell, then tumult through the halls again. I saw many of the same people who had been at the Laguna Beach conference, but whereas that gathering offered the guise of discussing great industry issues to cover the naked grab for money, this conference pulled away the curtain entirely. We were all here, if we were lucky enough to be invited, to pitch, nakedly.

It was a weird marketplace, a bizarre mating game. It was a morphing exercise. By the process of mergers and acquisitions, we would each turn into something else, partly into one another but, then again, into something further, stranger. This was some kind of cellular process, evolutionary, Darwinian, but absurdly random, too. There were no boundaries. There was a great symbiosis. The outcome would either be predictable— Microsoft hovered at the side—or, as likely, unimaginable.

In the hotel lobby I ran into Seth Godin, the Internet game show impresario who bore the unflattering resemblance to me. I'd last seen him at the Laguna Beach conference.

"Hey, I've been talking to your guy," he said.

"My guy?"

"Rubin."

"Yes," I said neutrally.

"Smart guy. Very sharp. We were really thinking about doing something with him. He really wanted to invest in us."

"He mentioned you were talking, yeah . . ." I was racing to understand the implications, if any, of Rubin having conversations with Godin.

"But we've decided we're going with Softbank on this. But you've got a good guy there. Very sharp."

"Oh. Very, very sharp."

I had a paranoid moment of clarity. If I were Jon Rubin, if I were a boy wonder with millions at my disposal and eager to make my business bones, I'd go after these underfunded companies, get control of them for the price of a preferred minority stake, draw them all together, and roll out an offering. Was that the game I was in?

The lobby was filled with people I knew. I saw Bruce Judson. He was sitting on a panel with Benoît, our aromatic twenty-something, the kid who had been our tech support telephone person less than a year ago but who was now an executive at a major public Internet company. I saw the people from Patricof. I ran into Seth Goldstein (known as "the other Seth"), my twenty-five-year-old assistant who had quit his job to start a company called Site Specific, one of the new breed of Internet advertising agencies. "If you mention me in your speech," he said, "I'll mention you in mine."

Our $40,000-per-month PR firm was everywhere in evidence—silent, eerie women in black suddenly at your side, whispering in your ear.

I saw Jon Rubin with his technology advisor cross through the lobby.

Three or four presentations went on at once. It was a minicompetition. Who would get the audience? I went upstairs to see if we were popular today.

We were doing well. Better than the online sports company in our time slot. Better even, I thought, than the Motley Fools, AOL's hugely successful investment advisors, who were also in our time slot.

I was pleased. Our room was filling up. I knew this crowd.

There comes a moment when you know an industry well enough. You know its personalities, its moods. You're like a good politician who knows his voters, his town.

I had been thinking this through. I had an idea that I could push the electorate. Change their thinking. I had an idea of how to break through. It was an industry that wasn't much more than a year old. It had to be looking for some meaning.

Most presentations were by the numbers. With low-tech slides or overhead transparencies or, for the snappy people, Power Point. CEOs walked the audience through assumptions and projections. It was preparation for an eventual road show. That was partly what the VCs were looking for—

not only companies selling good ideas but companies with showman CEOs. Who can talk the talk?

I dispensed with charts and numbers. I came around from the podium. I showed myself. I made eye contact. I looked for the heart of the audience.

I knew how important this presentation could be and wondered, briefly, if this was my Checkers speech and whether or not it could save me.

I began: We were building an industry on what we—the people in the industry, the people in this room—cared about. We were building an industry not only with technology but about technology. It was an industry that day by day became more inbred, self-referential, obtuse. We had better recognize, if we were to build a consumer business, a new mass medium, that America—my mother, my doctor, my real estate agent, my children's teachers, my insurance salesman—didn't care about technology, didn't find it thrilling, didn't find it endlessly interesting, didn't find it sexy. In fact, quite the opposite. They found it boring. Mind numbing. America, I said heretically, doesn't care about what Microsoft is up to.

As I spoke, the room filled up. The usual-size crowds of thirty or forty grew to at least a hundred. The room overflowed. In a sense, this made my point. People wanted a story. People wanted a point of view. Also, people like to be attacked. They liked the whip.

And I finished:

"In 1945 my father came home from the Pacific theater and found himself in the television business. I grew up on stories of the rise of CBS and Mr. Paley and Frank Stanton and remember the evening Mr. Sullivan came to dinner. Looking back, I realize the enormous uncertainties that must have pervaded that time, but in hindsight what I really see now is a pattern of inevitability. Likewise, in the four years I've been in the Internet business—making me something of a statesman—I can see that the pieces are falling into place in a way that has certainly already transformed my life and business and that will transform all our lives and the workings of this economy before it is finished. In 1949 the total amount of advertising dollars spent on TV was fifty-eight million. By 1955 that amount had reached one billion—that's eleven percent of the total consumer advertising market—achieved on the basis of a sixty-five percent television penetration of U.S. households. Work with me here. When do we reach a sixty-five percent Internet penetration? If we include office access, we reach it by 1998. On just households alone, the year 2000 looks good to me. Let's live a little and extrapolate from that eleven percent figure. That would mean a twenty-two-billion-dollar payload for our industry in the year 2000. That's not including transactions, that's not including subscriptions, that's not including premium services. Just advertising."

My autobiography was as tenuous as my numbers.

"None of this will happen, none of these numbers will be real, if we fail to create an industry capable of speaking to people who don't, and never will, give a damn about how this thing works. Trust me, they have more important things on their minds than what you're thinking about."

Judging by the noise level (the room was near silent) and the direction of all eyes, ahead on me, I guessed that my aim had been true.

Presenters, after they'd finished, were shown into small conference rooms to await follow-ups from bankers, VCs, and CEOs of other companies, who might want to come by "just to say hello," with a business card exchanged like a tip in a hotel.

Expecting to be mobbed, I was startled by the loneliness of my room. I checked the number on the door with the one that had been announced. No one.

"You stole all our business," said one of the guys from the sports online company, good-naturedly, in the next room. "You're hot." But the sports people had a steady stream of important well-wishers.

All we were getting were the foreigners. Europeans two or three generations behind where the business was. They would talk to anybody who would talk to them ("*Cheeberspazio*," the Italians say).

Of course, what was I thinking? I had just told the software industry, self-righteously, preacherlike, that they lacked the ability to command an audience. That they had no people skills. In my mind, I had thought (really) that they would say, "For sure, he's right!" and turn to me. But in the hard light of one of these little rooms, I had a new sense of the world. Software people, quite likely, did not want to be in the software business. They wanted to be in the pop culture business, too. They wanted to go Hollywood. They wanted to wrap America around their little finger. What was the fun of being rich and successful if you couldn't get girls?

Slowly, though, we began to attract a few visitors. The marketing vice president from Excite came by. I thought he was extending a feeler or two ("The next time you're in Mountain View . . ."). There was an East Coast representative from CNet who seemed to like what I had to say. "You were right on. We really have to talk."

Toward the end, as I looked at my paltry haul of business cards, I noticed two last-minute loiterers.

In the mythology of such conferences, it's the people right at the end, out on the edges, hanging back, the people who don't want to call attention to themselves, don't want the competition to know what's on their mind, that they're interested in you, who are the really serious fellows.

The first clerk-like-looking lurker introduced himself as representing Ameritech. The RBOCs are among the most prestigious and most stupid money around. Prestige money, of course, does not have to be smart. It just has to be endless. The more money, the more prestige. Of course.

"We were very impressed by your talk. Are you looking for financing?"

I demurred. "We're looking for partners."

"What we like about what you're doing is that you have a real feel for the consumer. Our customers are not technologically oriented."

"Well, we're a technologically sophisticated company that doesn't particularly believe in the virtues of technology. At least not for technology's sake. We believe that the Internet can succeed only if it can draw an audience. Drawing an audience, holding its attention, making it—" (The first rule of business is just keep repeating yourself.)

"Yes. Yes!"

Then the exchange of business cards.

Still hanging back was an older gentleman. He sprung then, seconds before our time in the private room was up. He was so-and-so, a name I didn't catch, from the Washington Post Company. "We'd like to set up a follow-up meeting with you. Very good presentation. I'd like to have someone call you." Fumble. Card. Mine. His. Exchange. Done.

Ameritech. The Washington Post. Maybe CNet. Respectable. Very respectable.

The game, now, was simple. I had managed to take Rubin's loan without agreeing to his terms; I could not predict the firepower of his response. But if there was a possible deal that emerged from the conference, the preferred holders would be forced to hold their fire. Any disruption on their part would doom a deal. They couldn't throw me out—not yet.

We had precious little time left, though. I wasn't taking Rubin's calls. I was avoiding increasingly strident messages from the factotum, too. There are x days of unreturned phone calls, which can arguably be justified; $x+$ days, which can no longer be justified but which you can cover with a variety of defendable technicalities (sick children, just got in *so* late, etc.); $x++$ days, a period in which all concerned understand that calls are flatly, defiantly not being returned but a period still in which one might cure;

and then, finally, past $x+++$, where you are beyond the psychological point of no return, when an act of total fuck-you is evident. We were now at $x++$.

By avoiding all calls I had crafted a kind of demilitarized zone that was safe and almost restorative.

Within hours, it seemed, CNet wanted to talk. There was a fit, they said. CNet had a vision to which we might lend an interesting dimension. There was a paper compatibility. Worth exploring. Why not right away? urged the CNet execs. (The disregard of the time–space factor between East Coast and West Coast is a bizarre conceit that I kept thinking would shorten numerous lives in the coming years.)

Rubin, growing ever more restive that he couldn't make contact with me, insisted upon attending the CNet meeting.

I got a message: Rubin had booked the rooms for us in San Francisco. Smart, I thought.

I flew into San Francisco with our EVP. It was a pleasant business-class flight. My surmise was that it would *not* be a very pleasant circumstance when I arrived at the hotel. Rubin, with his reservations ploy, had laid a trap. He would be waiting for me. A confrontation was on the schedule.

But he had apparently gotten hungry and left his post, allowing me to check in and go out for dinner myself.

In the morning, I had breakfast in my room. Before coming down to the lobby, I retrieved an e-mail message from the treasurer of the Washington Post Company, who wanted to set up a meeting, and from Ameritech—its investment committee wanted a meeting, too. This was good news. I could use it on Rubin as a sort of tranquilizer dart.

"The Washington Post wants to meet with us as soon as possible," I said to Rubin, firing my dart as I carried my luggage through the lobby. "They seem really eager to talk."

He seemed taken aback—"Kay Graham is a very good friend of the family"—but respectful.

"Ameritech wants to set up a meeting, too. They're really foaming at the mouth! You should see their e-mail!"

He wanted to ask what the e-mail said, I thought, but he also wanted to maintain the chill between us.

The cab ride over to CNet was strained but businesslike. Rubin, the EVP, and I discussed the probable scenarios for the meeting: In the ideal scenario, we'd skip the prefatory dance, admit the logic for a business combination (the deal), and start to talk what-ifs and hows. Barring that, we ought to be prepared to offer a preface that would set out the logic of a business combination. In the worst-case scenario, we'd have to make our pitch from scratch, but, we figured, you don't tell people to get on an airplane because you don't know anything about them.

CNet had built a wonderful stage for itself on the San Francisco waterfront. It was one of those weird reality upsets. Take an office and turn it into a television set. Take a television set and turn it into an office. I had been here just a few weeks before as an interview subject. CNet had created a talk show about technology with a kind of midday sensibility. Television had a weird draw on the computer world. In addition to CNet, Wired, MSNBC, and Ziff were trying to smuggle computers onto television and into the heart of America.

"Good spot the other day," said Shelby Bonnie about my recent CNet appearance. CNet's CFO and largest shareholder was a pleasant-looking young man, affable, forthcoming, networky—and ready, I thought, to make a deal. "Were you given the tour?" he asked me. "Would you like to see the space?" He turned to Rubin and the EVP.

Jon Rubin chatted with Shelby. They both seemed like socially adept young men. Expansive. Knowledgeable. Polished. Why can't everyone be like this? Possessing such smoothness, such ease.

As for me, I tripped on one of those intrusive structures you find in broadcast studios with a thud that shot a skeletal vibration down my back and legs. Assistant producers and key grips scurried toward me. "No, no, I'm fine," I smiled tightly.

Halsey Minor, CNet's CEO, whose talk I had heard at the Laguna Beach conference, brushed past me in the men's room, oblivious to my expression of familiarity and complicity and shared status.

While I had had a natural antipathy for Halsey Minor at the Laguna Beach conference, I was now, given that he had invited me to San Francisco to make me a millionaire at the very least ten times over, strongly predisposed to think of him as one of the industry's real pioneers.

CNet was reconstituting itself as a publisher in this new medium, stealing the ground from under the print publishers. It had invented itself as a publisher without print. It was creating a coherent information brand without the cost and headache of paper and distribution. Sort of.

CNet's play was not too different from ours. It was just larger by a factor. And CNet, too, if it did not reverse its fortunes or raise more capital, would run out of money.

It was odd. The meeting didn't know where or how to start. It was in Minor's office, which seemed too small for how he wanted to project himself. He seemed embarrassed by it, uncomfortable.

I was sorry we were seeing him like this.

We sat in front of his little desk in low-slung couches.

"What do we have here?" he said, looking to Shelby (Halsey and Shelby . . . hmm).

"We talked about this," Shelby said, frowning.

Halsey stared at papers in front of him. "You did the show recently?" he said to me after a moment, as though a veil were lifting.

"Yes," I nodded like crazy. "Good show," I said. "I had a good time."

Halsey looked at his watch.

Just as you can get a sexual vibe, you can get a business buzz. Or not. I knew immediately that something was fouled up here.

I said, grasping, "We met, just briefly, at the Laguna Beach conference."

"Umm."

"All right," Rubin said, impatient.

Everyone looked at him, willing to have him seize the floor.

"You know the company," Rubin said. "You know how we've been trying to position it. We apparently have points of intersection. We may be ahead of you in some areas of development."

"I'm only vaguely familiar with the company," Halsey said.

Rubin almost stamped his foot.

"I'm sorry," Halsey said.

"Did you have time to look at any of the material?" Shelby asked Halsey.

"This? No. Should I have?"

I had been in this meeting numerous times before. I had been in this meeting at Microsoft and AOL and companies up and down the Peninsula. It had a fraternity ambiance and a Mafia social club atmosphere. It was Hollywood style, too. It grew out of a kind of princeliness, a feudal sensibility. "You're calling on me in my lair. I don't think I will even bother to raise my head."

I, the soul of control, affability, and good sense, said, "Why don't we just start at the beginning, and I'll take you through the story of the company and why we think we're going in the same direction that you guys are heading."

"I don't think we have to go through that," Halsey said, making a kind of Windsor-wave gesture. He glanced distantly at our materials. Vagueness seemed like an affect or personality trait of his.

Rubin rose from his seat. From his body language, it was obvious that he just didn't want to be contained anymore. He wanted a higher ground. He was rich, after all. He didn't have to be sitting with us in a sinking couch.

"Listen, this is the opportunity for you guys. If this company is doing what you are going to be doing, then you have the opportunity to buy with paper what otherwise you'd have to pay cash for. You just have to decide if this company has built what you might have use for." He paced.

"Hmm," Halsey said.

"There's a lot of interest here," Shelby said, but passively.

"Great, how do we move it along?" Jon Rubin prodded.

"I don't understand these books," Halsey Minor said, holding up one of our books as if it were a recent and unpromising invention.

Selling out my career and education, not to mention much of civilized history, I said, "You really shouldn't look at them as books but as just another outlet of a content business. We create content. Whether books are an efficient expression of that content is an opportunity that we have to continually evaluate. So far, we've found that books are a successful adjunct to an electronic business."

"Online users of tomorrow are in the aisles of Barnes & Noble today," said the EVP, repeating a line that I'd come up with that seemed more and more sinister in its implications.

"I'm just not sure anybody is going to value books," Halsey said, but he was flipping the pages as though interested. "Books," he said, as though in a private meditation.

"They work," I said.

"It's not going to help our share price. It doesn't make much sense for us to buy your content for more than we'd pay to create it ourselves." That logic seemed crystal clear to him.

"But—" I said. "I mean, obviously we have an audience—"

"It's an audience but it's not traffic. Wall Street doesn't value a book audience very highly."

"And then—I'm not sure, really, that it would be economical for you to try to recreate our content."

"What do you pay for one of these little reviews? What do you use, freelancers?"

"I'm not sure the specific cost per unit is what's really relevant."

But we were gone, I knew. This was not a point of departure that would ever get us to where we wanted to go. Now it was just a matter of getting us out of here with some dignity.

"Shelby wants us," I said as Rubin, the EVP, and I walked through the lobby of the CNet building.

"Halsey's such a prick," Rubin said.

"I actually think there's something here," I said. "I do. Really. I think when they think about it—"

We went out the door into the San Francisco mist.

"Michael?" Rubin reached for and held my arm. "I need those papers."

"Did you get comments from Alison?"

"Michael, I need those papers signed." It was not just anger in his voice. There was panic. He was afraid of Jesse, too.

"I'm ready to sign," I shrugged. "As soon as you're okay with Alison's points. There's no issue here, Jon." I paused. He let go of my arm. "Anyway," I said matter-of-factly, "I'm on my way to San Antonio. I'm speaking to the newspaper editors of America. It should be an interesting conference. I sent you an e-mail about it."

"I want to talk tonight," he said. "Tonight!" he repeated, threateningly.

I was moving down the stairs to the street. "I have a really bad flight. Through Denver and Houston. I should get to San Antonio by eleven or so."

Rubin's car and driver were waiting. Our call-a-cab got there just then, too.

On the one hand, you had to be tough, I thought, to play this game; on the other hand, if you just kept going, not thinking too hard about the implications of any one particular move, it wasn't that hard to play.

My room in San Antonio overlooked the Alamo.

There were half a dozen messages from Alison and another half dozen from the office. Otherwise, no one else knew where I was staying.

"Jon's been calling at least once an hour," Alison said. "I finally just left the office. It's bad."

"Well, how bad?" At this remove, even here above the Alamo, I wasn't feeling very vulnerable at all.

"My guess? He hasn't told his father or Jesse that he gave you the money and somehow didn't get you to sign the papers."

I giggled.

"When he does, that's when we're going to have problems. They'll just be looking for blood. They'll sue us, I'd guess, right away. We could get buried pretty quickly in litigation."

"You sound calm, though."

"We have a little advantage now. Jon will deal, I think. If he fesses up to his father and Jesse, he looks like a jerk. If he comes back with an agreement, even with some important modifications from the original position, he can argue that out on a business basis."

"Uh-huh." I wasn't eager to start negotiating. I was quite comfortable with a straight fuck-you line.

"We can give him an illusory control," Alison proposed. "We'll let him have control of the board but we'll maintain our seats and we'll go for the right to pay back the loan, hence restoring control to the common share-holders. In other words, we will have put him in the squeeze he's put us in. For a hundred and fifty thousand dollars we can have control of the company. It's actually sort of wild," she said. "We'll have none of the disadvantages of control, the responsibilities, liabilities, risks. But we've effectively reserved the right to buy back control at any time with his money."

"And he'll agree to this?" It seemed doubtful to me that he would.

"I'll fax him a red-lined version tonight. I'll really mark it up. He'll go through the roof. Then we'll settle for our two points."

▃▃▃

At their conference in San Antonio, the newspaper editors of America were not looking good. The newspaper business had been savaged first by the broadcast media and then by sweeping demographic changes (young people don't read newspapers) and was now looking at a new information medium coming into people's homes.

It was a cross section of Middle-America that I saw in the audience. Two hundred or so inartfully dressed average Joes. They had a far different look from the software groups and technology business audiences I usually found myself in front of. The newspaper editors lacked an edge. They seemed to be looking for a way not to be noticed whereas those other groups were strictly a "shine that light over here" bunch. Newspaper people had fallen way behind the technology curve. Their management, fat on monopoly profits, had no incentive to make the investment in the resources that technology demanded. It was a sad state. Newspaper editor was a job alongside schoolteacher or bank teller. It was a small-town job, underpaid, underskilled, inexorably being downgraded from profession to back-office function.

I was pleased to be able to escape my own problems for a moment by addressing theirs.

After my talk, ·explaining why they would all soon be toast, I stepped from the symposium out onto the lawn and switched on my phone to call the office. Instead of sending, I opened the line and got the factotum.

"Where are you?"

"I'm in San Antonio. Where are you?"

"I'm in the office. I've been calling you nonstop. There's something wrong with your phone, I think. I've been trying to get you since yesterday."

"I'm in the middle of a panel discussion," I said, "about the future of newspapers in America. Not a very pretty picture. There but for the grace of God—"

"We have a problem."

"We do?"

"You took the money," he said censoriously.

"No," I said with pointed innocence. "I didn't take the money. It was wired into our account."

"You have to sign those papers."

"That's sort of the point," I said calmly. "I don't have to sign those papers."

"That's completely unethical!"

I blinked in the Texas sun. This former Drexel Burnham investment banker, now a managing director of one of the most hard-nosed investment firms in New York, whose office I had sat in for the better part of a year listening to the ins and outs of how to get the better of this or that fool, was telling me I was unethical. "Isn't it wonderful," I said.

"I don't think sarcasm is going to be helpful."

"Listen, let's try to move this forward." This was a favorite rhetorical tactic in business: no matter how obdurate and disruptive you were trying to be, always advocate returning to a positive basis of discussion. "I suppose I should ask if you're speaking as shareholders of the company or as bankers, and if you're speaking as bankers, who do you represent?"

Pause. "We represent the board."

"Good. Then the board hereby directs you not to communicate with any of the preferred shareholders." I savored my directive: projecting authority feels close to having authority.

He maturely decided not to challenge me. "I'm trying to help you resolve this. I've spoken to Jon. He's basically said that we have twenty-four hours to get this resolved. Come on. The Rubin family controls billions of dollars. If the choice is between writing off a few million dollars or dealing with a person they don't want to do business with anymore, they'll write off the few million. I'll guarantee you that. And don't think they won't make your life miserable to boot. Do you have any idea what these people can do to you?"

"Are you threatening me now? Or is Jon threatening me?"

I wasn't exactly enjoying this. But the adrenaline was certainly pumping.

"No one's threatening anybody," the factotum said wearily.

"Okay. Let's try to find a reason, other than your idea of an ethical life, for why I should sign this deal. It's obviously not for the money, because I have that already. So I would do it only to preserve a working relationship with Jon. Now, that may not be possible at this point—"

"I think it will still be possible."

"Sure thing." I laughed, then said, getting down to business finally, "Alison has provided Jon with a marked-up agreement. That's what we're willing to sign—"

"Michael—" the factotum interrupted, frustrated.

"If Jon has another suggestion for how to make this agreement acceptable to us, of course we're willing to listen."

Pause. "I'll get back to you."

"Right."

The second I was free, the phone was ringing again.

"Michael?"

"Jon," I said weightily. With only the briefest pause, I switched to nonchalance. "Have you received Alison's comments?"

"I'm not renegotiating! You gave me your word!"

"And I believe," I said, formally articulating the terms of the battle, "that you gave me *your* word, that you gave it to the whole board, about the terms for putting in five hundred thousand dollars."

"Is there an agreement? Show me an agreement. We've discussed many different financing options with regard to this company."

"Fine, Jon."

"You're fucking me over! You're screwing me. I've been up all night trying to get you on the phone. You don't have any idea what you're doing! You're just fucking me!"

"Jon, I'm in the middle of a panel discussion—"

"I don't care where you are. This isn't between the two of us anymore. You let it get out of my hands. It's too late. You are going to be fucked, Michael! Do you hear me?"

For a second, I thought the cell phone had, as usual, cut out. But then I realized that he had hung up on me.

"He just lost it," I said to Alison, reporting the conversation.

"Really? Wow."

I think we were both a little frightened.

It's easy to start to think that your own behavior is extreme when carefully composed, highly analytic, proudly reasonable businessmen start to scream at you. How far out on a limb was I? How much had I defied ordinary business conventions and manners by what I had done? It seemed to me I was just negotiating. Being tough was supposed to be a business virtue. But I was beginning to feel like an outlaw. No doubt, this is what your adversaries want you to feel. The context is dominance and submission. Money is dominant. Or believes, however irrationally, it should be dominant.

Part of money's job is to control the entrepreneur. In business mythology the entrepreneur is a breed apart. The entrepreneur is neither capital nor labor, neither investor nor employee. While the entrepreneur is the inspiration, the visionary, the leader (i.e., the unreasonable risk taker), the entrepreneur is also the unstable element.

The coming together of an entrepreneur and capital, with the attendant participation of lawyers, bankers, and other lesser interests, is an economic and political bargain of the most opportunistic sort. Conflict is inevitable. In most cases, the entrepreneur will be "dealt with." Sometimes though, if the entrepreneur has particular reserves of nerve and wile, well, the outcome might just be unexpected; the entrepreneur might turn the tables.

I was now functioning under this burst of hubris.

As I went back to my panel discussion on the future of newspapers in the brave new world, I considered all of the various elements conspiring with me or against me:

1. We had just released a good product. *Business Week* had praised it; *USA Today* had profiled us. Traffic was growing. It was a hit. What's more, it was useful. We had built, potentially, that mythical user-friendly front end.

2. We had real live prospective buyers lining up, heavy hitters, major names. The Washington Post Company. Ameritech. Yes, there was clearly a market for us.

3. It was hard to get rid of me. I had plastered my name over everything. I had an author's pride rather than a developer's team spirit.

4. Patricof had begun to push out in front of other New York investment firms for East Coast Internet deals. They needed ours to hold together.

5. The last thing Rubin wanted right now was for us to blow up in his face.

The last point, I realized, was probably the most important one. Rubin was not going to want to do anything to screw up his carefully choreographed efforts to take his online transaction company, First Virtual, public.

First Virtual was an anomalous little system conceived in the earliest days of privacy worries and credit card anxieties. You could buy merchandise online with a password connected to your credit card, but you would never have to expose your credit card to the open Internet. Every purchase you made would be confirmed by e-mail. Unlike credit cards, which charged merchants a 2 or 3 percent transaction fee, First Virtual charged 15 percent. It was not, therefore, particularly attractive to traditional merchants. But it actually achieved quite a wide use among porno dealers. (One of its early successes was individual photos, priced at $1.25 each, of Inga, the girl from Denmark, in various poses, complete with a description of each photo in a charming broken English, the entrepreneurial brainstorm of a student at Haverford College.) Bear Stearns, along with two other brokerage firms, was preparing a public offering of First Virtual, a company that had never topped $700,000 in annual revenues, and had losses of more than $10 million, which they hoped would value the company at almost $100 million.

While there were men rich enough to kiss off the $5 million invested in our company, there may not have been any so rich as to kiss off $100 million.

By the time I arrived back in New York from San Antonio, Jon Rubin had agreed to the two paramount changes we were insisting on: Alison and I would remain on the board, and control of the company would be returned to us as soon as we repaid the outstanding $150,000 loan.

Alison was right, he could not have done otherwise.

Still, all we had really managed to do was to draw the battle lines.

Almost immediately, I turned around and headed to Washington for our meeting with executives of the Washington Post Company.

The factotum, the EVP, and I were shown into Mrs. Graham's office—a gracious, frozen-in-time tableau, set off by black-and-white photos of the Kennedys and other pantheon-worthy politicians—which looked onto a serene outdoor terrace. I had left vague and shifting messages regarding the time and place of this meeting for Jon Rubin and idly hoped that he would miss it. With no such luck, he arrived as coffee was being poured into Mrs. Graham's china.

"I understand Kay's hip replacement surgery went very well," Rubin said as he joined the meeting. "My father had the same surgery last year, and he's been coaching her."

These were ranking executives from the Post's business side, financial side, and editorial side, but they did not seem to feel they were senior enough to idly chat about Mrs. Graham's health and soberly avoided comment.

There was a deep seriousness to the meeting, almost a grimness. The Post was already feeling a bite on its classified advertising from Digital Cities, AOL's Washington, D.C., Web guide. In addition, the Post could look forward soon to having Microsoft as a local competitor. The District of Columbia was a target market for Microsoft's Sidewalk project, another online city magazine dreaming of a windfall in local advertising.

"With our cash flow I wouldn't exactly say we are afraid of AOL," said Chris Schroeder, treasurer of the Washington Post Company and the company's primary acquisition executive. He added pointedly, "I'm not sure, though, we'd have the same feelings about the man in Redmond."

A boyish finance-oriented executive out of the Bush administration, Schroeder was a self-consciously styled straight shooter. Virtually everything he said was couched as bad news or less than good news.

"We think you've built an exciting company," he said in a halting and pained cadence. "I think the synergies are evident to everyone here, operationally and philosophically." He twirled a pen in his fingers. "I will be honest that we have looked at substantial numbers of Internet-related ventures. While we are, obviously, continuing to evaluate our strategy and strategic interests in this area, I think I can reasonably say that yours is the company that we are most interested in. Having said that, I want to caution you that we are continuing our discussions internally and that our timetable may not be your timetable."

I took note that this was clearly a prepared statement. Obviously, too, it made sense that if they had prepared this far, they knew where they were going. I began to compose the press release:

WASHINGTON POST COMPANY
ACQUIRES WOLFF NEW MEDIA
Deal Valued at $62 Million

I cleared my throat and made my statement: "We believe that we are looking toward a period of rapid consolidation within this industry. It would be my supposition that if we attend the conference where you saw me speak next year, we'll find far fewer and far less exciting independent companies. The decision in front of us is, Whom do we embrace and what is the nature of our relationship? We are in the interesting position of having two clear directions, two distinct choices. We can partner with a technology company, or we can partner with a content-oriented media company. I think most of you people here know my background as a journalist. While I've spent a lot of time recently on the West Coast, up and down Highway 101 as well as in Redmond, I'll be honest that it is hard for me sitting in this office—particularly this office—not to feel that I am home."

They liked my attitude.

The senior editorial executive said, "I think it's clear that we understand each other on an editorial level. We're not in the software business, we're in the journalism business: the Washington Post Company and your company." Disconcertingly, he added, "if I had the money and the resources, I'd create the kind of site you've created."

"Perhaps," I said, "we should acquire you."

A touch of laughter.

"We'd like to present three directions to explore with you," Schroeder said.

Moving right along, I thought.

"We can enter into an alliance that I think could be valuable for you in the short run wherein we would be an acquirer and perhaps distributor of your content. We can begin to talk about this relationship almost immediately."

This was the "let's be friends" approach.

"We can make an investment in your company."

A mutually satisfying sexual relationship.

"We can acquire you."

Marriage.

"And which," the factotum asked, "is your preference?"

"I have no preference," Schroeder was careful to point out. "And I don't know what the company will prefer. But I think I can share with you my sense that it is probably easier for this company to act within your timetable if we were to discuss an acquisition."

We, on our side, reacted with appropriate poker-faced consideration.

"Of course, the Post Company is not going to offer an IPO value. I can tell you that."

WASHINGTON POST COMPANY
ACQUIRES WOLFF NEW MEDIA
Deal Valued at $40 Million

"What was the value of the last round?"

"Approximately ten million dollars," said the factotum.

Schroeder raised his eyebrows.

"You're looking at needing another five to reach breakeven?"

"Approximately."

Schroeder tapped a pen. "Do you have a price?" He asked but did not really expect an answer.

It felt, now, like $25 million to $30 million to me. My take would be $15 million. Of course, I hesitated. It was $15 million versus letting the chips ride. Having practiced, on the bourse of my dreams, the strategies for trading up to vast sums, I knew that the way to play this was to get the Post Company to invest $5 million at the $25 million valuation (in other words they'd get 20 percent of the company, leaving me with—my math was failing me but I could expect to get, later in the day, a computer run on relative share value from Patricof) and then to go public in the hundreds-of-millions-of-dollars class.

"I think what we have to do is discuss this on our side and then let you know if we are ready to proceed. I think I can have an answer for you on that in forty-eight hours," Schroeder said.

And that was that. It was a smell-test meeting, and unless we were inured to our own stink, we had passed the test and a deal was there to happen.

I could well imagine the contentment and rosy glow and power aura of having sold my company for a personal take of $15 million. The fantasy was different from the $100 million fantasy, but there was a satisfying modesty to the $15 million. One's life was enhanced, improved, made qualitatively better, but it was not irrevocably changed, as it would be in the $100 million deal.

⚏

"Do you want to have lunch?" Rubin maneuvered me aside as we came out of the Post building. I was ready to deflect a meeting, but in the way he held my arm and looked me deep in the eye this was clearly a makeup lunch. I could feel the emotion here.

It was a casual lunch. We went to a barbecue joint. There was a little talk about Kay Graham and the dinner his parents had recently had with her. Then he said, taking a breath, "This has been a difficult period—"

"It has been," I agreed, and added, "I'm glad we've been able to get through it."

"Honestly." He crossed his arms and looked at me intently. "I think you have used extremely bad judgment."

I was nonplussed. It took me rather a long moment to realize that we were apparently not making up. "Hmm." I looked at him closely but had no idea what to expect here. I was curious, though. "Obviously," I shrugged, "I disagree."

"I think if you thought about it, you would agree that you made a bad decision."

I wondered if there weren't perhaps some official eating crow that was expected of me.

He pursed his lips. "You made a bad decision. The reason I wanted to sit down with you is to tell you that I don't feel I'm in a position to work with you any longer. I think you made a bad decision, and I don't think we are going to be able to recover the trust that clearly needs to exist in a working relationship like ours." How had I ever missed that this was coming? I wondered. Either my head was totally in the clouds, or his demeanor was far off message. Then he said that what he wanted to do was have his technology advisor step in as CEO and the EVP step up to COO.

"This is what you want me to agree to?"

"You made a bad decision. My concern is for the company and how we get it running again."

Having never been fired before (having hardly ever had a job before), I briefly considered the nature of the experience of having the kind of comprehension delay that I was encountering, before I fully processed the fact that it was really not so easy to fire me. The ties that bind capital with an entrepreneur are tightly twisted ones. I could, and I imagined I probably would, make it as difficult to shake me as it would be to shake a woman seriously scorned.

"As you know," I said, "the terms of my employment contract provide for termination with cause only in the event of a felony conviction."

"Indictment."

"No, I'm quite sure I have to be convicted."

He seemed sour about that.

"At any rate," he said methodically, "we don't have to talk about termination. We think an appropriate role for you will be as vice chairman and to remain involved on the creative side of the company and as its spokesperson."

All across the technology industry there are entrepreneurs whiling away their middle years as vice chairmen.

I quickly analyzed the cycle of dependence. Because my name was plastered all over the company, my presence was required to maintain the company's value, at least in the short term. It would be unlikely, I weighed the bet, that the Washington Post Company or CNet or Ameritech or anyone else would do a deal for the company if I were blowing raspberries on the sidelines. On the other hand, it was possible that the Rubin interests, having achieved at least temporary control of the company, had no desire to do any of these deals but, rather, to solidify control and to use the company for other purposes.

I knew that a good businessperson, a true businessperson, would look at this strategically and economically. I tried to imagine what Alison's advice would be. I could almost do it, too. Her counsel would be to figure out where I wanted to be at a reasonable point in the future. Did I want to get as much money as possible and be free of the company? Did I believe that if I held on, there would be infinitely more money to make? Did I want to stay running the company, building it, helping it grow, working with the people I'd brought together? Define the goal and work backward, she would say. Develop a strategic and tactical path to get where I wanted to be.

But, honestly, for what seemed like a long period—minutes, not seconds; ten minutes, twenty minutes maybe—I weighed the pros and cons of just hitting Rubin in the nose. There was no question that I could do it. It would be the first time in a long time, but not the first time. A surprise fist would take the day.

That's not what I did. But I didn't much follow the path of my economic interests, either.

"No," I said. "Fuck you. No accommodation. No nothing. I'll bury this company. I'll bury you. I'll bury anything else you're trying to do in a firestorm of publicity and litigation. I want you out of my company. You're a lightweight and a snot nose. Get out of my company. The longer you stay, the more money and pain it will cost you." I tried to remember later what I really said here, how close it came to those words. I think pretty close.

I don't believe I'd ever seen a face change so dramatically and rapidly without special effects. His color drained and then was replaced by a red and purple hue. A muscular reaction seemed to almost flatten the upper and lower jaws. The nostrils were like a bull's. The veins on the front of the neck seemed sculpted by Michelangelo.

I thought that he was going to hit *me*—probably an ideal outcome.

But again his face changed, almost as dramatically, as he forcefully recomposed. It was a masterful job of regaining control.

"I am an investor," he said. "I will have investments that work out and other investments that do not." He was breathing very heavily. "When they don't work out, I will, like all investors, go on to the next opportunity. You, however, just have this company. It carries your name. If it goes down, you go down with it."

"Actually," I said, suddenly appreciating what had been something of a disadvantage, certainly an oddity, in my business life, "I'm a writer. If this company goes down, I will continue to do what I have always done, which is write. Perhaps about you."

He stood, calmly. Emptied his wallet on the table. And walked out.

■■■

It's amazing how few things actually change when you're expecting everything to change. You wait for the roar, the flood tide, and nothing happens. The work keeps getting done. More desks keep coming. The Internet becomes a household word.

Ameritech came in to see us and seemed to be head over heels impatient, in a midwestern sort of way, to invest its money with us.

We had said to both the Post and to Ameritech, in a kind of Internet white lie, that we were doing, oh, about seven million impressions a month, give or take, and that we were scaling up quickly, that in a year we'd hit twenty million per month, certainly.

There were, fortunately, only a handful of people in America who understood Internet numbers, but there was an emerging math. For each impression, generated by each set of eyes that saw the page, an advertiser would pay $.02. So if we had five million impressions a month, we would be making $100,000 every month.

I was fairly confident I could make us a deal and get us an audience, or at least get us impressions.

The EVP and I flew out to the West Coast to make the deal that would give us the numbers we were proposing to sell to Ameritech and to the Washington Post Company.

Because in an astoundingly short period of time—hardly more than twelve months—the Internet had gone from a utopian moment, wherein the Web had created a new era in publishing with a new technology and a new economic model—as profound and as democratizing as the advent of movable type—to a system on its way to being as monolithic and as unbeatable as the television dial; if you wanted traffic, you had to make a deal with a search engine.

Yahoo, Excite (which had bought Magellan), Infoseek. Up and down Silicon Valley on Highway 101. And Lycos, too, in Boston.

We had meetings scheduled with everybody, but I liked Infoseek best. Robin Johnson, Infoseek's CEO, was out of Time Warner. He had a background in the media business. I had more in common with him than I had with the software developers and executives at the other search engine companies.

The EVP and I met Johnson in a windowless interview room at the San Francisco airport. He was heading east, just as we arrived out west.

Since the conference in Laguna Beach, Johnson and I had been talking about a deal that would introduce our content to Infoseek users. We would be the cream on top of Infoseek and, hence, get a share of Infoseek's one hundred million monthly impressions.

I hoped we could do this deal with Johnson, but I knew that he was almost as embattled an executive as I was. Infoseek's stock was trading at half its offering price. Someone had to be blamed. (We'd had one meeting with Johnson during which he left for a lunchtime board meeting and returned a different man. "He was chewed up and spit out during lunch," observed the factotum, obviously familiar with such boardroom dining habits.)

But maybe we could help each other out.

During the flight west, the EVP had been intently crunching numbers. Now, in the fluorescent-lit interview room at the airport, he took Johnson through the spreadsheet, analyzing the ebb and flow of traffic through Infoseek's search results and through our more narrative content. There it was: a visitor to Infoseek registered an average of 3 impressions—3 clicks—per visit whereas our users, appreciating, it would seem, our wit and opinions, registered 5.5 impressions.

While 5.5 clicks seemed paltry and unsatisfying to me, both Johnson and the EVP were taken with these findings. Our user was worth almost twice what an Infoseek user was worth.

What this user or these impressions were really worth was another issue entirely. We had, for instance, a book we'd published about online investing. We were able to buy the search word *cigars* on Infoseek, thinking the cigar crowd would be men with an interest in money (most of the other money-related words were taken). The cost was $.02 for every person who typed in the word *cigar*. What you, the Web surfer, would see, in addition to the forty thousand or so references to cigars on the Web, was our horizontal ad across the top of your screen. Because this space was so cramped and abbreviated, in order to get the full significance of our message you would have to click on our ad and be transported to *our* Web site, where we would tell you about our book and give you an opportunity to place an order. In general, three percent of the people who searched on the word *cigar*, for whom we had paid $.02 apiece, clicked on our ad. In other words, instead of a cost per thousand of $20 for people to see our ad (about the same as is charged by personal-finance-related magazines, for instance), our real cost was something like $666 per thousand. Of those people, .005 bought a book—a $22 book. In other words, for $666 we generated $110 in sales.

Still, for the moment, I was happy of course that we were operating in our own little world.

"Let's do a deal," Johnson said.

###

Finally, we received proper and formal, and uneventful, notice of a board meeting to be held at the law offices of the hated and feared Jesse Meer.

As backbenchers now at our own board meeting, we in fact had no idea of what was to transpire. I could be fired. The company could be reorganized, sold, merged, repurposed. The unknowns about which the Rubin side had to be concerned had to do with whether or not I was ready to negotiate sensibly and whether or not I was a crazy man without the sense of his own economic interests. How can you predict what a crazy man will do?

Obviously, too, it complicated their plans that Rubin, having gained control for a mere $150,000, could lose it back to me for the same mere $150,000. It was an unnerving balance of power.

Alison had prepared me for the meeting, as a doctor with a good bedside manner might go over all the possible points of pain and trauma for a surgical procedure.

The worst case, for all concerned, was an all-out exchange of retaliatory weapons. They could fire me. I could respond. We had a press release in the fax machine; we had lawyers poised to file motions.

Another possible denouement was an attractive offer. In some ways this one seemed like the most difficult to deal with, but Alison assured me that I had a price and that the world would not think less of me for it.

But the most likely outcome, according to Alison, was a set of steps designed to curtail my authority, frustrate my relationships with other managers, and isolate me from the operations of the company. In other words, I would be made vice-chairman in fact if not in name. I was to expect, too, according to Alison, a set of measures meant to punish me through small humiliations—lesser office, curtailed expenses, loss of my cell phone.

"They humiliate you," she said, "because it's the kind of stuff that brings on the emotions, that makes your voice break. When that happens, forget it."

So most of all, as we went into the meeting, I was afraid of crying.

Jesse Meer's law firm was, like every law firm in midtown Manhattan, made of expensive wood veneer, glass, and granite. You would not single it out as particularly son-of-a-bitch decor.

The Patricof people were subdued but genial.

The firm's creditors' rights partner, who came out to greet us, was gentlemanly enough.

Our CFO and EVP, who would be waiting outside during the meeting, were fine with pretending nothing much of moment was going on.

Even as Jesse Meer, Jon Rubin, and the technology advisor, who had been added to the board, entered the conference room from a side door, it was still a businesslike air. Any additional tension was hardly perceptible. It was almost possible to imagine that everyone here had a reasonable working relationship.

It was only Jesse who met every glance coldly and maintained a sort of cell-block expression.

"Some water?" Alison indicated the carafe on the sideboard.

"Yeah, it's water. At least she understands that," he said, to no one in particular.

For a second, I almost reacted. It was the first time in a business context I ever felt a spousal defend-and-protect reflex. It threw me.

"Let's get to it. We'd like to keep this as short as possible," Jesse said. "Some of us here have other things to do. Would the chairman of the company like to call the meeting to order?"

I had a physical response to someone else taking over, a flush that began in my mouth and rolled down to my stomach. Remorse and regret followed for having taken someone else's money in the first place. Investors. Venture capital. I looked around the room at the wood and glass and granite. How could I have been so stupid? So greedy? What could I have possibly been thinking? Obviously, this was going to end in tears.

"Let the meeting come to order," said Rubin. "Housekeeping issues first."

What a schoolteacherish word, I thought, with contempt.

"I'd like to move," Rubin said affably, "that Alison be replaced as board secretary."

Alison, who had already begun taking the minutes of the meeting, stopped, or froze, and, caught so unaware, flushed from the neck.

It was so moved, and the technology advisor thereupon became the board's secretary.

Alison pushed aside her notebook.

"I move," Rubin said, comfortably, in control, "that Jesse Meer become the counsel to the company and that Alison be directed to prepare a memo itemizing all prior and ongoing matters."

Alison faltered slightly but then said, "There are matters, because I have acted in both a business and legal capacity, that it will be hard for me to disengage from—"

"I don't think the board will have any problem with you continuing to work on these matters, reporting to and under the supervision of Jesse Meer and his colleagues," said Rubin.

If the company was taken away from me, I realized, I had a certain amount of recourse. I could fairly say, and it might even be believed, that I had been robbed. But Alison was in a much less certain position. There was really no company without her. She had acted as the free lawyer, deal maker, CFO, COO, personnel director, health plan administrator. Without official position, salary, or ownership interest, she had built the company. What's more, she couldn't walk away. I had no company if she walked away. The leverage of my need for her was being used here to reduce her to Jesse Meer's underling.

"Many of these matters . . . I have been personally—"

"Work them out with Jesse, Alison."

"I'm not sure, Jon, that you appreciate the way we have worked the legal and business affairs functions of the company," she said slowly.

He looked at his watch. "Discuss it with Jesse. Are you comfortable with that?" He turned to Jesse.

"Give me a memo," he shrugged.

"I am not going to—this is not how we've been working. How do you propose even to compensate me?"

"What's our arrangement now?" Rubin asked, shifting papers, impatient.

"It's only been a minimal—"

"Fine. We'll continue that. Let's move on."

"Jon . . . this company . . . you don't understand . . . my relationship . . . I'm sorry," Alison said, turning to me as the tears started to roll down her cheeks.

I have played this moment over a thousand times. Even in the all-powerfulness of my imagination, I don't know how to respond. I even find myself feeling bad for Jesse and Jon, who looked caught out and ashamed of themselves.

We were all saved by the factotum's cell phone.

"The Washington Post Company," he said, "wants to proceed with an acquisition or investment. They'll come up with a team early next week."

Jon briefly conferred with Jesse. "Why don't we adjourn the meeting then?"

So I was still, it appeared, running my company.

Chapter Eight

The Twenty-First-Century Corporation

In November 1996, a little before Thanksgiving, Jon Rubin found himself holding the missing piece. He was sure he had masterminded the salvation of our business. It changed him, too. It was as though we had never been antagonists. It was not only the renewed promise of great wealth that spread this sudden good cheer (although that will do it every time) but a personal satisfaction that he wanted other people to share. He was proud of himself. Rightly. He was about to do it. He was on the verge of putting it together. So he needed harmony, he needed an audience. He wanted everyone to appreciate the neat trick, this bit of matchmaking, that he was about to pull off: he was getting us into bed in a serious way with AOL.

I had been here many times before, without Rubin's help. Who in cyberspace hadn't? "Where are you with AOL?" was a question as prevalent in the Internet industry as "What's your business model?" Against all odds, AOL, the most dysfunctional company in America (while everyone says that about their own company, the AOL pathology was something else again; it was comic book as much as textbook), had become the big cheese, the mightiest enchilada.

Alan Patricof, who had been an early investor in America Online, back when it was a series of chat services—QLink for Commodore, PCLink for Tandy, AOL for Apple—was supposed to smooth our way to the highest levels in the AOL organization. But he was not remembered fondly, and his entreaties got us nowhere.

Through our own efforts and connections—impressive ones, too, I am told ("definitely a decision maker")—we arranged meeting after meeting, approach upon approach, with the "right" people at AOL. But to no real avail.

Rubin's technology advisor, shortly after Rubin made his investment in our company, took me aside to tell me he knew the secret. The technology advisor had paid close attention to how Candace Carpenter, the CEO of iVillage, creators of Parent Soup, forged one of the most successful relationships of an entrepreneur with AOL, and, he said, he'd gained an intimate familiarity with the nuances of the way AOL really worked. The petitioner, the supplicant, the entrepreneur who needed AOL, had to supply the functionality, he explained in technology terms. Had to coordinate communications between AOL executives and fiefdoms. Had to route e-mail. Had to organize meetings in Vienna, Virginia, where AOL was located. Had to ghostwrite the internal memos justifying a deal. Petitioners had to put it together themselves, because there were no processes or procedures at AOL for, well, making a decision. You had to hand it to them all wrapped up. But, after months of trying, the technology advisor's efforts and insights produced no results.

We got plenty of advice from the many AOL content "partners" whom we talked to all the time and advice from AOL executives themselves. We followed it all. We showed up instead of calling. We sent instant messages ("IMed") over AOL instead of sending e-mail ("Hello? Hello? Are you there?" I typed with no response. Nothing, nothing ever. "Well, if you're reading this . . ."). We stayed on top of the change of business models. We got to know everyone whom anyone said we should get to know. We even considered golf (odd, but true, that this game of the 1950s corporation was the official pastime, even obsession, of this self-styled first corporation of the twenty-first century).

It was as though you were dealing with an unstable government in a country with business customs incomprehensible to the Anglo-Saxon world.

But several times a week, Rubin took the shuttle from National Airport in Washington to LaGuardia Airport in New York. In addition to the many politicians and national news stars, the shuttle now transported a new power elite: AOL executives, commuting between AOL's Virginia offices and AOL's Manhattan base of operations in the Seagram's Building on Fifty-third Street and Park Avenue.

On this trip up to LaGuardia, before Thanksgiving, Rubin sat next to one of the executives charged with transforming AOL from the many businesses it had been before—a software company, online service, information business, communications concern, shopping center—into a media empire.

They were on passingly familiar terms. The AOL executive knew that Rubin had substantial investments in the Internet industry and that Rubin came from a wealthy politically prominent family. Rubin knew that the executive was an AOL star, a player on the AOL media team. In other words, it was a felicitous and serendipitous seating arrangement. Kismet. Two new media power guys at the end of the day humping it home to New York.

So they talked and everything fell into place. Just like that. A little personal juice at the right levels.

"Done. He'll do a deal," Rubin said to me, calling as soon as they parted. Rubin was cool, dispassionate, cynical almost. But then, in spite of his practiced hauteur and the near blood score between us, he lost it: "Really. He'll do it. I'm not kidding! He loves it!" His excitement almost turned to joviality. It shocked me to hear him so buoyant on the phone, so charged up, so easily tossing off his corporate enmity. Perhaps business really isn't personal, I thought.

"What kind of deal? How did this come up? How did you cast it?" I pressed.

"He knows about the company. He's into it. He's pissed off that you've been getting the runaround. He says the entire AOL organization is super fucked up. But he said he'll do it, personally. He'll shepherd it. If we can put a deal together, he guarantees he'll get it done. He's ready. He'll come into the office and do it. So let's do it. Let's set it up. Now!"

"Okay. Great. Yes. Wow. What else did he say?"

"He said he's got his coke problem under control, and now he's working on his fidelity issues."

<hr/>

I never really wanted to do a deal with AOL. At best, AOL just watered down the experience of the Internet and network technology; at worst, it was in some other business—it was a direct marketing organization, infomercial shit.

I never knew anybody who took AOL seriously as an Internet company.

I never knew an AOL customer who didn't feel seriously abused by AOL.

I never knew an AOL information provider who didn't feel that AOL was about to start turning the screws.

I never knew an AOL executive who didn't think he or she was playing a part in a very serious shell game that, ideally, would end in an acquisition of AOL by a reputable company.

I never knew anybody who really wanted to work for AOL, located in true Nowheresville, Virginia.

And yet AOL had become the most important company in the Internet business. It had moved into a nexus of the media and technology and communications businesses. AOL had emerged as an odd, unlikely alternative to both news organizations and communications companies. Certainly, the possibility of a deal with AOL would influence our negotiations with the Washington Post and with Ameritech. With a little critical interpretation, AOL was now the biggest newspaper in the nation. The real *USA Today*. What's more, it had become the largest provider of Internet connections in the world. It was doing the straightforward hardware/technology connection job that Ameritech and the other RBOCs and long distance companies should have been doing.

Of course, while it continued to take beachhead after beachhead in the American economy, it still had never made any money.

It was a company, both AOL supporters and AOL critics said, in perpetual start-up mode. The former meant to say that AOL had the rare corporate ability to reinvent itself, overnight, if need be; the latter were saying, derisively, that it was a fraud, a pyramid scheme, that before people caught on to the fact that every business AOL had ever tried had failed, it was on to another one.

Go back to 1992, say, when Patrick Spain, the CEO of Hoover's, a small publishing company that had the idea to take the kind of business information that Dun & Bradstreet sold for thousands of dollars and make it available to ordinary consumers in $19.95 paperback books, first signed up with AOL. AOL had about 150,000 members then, $26 million in revenue. There were AOL and GEnie and Delphi, the not very meaningful players in the online game, and then there were Prodigy and CompuServe, at the million-member level, who were kings of the online world.

On AOL you could get information from companies like Hoover's and Nolo Press, which offered legal information to laymen, or you could read the *Army Times* or check out a database of country inns. You could not, of course, get information from companies like Time, Inc. or the New York Times or Dun & Bradstreet. How could—and why would—an information company, a real information company that made money from its information, make its wares, its content, available online cheaper than its customers could get it offline and do so with no advertising opportunities to boot?

This was certainly not the way CompuServe worked or, for that matter, the important information database providers like Dialog or Lexis/Nexis. They charged users a premium price for getting the information in an efficient digital form, and this made it worthwhile for the information provider.

So AOL went to off-brand and no-brand information. For the AOL customer it didn't make much difference. You were paying the same amount for your time on AOL, anyway. You weren't paying more for Hoover's. It was, or seemed like, free information, as AOL kept saying. You were paying for connect time, according to AOL, but the information was free. It was a point of pride at AOL that it had no premium pricing plan. Chances were you were there to chat, anyway. AOL *really* was CB radio. *Hey! Hey! Hello! What are you doing? Chillin. You? Yeah. Chillin too. So? What are you wearing?* Information—content—was just gravy.

AOL's membership base began to expand at a faster rate than that of Delphi or GEnie. AOL had done a public offering as a technology company, which gave it lots of financial resources, but it was really operating like a magazine company. It hired Jan Brandt, who was a circulation specialist in the magazine business. She started building AOL's audience the old-fashioned way: through the mail! A start-up magazine company would never have been able to go to the public market for funding. But AOL, ostensibly a technology company but one that would gain subscribers exactly as magazines do and, in addition, would offer magazine-derived content, could. And did.

Jan Brandt sent out a billion disks. More than three disks for every American. It was pure magazine circulation strategy. Renting lists. Targeting groups. Measuring response rate. On an offer for a free ten hours a .002 percent sign-up is not acceptable; kill that list. A .004 percent sign-up is— but watch the conversion. How many from that list go into billable hours? How many from that list are still here in three months, six months, a year? Just like magazines do it. Mail. Blow-in cards. Everywhere you look, a dirt cheap offer. The AOL disk-blitz! The disks sit next to coffee cups in America's kitchens, get jammed into the backs of people's sock drawers. Even people who don't have computers have found some use for an AOL disk.

But AOL wasn't a magazine company. Wasn't small-time like that. Wasn't constrained by a magazine company's value (a one times multiple of revenues, whereas AOL was trading at thirty times revenues or need for profitability. It was a technology company!

One of the things that AOL did, that software companies do, was assemble a board of well-connected and powerful friends.

Alexander Haig sat on AOL's board (his presence, plus the company's roots in northern Virginia, helped spur continual speculation about AOL's defense and intelligence industry connections). As did Doug Peabody, a venture capitalist who funded media companies. As did Chris Meigher, the second-in-command at Time Inc. (Meigher and Peabody are now in business together), which brings us back to the magazine business.

AOL dramatically changed when it recruited *Time* magazine in 1994 as its first big-brand information headliner. Suddenly, AOL was a media enterprise.

It became "media" at the expense of the media.

Time entered into a peculiar economic relationship with AOL. It devalued its own product. For all practical purposes, it gave it away. And then, within the year, almost every other consumer information provider began to experiment with this new distribution method that, at least for the time being, offered no economic viability.

While this did not immediately damage the traditional information providers, who continued to make money the old-fashioned way, by printing on paper, it had a profound debilitating effect on the high-priced providers of online information like CompuServe, Dialog, and Lexis/Nexis—the only companies, ironically, that had ever made any money in the online business. (Three years later, AOL would acquire CompuServe's online service—Worldcom acquired CompuServe's telecommunications network—in something near to a fire sale.)

Then in 1994, Paul Allen, the cofounder of Microsoft, who had retired from the company in 1984, the second-richest man in the technology business and the only vaunted figure in the industry with enough leisure time to take an interest in the online world, expressed his interest in acquiring AOL. (He had been buying stock in the company since 1992, holding close to 25 percent of AOL by 1994.)

Allen's interest provided AOL with instant credibility in the technology community, which had never paid it much attention before (AOL, after all, was not really a technology company; it was no more a technology company than was any bulletin board service), and in the financial community, which had heretofore treated AOL as a money-losing mid-tier player in a niche business. Its share price soared.

Even more importantly, there was an internal sea change. As AOL's board debated the Allen offer, a consensus emerged that what had been, indeed, a niche play suddenly had a sky's-the-limit potential.

"We sat in the conference room in the AOL office in the Seagram's Building and had to almost physically restrain Steve from jumping into Allen's arms. You dumb son-of-a-bitch, we had to say, you don't know what you've got on your hands," recalled a board member.

The thirty-something Steve Case, AOL's chairman, was an unlikely mogul and an even more unlikely visionary. He continued to look like the P&G product manager he once was—an affable, nondescript, chinos and button-down guy with a layer of baby fat. His brother, Dan Case, who runs Hambrecht & Quist, one of the leading West Coast investment banks, is the handsome brother, much more the BMOC. "He struck me as very shy, almost embarrassed in an adolescent way," described a technology reporter who saw Steve at a White House correspondents' dinner in Washington shortly after AOL was forced to disclose that he had left his wife for Jean Villanueva, AOL's longtime PR director.

Case's role in the company began to change after the board rebuffed the Allen takeover bid. Case became Chairman Steve, and one of his most important functions became recruiting the talent to run this company that had somehow stepped to the forefront of technology and media.

AOL, with its stock rising, was able to acquire a California-based multimedia promotions company called Redgate—not so much for the company itself as for its chief executive, Ted Leonsis.

Case became the administrator—the suit—and Leonsis became the visionary. (Leonsis, it was said, put the first CD-ROM in a book; Leonsis, it was also said, in spite of a host of other pretenders to this claim, coined the phrase "new media.")

Case receded and Leonsis stepped to the forefront of AOL.

In the Leonsis era, from late '94 to late '96, AOL went from $104 million in revenues to over the billion-dollar mark. Leonsis became AOL. He could talk the talk, he could sell the vision thing. He was creative, motivational, combative. He was everywhere—before the technology industry, the New York media business, the Hollywood entertainment community, Wall Street analysts, the VCs—insisting, furiously insisting, that AOL was what he wanted it to be, rather than what it was.

People believed him, a fat man, an ugly man, sweating like crazy. You couldn't help thinking that what he was saying had to be true, that otherwise he'd never have the guts to stand up there and say it and huff and puff like that.

AOL was an online service, no different from every other online service that would go out of business during the next few years. What Leonsis said AOL was, was media; in fact, what he said it was was something near to, or next to, or at one with TV. It didn't matter that AOL didn't have the technology or the audience to remotely compare itself to TV. Leonsis said it was so.

This is what he said: On Thursday nights, between 9:00 and 9:30 EST and between 9:00 and 9:30 PST, AOL's usage goes markedly and reliably down. Why? Because AOL's audience turns on *Seinfeld*. Ergo, AOL has the same audience and is providing the same function as television. Double ergo, AOL's competition is TV, and not just TV but the most sought-after of TV—*Seinfeld*.

AOL wasn't Prodigy (yuk) or CompuServe (ho hum), it was mass media entertainment.

Wall Street believed him. The media community believed him (in fact, there became a competition among mass media brands to go online through AOL). And the AOL organization believed him.

The Internet became, by late 1995, an irritant in Leonsis's plans. He fought it, too. Defensively. The Internet wasn't for AOL users. The Internet was a jungle, a fetid swamp, a stormy sea, whereas AOL was a safe harbor, a nice neighborhood, a controlled environment, a planned community. He tried to articulate the difference between an online service and the Internet. And failed. But unlike his counterparts at CompuServe and Prodigy, he gave up trying to fight the Internet; he let the Internet, or really the myth of the Net, become a new engine of AOL's growth.

AOL recast itself as America's gateway to the Internet, which was fairly audacious considering that you couldn't get to the Internet from AOL. But no matter. In a highly interesting bit of semantics and dialectical legerdemain, AOL even began to present itself as the Internet. "I'm on the Internet," a good portion of modem-empowered America would say, though in fact they had never made it outside the confines of AOL.

Leonsis, while very good on the big picture, and superb on the vision, was not so good on the details. He had a getting-stuff-done problem.

"That's hypergrowth," AOL execs took to saying.

"Hypergrowth" was a good cover. It was almost okay not to get things done if you were soon going to have to do it differently, anyway. In fact, if everything was going to change, which you knew it would, it made sense to commit to as little as possible. Hence, the average contract turnaround time at AOL began to run at about nine months.

Eventually though, even pedaling as fast as you can, shit catches up with you.

The backlash was evident at AOL's fabled partners conferences. Its information suppliers were not vendors but "partners," and they were invited twice a year to discuss problems and ideas and issues of mutual interest at a resort with a good course (Ted was among the most ardent of golfers). By mid-'96 the mood was getting uglier. It was clearer and clearer that AOL, which the information providers believed had built its business on the backs of other people's brands, was distancing itself from those brands. AOL was busy building its own brand. AOL was the kahuna. Its "partners" were, well, not really partners. (AOL argued that customers came to AOL to chat and then look at the information. The info providers argued the opposite, that customers came to get news or make travel plans or read a magazine. Given that the vast majority of time on AOL was spent chatting, AOL was probably right.)

In an effort to deal with mounting disarray and animosities, Case hired William Razzouk from Federal Express to bring order to this chaos. He prescribed early morning meetings and precise executive apparel rules. Corporate organization was no match, however, for chaos, and within weeks he announced that, on second thought, he really preferred Memphis.

If AOL wasn't Federal Express, then perhaps it was—why not?—MTV.

Chairman Steve hired Bob Pittman, MTV's founder. Leonsis was sent off to run something called the AOL Studio, where, with any luck, he would think up an *I Love Lucy* for AOL. But for now it was Pittman's show. (One of Pittman's recent assignments had been as the CEO of Time Warner's Six Flags amusement park; Pittman said that running AOL was just like running a theme park.)

And then, in the fall of 1996, came flat pricing. Responding (rashly responding, many people say) to the sudden new reality of the $19.95-per-month unlimited connect time offered by many ISPs, and the evident commoditization of online connectivity, AOL abandoned its hourly charges and signed everybody on at $19.95 for unlimited hours.

Bob Pittman and flat pricing. It was a cable model with a cable visionary. The move had profound and immediate consequences:

1. The AOL business model was turned on its head; instead of making more money the longer a person stayed connected to the service, now the longer a person stayed online, the more money AOL lost.

2. AOL became a household word. Because it didn't cost money to stay online, no one got off. Therefore, no one could get on. The hue and cry that went up from AOL's seven million customers, and was echoed by state attorneys general across the country, had the effect of making the entire country think it was missing something. People *without* computers called to complain that they could not get onto AOL.

These developments changed AOL's business. It was no longer in the business of selling connect time or selling information or selling service. Now it was in the business of selling its customers. In the classic media business model, having gotten the attention of the public, having brought it here through come-ons and gimmicks, now it would sell this audience again and again, over and over. It hoped.

We were in our conference room—Jon Rubin, the factotum, the EVP, the technology advisor, Alison, and I—waiting for the AOL executive to arrive.

"This is going to work," Jon Rubin said. He was in an excited, nervous mood.

Because that sounded to me like a jinx, I said, "You know AOL. We have to make sure everything is one hundred percent explicit. Everything has to be spelled out. Who's saying what to whom. Who's calling whom. The next ten meetings have to be scheduled and planned before we leave here."

"I have a very positive feeling," Rubin said. He was not about to have his good mood downgraded.

"What do you envision?" the factotum asked, with just the slightest trace of skepticism.

"I know where I'm taking this," Rubin said, not imprisoned by the factotum's literalness.

"Are you thinking about an acquisition, Jon," Alison queried, "or an investment?"

"This guy is not a finance guy, he's not a lawyer; he's a salesman, like everybody at AOL. That's your mistake when you deal with these guys," Rubin said to me, and for the benefit of all the other plodders in the room. "You want them to agree to things that they just don't know how to agree to, instead of getting them to sell shit that they know how to sell." Rubin paced.

"And the pitch is . . . ?" I prodded.

Rubin was working something out on a scrap of paper.

"How many of our books did you tell me they sold recently?" Rubin asked the EVP.

"Fifteen thousand. In one morning! It takes a year for Barnes & Noble to do that!"

"They made a mistake recently, too," I said. "They flashed one of the books on the pop screen, just one flash—we hadn't agreed to it yet—and instantaneously sold twelve hundred copies. They were very apologetic."

"We don't need an investment from them," Rubin said. "What we want is to lock into a distribution arrangement. If we can do that, if they'll commit to selling our books and our ad avails, if we can make it worthwhile for them to do that, we've made this company. Story finished. We'll have flipped from free fall to success."

He was envisioning the kind of underlying, symbiotic one-hand-washes-the-other arrangements that are, perhaps, the fertilizing moment of all successful businesses. He was imagining the way the cyber business was coming together. He was feeling it.

It depressed me, in a way. We had worked awfully hard just to become a part of AOL's grand strategy. *Strategy*, on the other hand, was not the first word you'd immediately associate with AOL. This was more of a random symbiosis, which seemed even more depressing.

Our glass conference room was positioned so that you had a bird's-eye view of visitors arriving at the reception desk. You had an opportunity to take an instant measure of your business opponents as they presented themselves to Ann, the receptionist. Almost all of the people (virtually all of them men) who arrived to discuss alliances or financings or M&A propositions (how many meetings like this had I had in a year? Three hundred? Four hundred?) arrived as delegations. To come alone was to be vulnerable, lesser, feminine. The message here is partly that a businessman is not alone but instead is a reflection of group-think, organizational concerns, market considerations. It was always interesting to watch the earnestness, the purposefulness, the gravity of these men of affairs as Ann helped them with their heavy coats and briefcases and as they composed themselves, used the men's room, and prepared to get down to business.

The AOL Exec, however, breezed in alone, carrying nothing, handsome, grinning. In a moment Ann was laughing, too.

Jon Rubin went happily to greet him.

Together, they came into the conference room with their heads bent over the AOL Exec's new cell phone (digital, micro, and just out on the market).

The AOL Exec was dressed in a dark tweedy, almost literary, style, except this was obviously the expensive version of the look, cashmere instead of wool. Contentedly, he put his feet in his half boots up on the table.

"What do you want to do?" he asked, grinning.

He was not only comfortable here with us, I guessed, but comfortable everywhere with anyone.

Overeager, I got the cue wrong and plunged into my standard windup song and dance: "Why don't I give you a snapshot of the company and where we think—"

"Don't bother, don't bother. If there's something I don't know, you'll tell me later. But I get it. No problem." Big grin (just for me).

It was nice not to have to go through the bullshit, but unnerving, too. Playing with the cool guys might be more fun than playing with the squares, but the rules are less clear.

Jon Rubin laughed. Chortled. "How fast do you want to go?"

"Fast."

"Do you have a proposal?" asked the factotum, a classic square guy without terribly much patience for the cool, ironic, handsome cats.

The AOL Exec put up his hands, mugged for the camera, for another audience somewhere, as if to say, who was this guy, the factotum, this square, come on? "Really," he said, "whatever you want. We should have done this a long time ago. I can't believe those putzes haven't put something together here. What fuckups. Who have you spoken to?"

I knew not to play this game, ratting out other executives, but he prodded. "Tell me. Come on."

I was naming names before I knew it.

To each name, the AOL Exec attached some shiv-like description, laughing at the incompetents and losers who populated AOL. Having had a brief period in Hollywood, land of the corporate shiv, I knew about companies like this. No one was in charge. It was just a hurtling fireball of separate embers of ambition. There were people on top and there were toadies and there were other people trying to get on top. It was also, probably, a little like prison. Maximum security. Hard time.

"Okay," the factotum said. "Should we be thinking in terms of an acquisition?"

"God, save me!" said the AOL Exec, throwing up his arms in mock horror. "Shit! You know, we have fucked up every acquisition we've done. But sure, we could do an acquisition. If that's what you want, we'll do it. But"—he rolled his hands—"let's think of something else. Let's be creative. Make it sing!"

"Okay," said the factotum, clearly not very happy with any of this.

"Look," Jon Rubin said. "We know what we have to sell, and we know that you can sell it."

"Great!" the AOL Exec said, happy.

I said, "We sold fifteen thousand books off the AOL pop screen in a morning."

The AOL Exec chuckled, truly chuckled; this was very amusing to him. "We could sell anything off of that screen. If we said click here for nothing, absolutely nothing, just nineteen ninety-five for *nothing*, we'd sell it. It's total, like, hello? What are you, stupid? You fuck!" He shook his head. "Who are these people?"

"Nevertheless," I tried to justify, "I think that our products—"

"Yeah, yeah."

Jon Rubin laughed. He was the only person on our side not particularly rattled by this wholesale dropping of business pretense and manners.

"You want a cigarette?" Rubin asked him.

"Can we smoke here?" The AOL Exec looked around happily, if furtively.

"Come on," Rubin said. "Come on. Let's go outside. Let's work this out."

It was embarrassing. The rest of us were left on our own to—what? throw spitballs? It did feel like the teachers had stepped out of the room. We tried to pretend we had something to do. The factotum propped open his briefcase and hunkered down with his cell phone.

"Do you know what's going on?" Alison asked warily.

"They're having a cigarette downstairs," I shrugged, annoyed that she might think I didn't know what was going on. I imagined them down in front of our office building, with all the other unreconstructed smokers, planning the future of my business.

"I don't get it. I just don't get it," she said. "What is the AOL explanation?"

***

The AOL explanation is . . . sex. It always surprised me that this was not widely known and appreciated.

I had often wondered, as AOL works to transform itself into a great, new American family-centered company, putting its product into living rooms and finished basements across the continent, what will happen if (what will happen when) the forces of reaction and hellfire and religious oppression and white bread get a clear idea of what's going on here?

How many reports do we need of a teen traveling from a chat room to an assignation in a mall and onto some not pretty picture described (almost gleefully) in *USA Today* for us to get the message? But most of us think of this, rightly I would guess, as marginal behavior and stop thinking about it there.

When in fact it is, at the same time, quite possibly the outermost manifestation of a whole new rich stew of social and sexual behavior, perhaps as momentous a behavioral development as the sexual revolution itself.

I mean, people talk about it. People are always saying, "Sex is an early market for new technologies." The home video business grew up from porn rentals; 900-numbers, cable, Hollywood, all sex inspired, of course.

But that discussion, that kind of long view, that I-don't-know-anyone-who-is-a-part-of-this position, doesn't begin to give the flavor of what's going on here.

There were almost 8 million AOL members by the end of 1996, with nineteen thousand chat rooms operating each evening, according to *USA Today*. Rumor (AOL is highly secretive about its numbers—about who goes where for how long doing what at what time) has it that as much as 80 percent of prime-time activity is spent in those rooms.

The irony is that AOL knows more about what an individual is doing at any given moment than any monitoring scheme that's ever been invented. Double irony: part of AOL's compelling programming is that it offers users the ability to know what other users are doing, which makes AOL something of a community of stalkers.

After logging on to the service, AOL members descend, Dante-like, from the cheerful, servicey, slightly vapid airline-magazine tone of the opening screen to the People Connection, a level with a kind of mixer atmosphere of off-color, tongue-hanging, "let's get friendly," boy–girl, girl–boy, girl–girl, boy–boy humor; to the member rooms, which present a series of doorways into Fellini-like fetishes, and down deeper into private rooms, where autoeroticism rises at least to the level of pulp fiction if not to some new form of entertainment or even twenty-first-century sexuality.

Then there's the member directory, a remarkable tool. From this you can know what secrets lurk in the hearts of man. Really. Want to know how many women are dying for a spanking in Phoenix? (Spanking—a cultivated and esoteric interest, one would think—seems all the rage in cyberspace.) Want to find one of those Phoenix spanking women right now? She's in the Strict Parents chat room, or if that room is full, maybe she's in SP Regulars.

Anyone can have sex on AOL. Many, it seems, do. Curiously though, recognition of this phenomenon has not yet become part of the overall understanding of what AOL is about, or part of the business analysis of what moves the industry.

But this, the sex stuff, is New Media. Everything else is largely a redistribution of media as it's always been. This sex stuff is, really, new—a paradigm shift.

For one thing, you have ordinary people, millions of ordinary people, engaged in a narrative enterprise. Writing dialogue, crafting descriptions, setting scenes, developing characters. You have real dramatic engagements. It's a new form of story, of the written word, of the way we communicate fantasies, desires, aspirations. I'm serious.

This is interactivity.

Then there's the social thing. I'd love to see numbers on this. How many private room dalliances shift to direct phone contact? How many phone callers take the next step to a Bennigans? My guess is that if a reliable study were ever done, the results would have a Kinsey-like effect on our worldview.

Okay. People like sex. Even baroque sex. So what else is new?

It's just that sex has not historically been a main motivator, to say the least, in the software business. So it will be curious to see what happens at this unexpected intersection. What happens when not only consumers but the technology industry comes to terms with the interesting fact that the cyber business is motivated by an itch. When Microsoft understands— duh . . . it's sex!

Perhaps it is exactly at the meeting point of technology and sex that mass media is created.

Now, although cybersex has been the mighty engine of AOL's hypergrowth, AOL has been trying maniacally to distance itself from this fact. There is the engine room and then there are the promenade decks, sort of.

Moving from its chat service roots, AOL, in the early 1990s, started to add content. The notion was to broaden the appeal of the service, to offer something to users who might not be as interested in spanking as in, say, country inns. But perhaps more important, the idea was to keep the spanker, then paying six dollars an hour for his AOL visits, online a little longer. Spankers, after all, might need to look for a country inn, too.

The cable business got a big initial push because it offered consumers a glimpse of things never seen before, perhaps hardly ever imagined, in an American home. But cable then proceeded to narrow and contain those offerings until they were only some late-night, low-rent oddity. AOL, on the other hand, grew its sex business even faster than it grew its "content" business.

You might not know it—and if you did know it, ironically, you could hardly admit to it—but underneath AOL's layers of *Time* and Disney beats a heart of astounding carnality. Indeed, without the restraint of hourly charges, AOL becomes the greatest sex business in the history of the world. A nonstop orgy really means something here.

This was, then, what had brought AOL, against all odds and logic, to the precipice of owning the industry.

···

Jon Rubin and the AOL Exec came back upstairs from their smoke in a playful good humor. Frisky almost. They were masters of the universe. They were above it all. We were all geeks whereas they were two guys who could cut a deal.

Rubin had not only set up the shot but now he was getting ready to make the goal, too.

Taking his time, prolonging the wait, enjoying the tension, he made a phone call first, languidly arranging his evening plans.

The AOL Exec had plans, too; he confided into his little phone.

Everyone else in the conference room was an afterthought.

"We're not going to be able to do anything with AOL," Rubin said to the factotum, grinning.

"It's such a shitty company, anyway," said the AOL Exec, having fun, too.

"You mean America On Hold?" said the factotum, taking his best shot at repartee.

"Okay," Rubin said, pulling a piece of scrap paper from his pocket and putting his foot on the chair. "Are you ready? Do you want to hear it?"

Alison, the factotum, the EVP, and the technology advisor each got out their pads.

I sat on tenterhooks.

The AOL Exec settled into a chair and put his feet back up on the table.

"This isn't complicated," Rubin said.

"No bullshit," the AOL Exec said. "No lawyers."

"Okay. Ready?" Rubin made us wait for another moment. "AOL guarantees us enough cash to cover our monthly burn rate," said Rubin. "On the first of every month we get a check."

He continued: "AOL recoups from selling our books on the pop screen at standard discount, plus AOL, which will provide us with traffic, becomes the exclusive rep for all of our ad avails."

"What's the term?" Alison asked.

Rubin turned to the AOL Exec. "Three years?"

"Sure."

"AOL receives nineteen point nine percent of the company and has a six-months option to purchase the rest of the company for forty million dollars. Okay?"

"What else?" the factotum said.

"That's it." Rubin spread his hands to indicate the ease of victory.

I looked over at the AOL Exec. "Beautiful," he said. "Tell me we don't need lawyers."

"We may need a few," said the factotum with his helpless literalness.

There was beauty to the deal. Symmetry. Proportion. By giving AOL part of our company, it would give us access to its audience. The monthly guarantee would force AOL to make good on this access; what's more, we were encouraging AOL with a solid profit basis—the more AOL opened its audience to us, the more money AOL made. Then, too, by giving AOL control of our ad sales, AOL would be motivated to open the spigot of its audience to us. Then, after having made us a profitable company, they could buy us for a relative discount; indeed, they would be motivated to make us as profitable as possible to increase the size of their discount. If they made us widely profitable, which they had the ability to do without much thought, Wall Street would be pleased that they could buy us for only $40 million and would then send AOL's stock up a notch or two, thereby paying for our acquisition. AOL would, therefore, be buying us for nothing.

I wondered if in this snapshot you couldn't see how industries are reduced to a few giant players. All the struggles, all the sleepless nights, and all that entrepreneurial zeal come to this, I thought with sudden nostalgia.

"If you," said the AOL Exec, looking to the factotum, "could put this into memo form—not long, two pages tops—that would be great. I'll just walk it through. Good deal. Perfect. Easy. No one's going to break a sweat here. Done." He took his feet off the table. He was ready to go.

"Let's not complicate it," Rubin said. He didn't want the factotum, or Alison, to start to ask the kind of questions that bankers and lawyers ask.

I didn't want them to ask those questions, either.

But I did want to do something. Having been here, I wanted to force it a little more. Apply some glue.

I said, "Are there any obstacles between here and closing the deal?"

"I know that you've had problems with us before, but I'm giving you my word. This is a done deal. Done! Absolute outside, end-of-the-year closing."

Forty-five days.

"Just," I said, "so I don't have to kill myself on New Year's Eve, are there any impediments, any at all, to moving this through the AOL bureaucracy and getting this signed, sealed, and delivered by January 1?"

"Only," he grinned, "if you doubt my abilities as a salesman." Is the Pope Catholic?

There was a restaurant that Alison and I went to sometimes. It was a place that might make you crazy with envy if all wasn't right with your world, but if you had put it together, if you had pulled it off, sowed and reaped, you could be very comfortable there. I called for a table.

A lot of business seems to be about ending up where you never wanted to go. It's about toeing the line. Accepting reality. Going with the power. The fact that the entrepreneurial impulse runs against that grain just means that you have to develop a sense of irony.

Early on, I had rejected AOL. What did they know, after all, about the information business? They were a computer bulletin board service, a

BBS; this was, really, CB radio stuff. It was AOL who pursued us, trying to buy an ad in one of our books. Who buys an ad in a book, anyway? Clearly, they had no idea how the media world works. We did, however, take their $5,000 for a page somewhere after the index (in a bit of AOL dysfunction, they sent us $150,000 instead of $5,000 for the page).

Then there was a snobbish thing, too. We were an Internet company. AOL was a "proprietary system." It had nothing to do with the Internet; it wasn't at all part of this grand new adventure in communication, community, and free information; it was uncool and headed, surely, to the ash heap of history.

But you could make money from AOL. Rosalind Resnick, formerly a reporter at the *Miami Herald,* was NetGirl on AOL, a cyber Miss Lonely Hearts, whose cut of the connect time, the pennies out of every dollar spent connected to the service and through to NetGirl, amounted to $40,000 every month. Then there were the Motley Fools, the irreverent investment advisors, whom AOL had turned into near stars. Then the Gay and Lesbian Forum, raking it in. And Hoover's (offering profiles of American companies), whose first monthly AOL check in August 1992 was for $123 and who by 1996 was netting more than $35,000 a month from AOL.

This was real money, in cyberspace.

But because what happened at AOL was so often unplanned for, inadvertent, a surprise to all concerned, a true algorithm of unintended cause and effect, it was hard to get the institution to respond with any predictability or logic or business process.

In the spring of 1995, I had gone down to AOL's offices with Pat Spain, the CEO of Hoover's, who had arranged a meeting for me with AOL executives.

Hoover's, then called the Reference Press, a book publisher in Austin, Texas, was started in 1990 by Gary Hoover, a retail savant who had created the first book superstore chain, called Bookstop, which grew in six years from one store to the fourth-largest chain in the country before being bought by Barnes & Noble. Gary Hoover was an information geek, with a small-college-size library of reference books located in a separate building on his Texas estate. He had hundreds of thousands of books about trains, books about war, books about travel, books about business. It was more or less natural that he would start a reference publishing company after he sold his bookstore chain. He figured he could take high-priced information and retail it at attractive prices to ordinary consumers.

It may be a meaningful footnote in the life of the book business that one of the real geniuses of retail book sales was not able to sell his own books in bookstores. Disappointed with the publishing business, Hoover let Pat

Spain, a disaffected lawyer and 1980s M&A guy and a friend from the University of Chicago, try his hand at running the company.

In many ways, what Spain began to do, slowly and inadvertently, was to create perhaps the first successful alternative to consumer print publishing. With the philosophy that "no deal is too small," he began signing up with any electronic information distributor that would take the information he had to sell. A skilled and patient negotiator, he was able to resist the one convention of the online business at that time—exclusivity. "In the end, we were too small for exclusivity to be so important. Besides we just wouldn't do it." The first deal was with AOL. Other pre-Web deals would include CompuServe, Dow Jones, eWorld, Lexis/Nexis, and Bloomberg. At one point, highlighting the contradictions that would soon threaten the old-line online providers, the same Hoover's info that would cost you pennies on AOL could cost you more than twenty-five dollars on Lexis/Nexis.

What Hoover's began to see was a distribution model that would allow it to sell its information for the same price and for potentially greater margins to the same audience it had hoped to reach in Barnes & Noble without unit and promotional costs and without the risks of returns.

In 1994, Larry Kirshbaum, president of Time Warner's Warner Books, looking toward the end of books in paper form, bought 30 percent of Hoover's.

In early 1995, in a further oddity of the relationship between books and bookstores and readers and information, our company published a book called *NetMoney* that featured Hoover's on the cover and doubled Hoover's traffic on AOL.

I went down with Spain to Vienna, Virginia, to AOL's unprepossessing faceless brick headquarters at the end of a road. Spain had done this trip innumerable times. He knew the routines and the rhythms. Just go. Just sit there. Purge yourself of ego. In the great maelstrom of history, of which AOL increasingly saw itself as a key part, the individual was of little consequence. Just be there when they needed you. Let someone else worry about the big picture, concentrate on the details.

We sat around a conference table. No one at AOL seemed to know what to do with us. "Did we know you were coming down today?" asked several affable execs. Spain took no offense. He just didn't move.

It took a little while, but before long we had a real meeting on our hands with nine or ten people (only one of whom looked to be out of college) with large titles and wide areas of concern—business, sports, entertainment. It was as though each of these concerns was being addressed for the first time. It was very much an undergraduate seminar mood. These were deep, broad, meaningful, as well as meaningless, questions being tended to.

Something was going on here. The online world had always had a pretty clear idea of mission and function. Its metaphor was a straightforward one. An online service was a newsstand. It was very happy with this metaphor because it was simple and it was businesslike, very clearly dividing up talents and skills. Newsstands brought you other people's information. Online systems did that and, in addition, made it possible for you to get this information with a whole range of technological advantages and added value. But an online service was not in the information gathering and creating and processing and packaging business. The online service was not in the content business.

But AOL obviously had plans. They denied it: they weren't content creators, they said. Except for look and feel. And except for navigational issues. And except for chat. And except for the opening screen. And except for celebrities. And except for news.

Still, while I was disturbed by this arrogance, this mix-up of roles, this changing of the rules, I was not foolish. Not only was the AOL payday real, but their interest in what our company might offer them, how they might put our content to use, as they put it, seemed genuine. They overflowed with ideas about how we might "work together"; it was a free-for-all of notions and ideas and opportunities for all. I left the meeting with point people assigned and follow-up steps in place.

"Thank you," I said to Spain. "I appreciate that. They seemed really receptive."

"You'll never hear from them again," he said.

I laughed. What he was saying, I knew, was that the follow-up was always hard. Follow-up, in fact, is everything. Most entrepreneurs will fail in follow-up. They don't press hard enough. Or press too hard. They get lost in the turnaround. Or lose the enthusiasm of the meeting. Or they find out their point person has been canned or promoted. A hundred things can go wrong. I knew that, of course.

But that's not what Spain meant. He meant that I wouldn't hear from them again.

Four months passed with absolutely no response to the variety of e-mails, phone calls, and colorful packages of books I sent in their direction.

"What do I do?" I asked Spain.

"Just keep doing what you're doing. It won't hurt, anyway. But you should probably go down again."

Then one day, very early on a Saturday morning when I happened to be grabbing a silent hour in the office, AOL called. "Just wanted to follow up, see where we are. Find out about the next steps," said the affable point person.

I was ready to play the game: "I'm going to be in D.C. at the end of the week. Maybe we can get some face time together. I can come out to Vienna."

"Great. Lunch?"

And so, only a season after my last meeting with AOL, I flew to D.C. and took a cab from National Airport through the Virginia foliage to Vienna.

At this meeting, with a large spread of cold cuts, there were almost twenty people, none recognizable from the last meeting except the person who had made the Saturday morning call.

Every encounter at AOL, I started to understand, is a process of starting over again, because an organization that is growing as fast as AOL is, from month to month, is almost a new organization. My history with the company, I realized, was now longer than that of most of the people at this table.

AOL wasn't pretending otherwise. It was an organization that begged tolerance. It was hard not to be tolerant as I looked around the table at the eager, flushed, young faces, all wanting to do well in their first job.

There was the enthusiasm here of wartime. A good war. People full of idealism flooding into Washington. "Let's do everything we can." "Let's run it up the flagpole." "Let's throw it against the wall and see if it sticks." And perhaps, in this, an absence of personal responsibility, because the individual is dwarfed by the forces of history. AOL was part of the tide now. AOL would happen. The online revolution would happen. New Media would happen. No matter what anyone at this table did.

I was assigned another point person. We agreed on a list of "action items." I was invited to the next AOL partners conference.

Then—well, nothing. Like there was no AOL. Like there was no Vienna, Virginia. Silence. Nothing. Nada.

So what you do is you send an e-mail and you say, "Oh, it just so happens I'm going to Washington, have a meeting with the President, and thought I'd stop by and see you afterwards. Maybe we can continue our discussions."

You show up and it truly might have been that all you'd find was a fragrant field, where, in your dreams, a company called AOL had been. But, no, you get there and find another conference room of eager, unfamiliar people wanting to talk about the great things you're going to do together.

You keep doing this. Why? Because it is just so weird. And then you get to talking to other people, other AOL partners and prospective partners, and you find out you're not alone, that this is the way you do business with AOL. It is like the government. And, like the government, it is not going to do anything unless you make it, force it. Work the halls. A thousand handshakes later, your company gets a tax abatement. Or something like that.

The Patricof people prepare the two-page document outlining our agreement with AOL and fax it to Jon Rubin, who is in St. Barts for the weekend, and deliver it by hand to the AOL Exec at his apartment in New York, by Fed Ex to his office in Vienna, by e-mail attachment, and—to be double, triple, quadruple sure—by courier out to the hotel in Arizona where the AOL partners conference is shortly to commence.

By midweek, the AOL Exec's secretary in Virginia confirms that, indeed, he hasn't gotten anything from us yet but that we should get it to him as soon as possible.

We deliver it all again.

No word.

Then, yes, confirmation.

Silence.

The weekend.

Day One of the next workweek with everyone in their respective offices.

Day Two.

Day Three.

"I'll call him," Jon Rubin says.

Day Four.

Day Five. "It's set," Rubin reports. "It's cool. There's an executive committee meeting on Monday. It'll be signed off on, and we'll go to contract. He'll call as soon as the meeting ends."

Alison and I take ourselves out to dinner again.

Monday. Day One of Workweek Two. Waiting for the nod from the executive committee meeting. Continue waiting. No word.

Day Two. "The meeting got pushed," Rubin reports back. "It's on Thursday. What can I tell you?"

Day Three. I send an e-mail. My tone tactically assumes that a deal is done, that we're working together, that we're all on the same team.

Day Four. Nothing.

Day Five. "Looking good," Rubin says.

"What does that mean? Are we going to contract?"

"I just got a message that everything was looking good, that's all I know."
Rubin is testy.

⚏⚏⚏

The technology advisor, the EVP, and I head out to Chicago for a meeting
with Ameritech.

Ameritech has the idea that it's going to become the Midwest's gateway
to the Internet, so it's more than likely we won't be able to do the AOL
deal *and* the Ameritech deal. We'll go with AOL, but obviously it will be
good to have Ameritech in our back pocket.

It's an easy meeting. Ameritech is at least eighteen months behind the
industry. Their enthusiasm is untempered by any experience. I've taken
advantage of this kind of condition before; I'm confident I can take advantage of it again.

We spend the day working with them through their due diligence. We
seem sound to them. They like us. And that's it. Yes, they'll do the deal, invest the money we need at the valuation we want. And they'll close it by
Christmas.

So there it is. Home. Safety. I've made it.

We deliver Ameritech into the factotum's hands. We'll have a deal
memo in days.

Now let's see if there are better options.

⚏⚏⚏

The Washington Post Company comes in again. They are having a slight
change in the way they are thinking about our deal. They are seeing it now
as a Newsweek deal—they own *Newsweek* magazine—rather than a
Washington Post deal.

"Okay," we say.

"But," the factotum says, "we should tell you. We have a proposal we're
considering from AOL."

This rattles them. Clearly. Our price is going up. Way up.

They'll get back to us next week, for sure, they say. In fact, let's set it up, let's
get all the appropriate Newsweek people in here. Let's get the dialogue going.

⚏⚏⚏

At the end of the third week, I place a call to the AOL Exec through the
Wildfire system. Wildfire is the king of all voice mail systems. It's one of

those Hal-like bits of technology that makes you say, "Whoa, this is enough!" The cool dominatrix voice. The machine's omniscience. It's universal reach. The way it expresses its lack of interest in you, the way it declares you unworthy of a connection.

My query ricochets through the AOL offices in Vienna and then up to the Seagram's Building in New York. It finds the AOL Exec in transit via cell phone.

He accepts the call, and Wildfire completes the connection.

"I would tell you," he says, "if there was anything to worry about. There is nothing. This deal will happen. I give you my word. Guarantee. We want this deal. This is a no-brainer. I'm sorry things got fucked up last week, but this is a fucked-up company. But it doesn't have anything to do with your deal. I won't let anyone fuck this deal up. Relax."

"Listen," I say firmly. "We have an offer from Ameritech. And we're going to get one from the Washington Post. We can't do those deals and do a deal with you. We want to do a deal with you. You're our choice. But we have to nail it down with you. And I mean now!"

"I'm telling you, we are nailed down. I don't want you to do those other deals. I absolutely don't want you to do those other deals. Promise me."

"I promise you if you do a deal with me, I won't do another deal."

"Done! Really, man, I'll kill you if you do another deal. I'll fucking kill you!"

"Listen, here's an idea. Why don't we all come down to Vienna. We'll come with our lawyers, you'll get yours there, and we'll just finish it. Close it."

"If you want to do that, fine, no sweat. But it's not necessary. The executive committee is meeting on Monday. We can do a conference call with lawyers on Tuesday. Then we'll make a game plan for closing."

"Okay. Let's schedule that." I am confident I have cleared the path to finishing this.

The executive committee meeting was put off until Thursday. Meanwhile, another executive, who in fact had previously worked as a consultant for us and from whom we had an outstanding bill for ten grand or so (and who, I imagined, feared his $10,000 might be in jeopardy if we didn't get the AOL deal), had been asked to prepare a business plan for our deal. This executive suggested that perhaps we wanted to do a draft. This was good, I knew. This was how you stayed in control. We were well connected. We were on top of things. We were working the organization.

On Thursday, Jon Rubin went out to National Airport and hung around the shuttle gates to run into, fortuitously, the AOL Exec on his way up to New York. From the exec, Rubin learned that the executive committee meeting had been held, all right, but something had come up and our deal had been bumped from the agenda. But the AOL Exec gave Jon Rubin his word. They talked about the frustrations of such high-growth organizations, of the certain sickness of opportunities that affects the organization, a real pathology, this need to grab for everything. And they talked about vintage Mustangs, too. They both dug them. Jon Rubin had one, and the AOL Exec was looking for one, too.

Jon Rubin was confident about the deal.

I wasn't taking anything for granted. I was shepherding Ameritech with great care. We were looking to close a few days before Christmas. We were on target. This was the factotum's real talent; he was a document guy. He would pull this together. I was checking in with him on an almost constant basis—two calls in the morning, two calls after lunch. There were no wrinkles. Say what you want about the boring Midwestern guys at Ameritech, they were steady. What you see is what you get. The factotum was totally confident about the deal. And he didn't have any doubt that we could bring it in right on schedule.

We were all a little less sanguine about the Washington Post Company. They weren't necessarily less interested, but they seemed all of a sudden interested in the wrong thing. They were interested in our book business. It was odd. They kept gnashing their teeth about the Internet, about what the Internet was costing them already, and about all the costs to come. And would it really happen, the Internet? How could you be sure? Books suddenly seemed like a great thing to them. Now, our books were a decent business—we pumped out a new guidebook to the Internet every twenty days or so, which provided a nice revenue stream and even a little profit—but because book businesses, no matter how profitable, tended to be sold at about a multiple of one times revenues, and Internet businesses, no matter how unprofitable, could well be sold at twenty to forty times revenues, the last thing that we wanted to talk about was books.

Ameritech was on the phone. I was on one end of the floor and asked for the call to be put back to my office at the other end. It was going to be a schmooze call. I was starting to like these guys and had begun to balance in my mind the relative value of AOL glamour, with its attendant dysfunctionality, against Ameritech's flat-footedness and its accompanying dependability. At the moment, certainly, AOL had the business by the tail. But that could change in a second, I figured, and you could easily see the RBOCs slowly, doggedly coming to control the Net. It was a pretty fundamental choice. Glamour on the one hand, infrastructure on the other. It was one of those choices that you could make either very right or very wrong.

When I picked up the phone, the guy from Ameritech, a very affable sort in his early thirties whom I had first met at the conference in New York and become friendly with during a fair amount of conference room time, said, "We're not going to be able to do the deal."

An echo chamber seemed to open up.

"I know that's not what you expected to hear. And all I can do is say that it wasn't what I expected to tell you. But a decision has been made to curtail all of Ameritech's Internet investments for at least the next quarter and probably two. It's terrible that yours was so close to getting done. I'm sorry. This is really a hard one."

"I understand. Thanks for calling."

"I'd like to stay in touch."

"Definitely. Definitely."

Our office was just down the street from the Museum of Modern Art. The museum was an awfully good place to hide from reality for a couple of hours.

Meanwhile, AOL, we were getting reports, was going through another transformation in the way it saw its business. It was probably the thing that most marked it as a new kind of company, a twenty-first-century company. It was not that AOL represented a new kind of media delivered through computers but that it was comfortable changing the fundamental nature of its business as often as need be—every other month, if necessary.

It had been a computer bulletin board service, an information distribution company, an Internet service provider, a direct marketing organization, a media company, and now, in its latest incarnation, it was trying to become something like a cable company; using the infomercial media model, it would sell space to direct marketers, to the Ginsu knife people, and on top of that would take a piece of each sale, too.

"There's been a rethink," said the consultant, to whom we owed $10,000, who had joined AOL. He was delivering a back-channel point of view. "If there's any way," he said deliberately, "that you can revise your proposal so that you're paying us instead of us paying you, the time to do that would be now."

AOL, apparently, had understood the implications of flat-fee pricing. As they continued to think about the no-win situation of paying information providers, they flipped this around and saw, clearly, that information providers should be paying *them*.

"This is my fault. I'm going to take care of it," said the AOL Exec. "This is what we'll do. We'll put everybody in a room and just get it done."

"And you still feel . . . you still feel that it will go through?" I prodded.

"Don't sweat it, okay? Don't sweat it. I would tell you if there were any problems. This is just a fucked-up company, and sometimes you have to wrestle people to the ground. Just get your guys together."

AOL was in physical transition, too, moving from its more modest, red-brick, down-the-end-of-the-road office to a corporate edifice, with atrium lobby, in a campus setting out near Dulles Airport in Virginia.

The meeting was scheduled in the new executive suite out at the "Dulles location," as it was being called in the transition.

Jon Rubin and the factotum swung by the Vienna office and offered the AOL Exec, who had not yet completed his move, a ride out to the Dulles location. The EVP and I went directly out to Dulles.

The EVP was a businessman's businessman. He was in the Halcyon Club of every major frequent flyer group; at Helene Curtis, where he worked after his stint at P&G, he flew to Asia twice a month. He bought every self-help inspiration business book—*God Is My CEO, Lincoln Is My Manager*, or some such. His head was always in *Forbes, Business-Week*, or *Fortune*. He was analytic to a fault. Paragraphs were for pansies, spreadsheets were for men. His desk was military neat. He snacked on Power Bars. He never wrote a sentence without a forward slash in it. He had a square head, a close shave, and UCLA shoulders. He was a constant reminder of the intrusion into my business of a sensibility—impersonal, managerial, literal—that I assumed dominated most businesses in America. He was the by-the-book guy in every army movie.

He was here, we both understood, to take my job. He had been promised it. He was the investors' stalking horse. He was their fallback—and their leap forward, too. He was one more way they figured they couldn't lose.

It was odd, therefore, that we got along. I thought it was perhaps a talent he got out of the self-help business books, some rule of modern business warfare. Kill the other guy with sincerity. We had nothing in common, except miles flown together. But perhaps this was not true. We had the cyber business, which had hit him hard. All the certainties of business (which, no doubt, was what appealed to him about business) had been removed. A whole business value system—successful businesses are profitable businesses; numbers don't lie; phone calls are to be returned—had been turned on its head. The hype was killing him. In the packaged goods business, where he had spent the formative years of his career, people, apparently, told the truth more often than not. In the cyber business, it seemed that no one ever told the truth. Sometimes it seemed that there was no truth. It was all bullshit.

As the EVP and I sat in the AOL commissary, he started to reminisce about the Procter & Gamble cafeteria. He confided: "When I was at P&G, I never wanted to eat in the cafeteria," he said, as if to tell me some secret about his character. "I always went out to a restaurant. Didn't care what kind of place it was."

I had an unlikely vision of the EVP walking down the road in Cincinnati, P&G's hometown.

Then he said, "I've told Rubin and the Patricof people that if we can't complete this AOL deal, I'm going to be leaving the company. I'm sorry. I just can't do it anymore."

I had found that one of the hardest things in business was that people leave you. Even when the people I didn't want in the first place tell me they're leaving, I choke up.

"I guess it's been rough," I said. "I'm sorry."

"I can't deal with people who aren't straight with you. Who do these AOL guys think they are?" he asked bitterly. "Do they just think they can screw around with anybody they want to screw around with? Maybe that's naive. I can't help it."

"I'm not sure it's a screw job," I offered. "I think it's more that nobody knows what to do. I think everybody is sitting on top of very precarious businesses. It's as likely as not that none of the companies we take for granted today will be here in a year or two. Not just us."

"You don't think you'll be here?" He seemed concerned.

"I guess I've never thought much more than a day, or a pay period, ahead. Which is wrong, obviously. We should be taking the long view and realize that nothing that we do today really matters."

He seemed shocked. "I don't think I could live if I thought that way."

"Well, it matters. Today it matters," I tried to comfort him.

"You think this will all be . . . " He waved his hand, trailing off.

"I think it will all be different, unrecognizable. Yeah. We're transitional. All technology is transitional."

"In the end, what? Time Warner or Disney or Murdoch or Microsoft buys the winners and runs it all?"

I shrugged. "I'm sure they're transitional companies, too."

"That's cool," he said, seeming to find some comfort in this notion.

In my experience, most meetings are hard to start. AOL meetings were particularly hard to get going. This meeting, however, which involved moving people—the penultimate people in the AOL corporation—not only around a new building but across northern Virginia, was the worst so far.

My father described World War II as four years of waiting around. Now I have an experience, I was starting to think, to compare to his.

It took a few hours for Jon Rubin and the factotum to round up the AOL Exec in Vienna and transport him to Dulles. They were all in a good mood, a fraternity brother mood, when they arrived.

It took an hour or more to have lunch again because they hadn't eaten.

"Where are we?" I asked, catching Rubin for a second.

"The deal is done."

"No, seriously."

"Really, he says there's nothing to worry about."

"What did you say to him?"

"I said if he got it done, I'd give him my Mustang."

"That's a joke, right?" (I had actually heard this before. If you were really serious in business, if you were really a player, you'd give a car.)

"Yeah."

But when the meeting did begin, it was pretty clear pretty quickly that we were a long way from a done deal here.

Indeed, we were starting all over again.

There were new faces.

There were new considerations.

Why were we here? What did we have to offer? Etceteras, etceteras.

People went in and out of the meeting.

The AOL Exec actually seemed to be in several meetings at the same time, working the hall.

"Let's do it. To me it's done," he said to his colleagues puzzling over the details. "Just figure out how you want to do it."

He left the room.

His colleagues, each in turn, left the room, got involved with something else, then returned to our deal again.

More meals were served.

Hours passed.

I saw how this would happen. I saw how it could happen. You could have anything you want, you could do anything you want. If you didn't make someone say yes. No big yes. No grand decisions. No one wanted that. Someone would have to take responsibility for that. But if it just started to happen, just began to move here and began to move there . . .

It *was* like the army. We were all in the army, the cyberspace army. And if we didn't make a big deal out of something but just figured out how to do it, or do something, without anyone having to make a decision that no one had the experience and foresight to make, then it would happen, and the war would be fought in the same condition of absurdity and occasional personal profit that all wars are fought.

We were left there in the conference room—with occasional visits and expressions of interest from the top AOL brass—to our own devices.

And I had the feeling that I could do it. I could move down the corridor, introduce myself, get a thing going here and a thing going there. Yes. Get a hotel room. Stay the evening. Come back tomorrow. I could do it. If I weren't so tired.

And I *was* exhausted. Beat. Beaten.

Well past evening, with no formal end to our meeting (Jon Rubin had long since left, and the factotum had gone in his own direction), the EVP and I got up to head back to New York.

"We're going to do this," the AOL Exec said, catching us on the way out. "It's a no-brainer."

Chapter Nine

Exit Strategy

I flew out to another conference in San Francisco, where I was scheduled to speak to beg for my future. More VCs mingling in the event rooms of a downtown hotel. More pastries. More fresh fruit. Many of the same entrepreneurs from the last conference, a few fresh from successful IPOs, a few with recent funding in hand, most running out of dough. There was a new crop as well, as determined as the old. And, as always, our PR people, our $40,000-per-month PR people in black garb, moving in their snarky fashion through the crowd.

Push was the word. *Push* instead of *pull*. Because users were not reliably coming—that is, being pulled—to most of the five million Web sites (or six or seven or eight million. They were growing in some weird Malthusian inversion: population grew arithmetically, Web sites geometrically) that resided in cyberspace, there was a new technology whose strategy was to push the Web to them.

"Destination is bullshit," my former assistant, Seth Goldstein, now cyber ad agency CEO, lectured me. "If you build it, they won't fucking come. Forget about it. If you don't got distribution, you don't got nothin'."

By which he meant, you had to get your Web site in front of people's faces—like television. PointCast was the company to beat in the push field; virtually everyone, including Microsoft, was trying. PointCast wired your PC to serve the Web up to you in your idle moments. The Web was your screensaver. Neat.

Except that it didn't exactly work. And if you did get it to work, the question people seemed to ask was, Why? Why do I need this? If I want television, I have a better one. People in the know were saying, "Push." People *really* in the know were saying, "Push is stillborn."

I had no opinion.

I do not believe I have ever been so tired. I looked at the cheese Danish in my hand and wondered how it had gotten there. I stood at the podium in front of the VCs in my little hotel conference room and thought it is not at all unlikely that I was going to throw up. I watched myself, out-of-body like. There I was. Precise. Sober. Elegant. Gray double-breasted suit. And about to deliver a projectile vomit.

"Need I say more?" I hoped I'd have the aplomb to say to the financial and technology community after my hurl.

Exhaustion, this kind of exhaustion, is not just what happens when you haven't slept enough. It happens when you've roamed the far reaches of your mind and experience and just don't know what to think anymore. There was no exit from the cell.

I was scheduled to go home on the red-eye, too.

I wondered how other people here, the people who were doing what I was doing, begging for money for months and months on end, did it. I sure hoped they weren't wondering how I did it.

After I did my pitch—by the book, with numbers on projected growth and return on investment—without an upchuck, I had a few hours to kill and decided to stop in at Wired. I found Louis's empire to be both profound and comical. A magazine, an electronic media company, a book group, many projects to come, 350 employees, real estate all over downtown San Francisco. He had achieved the commercial manifestation of exactly what he believed in. Of how many visionaries can that be said? But the financial prospects of the Wired empire were slim to none. He had failed at his second IPO. At the end of 1996, he had been forced to take money on terms perhaps even more onerous than the terms I had taken money on—$20 million with impossible-to-meet performance hurdles. I wondered if he thought he could yet pull this off. Certainly no one who knew anything about the rules of preference thought he could. What do you do when you know that you're fucked?

Louis looked even more tired than I felt. He sat in front of a big monitor doodling with his mouse. His eyes were deeper. His face gaunter. I would have liked to reminisce, to spend a moment remembering when there was no Internet, no cyber business, no millions to die for. A lot had happened in a short time, after all. That was worth something. More than just something. Many people would certainly be willing to regard Louis as heroic, if not entirely successful. I would.

He had made a revolution. Hell, me, too. In a way.

I suppose, though, it would be a little while still before we knew if it was a revolution in the way people think and communicate and relate that we had helped make, or just a revolution in the way people shopped.

I did not succeed in getting Louis to open up.

I went out to the airport and was back in my office in New York just a little after dawn.

I knew the rule. Just keep showing up. If they can't move you, if you just stay put, hang on, hold out, you become part of whatever gets built.

I can't place the exact moment when I started to question that logic. But I know that once you do, whether it's in a relationship or taking a test or running a race or building a business, once the willing suspension of disbelief fails, you're in big trouble.

Is this worth it? is a very subversive question.

Alison quit. She would help me, but she wouldn't work for the company anymore.

"You decided to go into business with people who you thought could make you money," she said.

"Make us money!"

"It wasn't relevant to you whether you liked them or trusted them. That seems relevant to me now."

"We made a business decision. This industry was moving so fast that we needed to get the resources to grow with it."

"Yes. That was your decision."

The Internet itself was also starting to close in on me, I felt.

We were publishing as many words a month on the Internet as a monthly magazine publishes in print. And we weren't stopping there. We were moving to a schedule where we would be publishing that many words every week. Given the speed of the Net, given its ability to deliver information at a speed that made television seem sleepy, we would be publishing more and more words faster and faster. Ever spiraling. Already we had five million words residing out in cyberspace.

We were building an audience, too. We were making our distribution deals. We were getting traffic. We were selling ads.

Because this was cyberspace, because this was server technology, because this was a revolutionary new medium in which we could monitor the interests and habits and behavior of our users, we knew something about the users of the Internet that I deeply, desperately even, wished I did not know.

Here is the incontrovertible truth:

No one reads on the Internet.

Not conventionally. Not as I read something printed on paper. Not as I write. Not in word, sentence, paragraph, article, and longer-version form.

We could see the "user" hover for a second, or a half second, and alight, like a bug, on a paragraph and then linger for a moment and be gone. Bolt. Vamoose. Vaporize.

I used all the tricks: screaming headlines, audacious jokes, in-your-face conflict. I used short sentences. Shorter sentences. Exclamations!

Nothing worked.

There were many explanations. We hadn't configured lines and pages right for the eye. People had to get used to monitors. People still didn't really know what they were doing on the Web. It was early. Behavior was still in flux.

But I knew. I just knew.

In some perfect irony, we had invented this new publishing medium, and no one read.

And no one would read. They would do many exciting things. They would be stimulated and informed in ways that we had not yet invented and could not begin to imagine. But they wouldn't read. I understood that.

I was lonely but not alone. I had Jon Rubin. He had me. We were each other's tar baby. His taking control of the company, a move that had made me feel something like a prisoner of war, was, I think, a big blunder for him. A version of the Soviet Union in Afghanistan. He was Andropov; I was a mullah. He didn't have the will or the attention span to effectively occupy what was now a sullen and rebellious colony.

As we battled—a kind of terminal bickering really; death by last word—over each decision, I disengaged a bit more and began to understand and accept that I no longer had the responsibility that bound me here.

His company, First Virtual, had made it out; it had completed its public offering. But instead of being a victory, it was a chastening experience for him. Two of the three underwriters had dropped the offering. The third, Bear Stearns, had held tight and completed the offering, albeit below the estimate, because of its connections to Rubin's family. The rich kid effect. Not the ideal way to play the market.

Rubin was starting to realize that he might be stuck with us a lot longer than he had ever intended.

One evening, after hours of disagreements and recriminations (God, we detested each other! We glared across the conference table, each, I think, truly astounded by the contempt he felt for the other), we were exhausted enough to relax a little and to take stock of our horrible relationship and the strange fates that had inflicted each of us on the other.

"You know, your friend Machinist promised me, absolutely promised me, no doubt, no question, he'd have me out in a year," Rubin said, his pain apparent. "You think I would ever have gone into this deal without that promise?"

I nodded. "He made me the same promise. He swore he'd get rid of you in a year. I would never have done this if I thought I'd get stuck with you."

He bitterly laughed. "God, that Machinist is a fat fuck."

While it was not always easy in the cyber business to distinguish between companies in good shape and companies in bad shape, I wondered if I couldn't glimpse the light at the end of our tunnel. In some sense, the discovery that people didn't read on the Internet was a profitable one.

The most costly aspect of a cyber business is content. If you could cut down the amount of content you were creating, and if you could cut down on the quality of the content you were creating, your costs would start to seem manageable.

That was the most depressing piece of good news I had ever received.

There were two new investors who came into the picture in the middle of February 1997. Let me call them Little One and Big One.

Little One was in his mid-fifties, a name-on-the-door partner in a mid-town law firm. Big One, in his sixties, was his principal client. Together they had gained control of some forty companies over the last ten years and taken them public.

Little One had a monkish haircut and a carefree manner; he tended to the details and conducted most of the business. Big One, a tall man with very large hands and a rubbery face (Walter Matthau–like) and a big fortune, did the smell tests. He'd step into a meeting, listen for a few minutes, and then make a decision. "Let's do it!" or "I'm in." Or ask a few questions: "What's the worst we can get fucked?" or "Any bad guys involved in this?"

They specialized in "undercapitalized situations in which a company's managers and investors hate each other's guts," according to Big One. He seemed to think this was amusing—amusing that it provided such a wonderful opportunity for him and for Little One.

Their play was to cover short-term capital requirements and then bring the company public. As soon as they possibly could.

"We don't fuck around," said Big One.

"We always get it done," Little One shrugged. "Don't worry about that."

They seemed to regard the Patricof people as white-shirt, risk-averse, fuddy-duddy players.

"Didn't I see Alan Patricof on the list of people who slept in the Lincoln Bedroom at the White House?" Little One asked, as though this suggested that Alan Patricof's interest had turned from making money to vain and idle things.

Little One and Big One had interests in several technology companies: an Internet provider, a city listings service, a nuts-and-bolts company that for $300 could make any PC a Windows-compatible machine. But they knew nothing about technology and did not particularly want to take the time to find out.

"I'm too old," Big One said. "But it's great, it's wonderful, all of it. I believe you. If you tell me it's Internet, it's Internet."

"We know enough," Little One said. "We do."

I said, "Tell me again why you think you can get our company out?"

"Most of our companies were in much worse shape than yours when we got involved. What? You lose a little money. So what Internet company doesn't? Look," Little One said, "you're just overstaffed. Cut back and you're almost profitable. Your problem is that you all hate each other. You had expectations. You were going to be on top of the world. Boom boom boom. Higher, higher, higher." He shrugged. "People get disappointed. People disappoint each other. Business is not so complicated. A fresh start is always good."

Little One invited me out to dinner. "No business. Just social. Now I want to get to know you. It's our relationship with you that's important here. If we don't like you, if you don't like us, then we shouldn't do it. But if we like each other, if the rapport is there, bingo. Bring your wife. We'll break bread."

Alison wouldn't go. I didn't try to push it.

I made an excuse—"Our five-year-old . . . a cold . . . baby-sitter problems," I mumbled—when I arrived at the Four Seasons and greeted Little One. I was introduced to his wife.

She was tall, blond, coiffed, expensively accessorized, and in her twenties.

I thought to myself, Why should I be judgmental about this?

She was actually very pleasant. Young people who spend lots of time with older people become mature fast. Their interests and concerns and style meet the higher water level, in my experience. I felt like the kid.

Little One and his wife talked about the theater, about restaurants, about politics, about city real estate and Hamptons real estate. They talked about her knowledge of the Internet—she was helping a charity group build a Web site.

What the hell? I thought. They weren't pretending they could run my business.

Little One explained to his wife: "Michael has a partner who doesn't have enough to do. He's gotten too involved in the business. A smart guy," Little One said about Rubin, "but you got to understand that putting up money is putting up money, and running the business is running the business. They're different things."

Now while I didn't believe that Little One actually believed that, or that Little One was describing anything other than an unattainable ideal, I did think, Well, at least I'll be starting over again. And now I have experience dealing with investors. I'll be smarter next time.

There was a lot of wine and Little One kept calling for more and refilling everyone's glass. I had to make a special effort not to drink too much, I realized, precisely because I *wanted* to blur this all a bit.

"Let's do it!" Little One said.

"Let's do . . . ?" I wasn't sure where he was heading.

"Let's go into business together."

"It really sounds great," his wife said. "It really, really, really sounds great. The Internet is going to be so important in our lives."

"Can you get Jon to agree to—"

"To take a haircut?" Little One laughed. "He has to give up his preferences, we'll deal with that."

"Do you know his lawyer, Jesse Meer?"

"Oh, Jesse. We've been in a couple of deals with Jesse. He's not so bad. A blowhard."

He went over again, sketchily, the terms of the deal they were prepared to offer me. He emphasized the thirty percent of the company I would be left with "at the end of the day," after he gave Jon his haircut and dealt with the Patricof interests ("I'll deal with Alan"). Still, of course, as you bring in more preferred money on top of the other preferred money you've already brought in, you recede ever further from your own piece of the action. ("The most expensive thing you'll ever buy," I recalled Bob Machinist saying, "is money.")

"Are you all right with this? Tell me if you're not. We don't want to put in time on something that the parties aren't happy with."

I nodded. The chance to get rid of Rubin seemed so sweet that I said, "Yes, I'm sure I can work with it."

"Then," he said, raising his glass, "to a deal."

"To a deal," his wife said.

Rubin wanted this deal. Making ten times his money no longer mattered to him now. I could hear it in the background, I picked it up in every break of his voice—Jesse and his father deriding his business acumen, his smarts, his guts.

He was desperate to get out.

I do not honestly know if it might not have been, in some part, just to torture him that I became Hamlet-like all of a sudden. To be, or not to be a businessman.

I said to Rubin, "I don't know if I can do this. I'm so tired. I don't know if I have a clear idea of what's happening in the industry anymore. What I see, I'm not sure that I like."

I was in an end-of-the-world confessional mood.

In some fine irony, Rubin thought I was negotiating. He began to reach out, to make concessions. He would sweeten my deal with Little One and Big One at the expense of his own if I would just do the deal and let him get away.

Ambivalence, I thought, can be a trump card; before, they had had me by the scruff of the business that I had built. The game changes, your own leverage changes, if you suddenly find you can take it or leave it. (That was something else Bob Machinist always said, which now I understood: "Never negotiate with a hard-on.")

Even Jesse called to play nice.

Rubin and Little One, calling from Little One's office, found me on the cell phone as I sat in a cab driving into Providence, Rhode Island, from the airport to have another talk with American newspaper people about the triumph of technology and the imminent demise of their world.

Rubin and Little One were very eager to tell me that they had cemented their deal. They told me how good this was for me and how all that remained then was for me to sign on. We could close almost immediately. Get back to work. Set this industry on fire. I expressed the greatest enthusiasm for the deal. I'm not sure Little One knew, but Rubin certainly knew that I was stalling.

I went on to my newspaper conference. It was noteworthy that I continued to be invited back to these meetings; I certainly never said anything reassuring. My role seemed to be the whip. To taunt them. It wasn't hard.

But this meeting was different. Times had changed.

I was to attend some seminars in the morning and then speak to the assembled group in the afternoon.

The seminars were workshops, a motivational laying on of hands to bring the reluctant managers of America's newsrooms into the cyber age.

I was startled by what I heard. The newspaper people of America, one after another, stood up to profess their faith in the Web and their acceptance of the end of newspapers as we knew them.

It had happened, apparently: in the course of six months or so, the Web had become a strategic avenue for every mid-size paper in the country.

The promise here, I heard from representatives of the great old names in American newspapers, was to be able to bring retailer together with customer in some new, wonderful, and efficient relationship. That was the future. Sixty billion dollars in local advertising was at stake.

There was real excitement. They had really gotten it.

Maybe it was my Hamlet funk. Maybe it was my increasing dread of Little One and Big One. Possibly, it was just the writing on the wall. All I could hear was that the Web—this great experiment—had become the catalogue business.

In the cacophony of Web analysis and instant analysis and overnight paradigm shifts, people were now insisting that what worked—the only thing working with any consistency, with any predictability, with any prospect for long-term business growth and profitability—was transactions. Shopping. More and more, with greater and greater confidence and comfort, people were buying stuff on the Web.

When at last it was my turn to speak, I said, "I usually come to these conferences to tell you that history has passed you by. But I think I'm wrong. I think you should go back to where you came from. At some point in your lives you made a career choice. Instead of choosing the retail business, you chose the newspaper business. But all I'm hearing today is that you want to put your papers on the Web because you'll be able to become a middle-man, you'll get a piece of the transaction. You can become retailers."

I was lashing myself as much as them.

At some point, you have to decide what you do for a living. What your skills encompass. I certainly knew that I did not have the talent for the re-tail business.

I didn't go over well. I strongly suspected I wouldn't be invited back.

I had an unpleasant epiphany: What if the Web, the Internet, this whole thing, wasn't, well, media?

Four years ago, at the dawn of cyberspace, virtually everybody not strictly in the technology business found themselves saying, "Wow, a new communications technology! Must be media. *New* media!"

There was a leap there that certainly seemed logical at the time, so log-ical that I don't recall anyone questioning it. But now, to me, it seemed glaringly untested.

After all, the telephone was a communications technology that never became "media."

Which begged the question.

For several days, trying to avoid Jon Rubin and Little One and Big One, I called everybody I knew and demanded to know their definition of me-dia and their opinion on whether or not the Internet was the media busi-ness.

I can't say that a lot of people thought this was the central question. "Call it whatever you want" seemed to be the general response.

But I found that I couldn't stop myself from thinking that I had gotten into the wrong business.

My business, my somewhat unique skill set, was to compose point of view and story and character in such a way that a more or less broadly de-fined group of people knows what I'm talking about and perhaps even thinks what I want them to think or feels what I want them to feel. Putting it that way, it sounds like a somewhat manipulative business. Well, it is. For good and for evil: Rush Limbaugh or the *New York Times*; *Sesame Street* or the Marlboro Man. There are literary messages, commercial messages, and political messages. But the message, whatever its particular legitimacy or integrity, needs to be delivered in a more or less coherent fashion if it is to be understood. You have to hear it the way the message creator wanted you to hear it, starting at the beginning, with the right music, with the right typeface, in the right setting (a message in the *New Yorker* has, quite likely, a different meaning from the same message in the *National Review*). What's more, it's usually relevant that you get the message in a controlled time frame—for example, this morning on the *Times* op-ed page, this evening on *Seinfeld*. The message is, of course, reinforced by the fact that other people you know have gotten it, too.

Something fundamentally *not like this* had developed on the Internet.

I'm not sure any two people came away from the Net having had anything close to similar experiences; that is, gotten the same message. Much like the telephone, the Internet was an instrument through which we were all finding we could exercise a highly individual and idiosyncratic control over the messages we were getting. You got it when you wanted to get it, not when someone wanted to serve it up to you (hence the bleak outlook for push technology); you controlled the look and feel; you entered into the message where you wanted to enter into it (hypertext's breakdown of the linear world); you could put together pages from a hundred magazines into a magazine of your own, defying the authority of context; you could, and I was thinking almost inevitably would, reduce the medium to a dataport enabling you to take in what you wanted, when you wanted, how you wanted. And lastly, and most importantly, you could, if you wanted, make your voice as powerful as any other. You could send your own message. Good for you. God save us.

⊟⊟⊟

Or was my angst just a tangled rationale for getting out of doing what I didn't want to be doing anymore?

⊟⊟⊟

I said to Little One, with what seemed to him no doubt like cunning frankness, an artful negotiator's stance, "I'm not sure that I should be leading this business anymore."

"I hear you," he nodded. "All right. I think what you need is a strong COO. We'll bring one in. If you want, we can bring in a CEO and you can be chairman. You won't have to do any shit, just be a visionary."

"I'm having some doubts about the business."

"Doubts about what business?"

"The Internet." I shrugged.

"What do you mean? It's the Internet. Today. Tomorrow. It will happen. Don't worry about it."

"I don't doubt that it will happen. What I'm thinking about is whether I belong in it. Whether the Internet is a natural place for what I do."

"What do you do? You do the Internet."

"The Internet, actually, was just something that happened to me. I never planned it."

"Yeah? And so? You seized an opportunity."

"This is hard to explain. I am really a—"

"Visionary. You're a visionary. You get the big picture. You see the future."

"Not exactly. In fact, honestly, I'm feeling like a relic. I'm a writer. And occasionally a publisher. With a little television and movies here and there."

"I know. Great! That's why you really get the Internet. You're so eclectic!"

"I am starting to feel, however, that my early belief that this was . . . that the Internet was a new kind of publishing system, offering a new kind of manufacturing and distribution economics, was misplaced."

"It is what it is. Don't get all crazy."

"No, no . . . what I'm trying to say—"

"Hey, we've spelled out a deal for you. It's on the table. If you have issues with it, let's talk. We're willing to press Rubin for you. We can squeeze."

"I'm not really negotiating. Honestly. Believe me. I think . . . I'm just not sure I can lead a company in a business that doesn't seem very interesting to me. I don't want to sell Ginsu knives."

"Who's asking you to? Don't sell Ginsu knives."

Even I could appreciate that I was acting strangely. Why was I pouring out my doubts to someone I didn't know? Someone I was in a business negotiation with. Logic said, therefore, that I was still negotiating. Perhaps, even unconsciously, I was. That was it. I saw my circle in hell: I would never be able to stop negotiating.

"I just deposited three million dollars this morning. I'm ready to write you a check. It's for you. I'm not going to give it to anybody else. I'm not going to give it to Jon Rubin. I don't want this company without you."

I nodded. "I appreciate that. I do. But does that make sense? Let's think about this. It's a promising company. It's ready to happen. It's ready to take off. What it needs is somebody who believes the Internet is the greatest business opportunity of our lifetime."

"Don't you?"

"I do. I do. There's no question it is the greatest business opportunity of our lifetime. It's bigger than the telephone. It's an incredible telephone. An unimaginable telephone. Not just voice, but now we can control the back and forth flow of data in almost every form imaginable. We're going to add robots and intelligent agents to this, and we'll occupy a new universe of data and information. It will change everything. Yeah, I believe that."

"Well, that's it then! You're there. Everybody's going to want to be there. But you're here already. You talk the talk."

"Yes, but I'm not sure I'm really suited to the telephone business, even an incredible telephone business."

"Oh, sure you are. God, this is great! Listen, I don't doubt at all that we can work out a deal. Don't worry about that. We want you to be happy. If you're not happy, we're not happy."

Alison was amused. "You only get what you want when you don't want it," she said.

"What should I do?"

"If you get rid of Rubin and Patricof, the faces change. But do the players?"

"Well, these guys would be less involved. Really. They seem to like me, too. Really."

"Come on."

"Anyway, they have a track record of getting these companies public. Outside, they'll get this company public in six months. And for a solid price. Twenty-five or thirty million."

"Only twenty-five or thirty? How the mighty have fallen."

"Seriously. Six months more. I get thirty percent."

"You won't have registration rights, so it won't be liquid. You won't be able to sell your shares when the investors sell theirs. Also, thirty percent is on a pre-money or predilution basis. You won't have a chance for a liquidity event, as Machinist would say, for close to a year. In that time, your interest could have shot to the moon or crashed to the ground. In other words, it's all meaningless."

"Then why is anyone doing this? Why have I even put in the effort?"

She thought about it for a moment. "Because it's interesting," she offered.

"May your life be interesting," I said, using the Chinese curse. "Really, would anyone do this if they didn't believe they were going to make a fortune?"

"I think it is interesting." She rolled the word around. "In a good way. Of course it's interesting. You have a bird's-eye view of the world changing. But the industry is consolidating. To really do what you're doing, to run a company in this business at this point in time, you have to be a serious, serious control freak. I mean a crazy person kind of control freak. You have to want to monopolize every detail, every relationship, every idea. Your main interest has to be in gaining control, in eliminating every other player. You have to do this both within your own business and within the industry as well. That's what you have to be driven to do. If you don't have that absolute drive, then it's probably not a good idea to be a CEO of an Internet business or of any technology business right now."

"In other words, in the end the world divides between Bill Gates and everybody else?"

"Between Bill Gates and the next Bill Gates and everybody else. I'm right."

"I didn't say you were wrong."

"So just walk away," Alison said.

Could I?

"Well, there's no such thing as slavery," said the employment lawyer Alison had me talk to. But that seemed clearly not to address the issue of personal responsibility.

I had gotten people to invest money in the company. There were other people whose dreams were part of this business, too.

"It's not the local factory," Alison said. "It's unsettling, but maybe it's good that a business can play out its destiny in a couple of years instead of a lifetime. I like that. It is good. It's the Internet business, after all. There's no assumption that you have today that you had a year ago, practically. Entities, corporate entities, should be able to shift, to transform, to transmogrify, to be shed, as well as paradigms."

In fact, the idea of having to do this for a lifetime, of having to do anything, let alone squabble with Jon Rubin and the Patricof boys, for a lifetime was a sickening thought.

I had a decision to make.

Little One and Big One truly seemed ready to write a check. I could do this deal. I could start another chapter. I just had to say yes—by the end of the week.

Here are some signs that you're having problems with your job: Your twice-weekly half-mile run grows into marathon training. You don't arrive at the office until noon. You're current with every major museum show in town. You don't feel guilty at all after an afternoon film.

Pounding through the park, I laid out my issues:

1. Personalities. I detested Jon Rubin, I distrusted the Patricof boys, and I had no reason to doubt that pretty soon I'd be in the same soup with Little One and Big One.

2. Exhaustion. There are limits, and without some new adrenaline rush—and it didn't seem that the renewed promise of potential millions was going to supply it this time—I had reached them.

3. The Internet. I just couldn't get excited about selling stuff, online or otherwise. Also, I was certain that if one more person said to me, "Have you seen my Web site?" I would scream. I was realizing that the success of the Internet, the astounding mind share it had captured and the ubiquity it had achieved, meant that it would necessarily be less interesting, less inspiring, less, well, mine.

4. Business plan. I didn't have one any longer. My business, after all, was to create content that would be interesting and useful to an audience reachable through the Internet. But, frankly, I was not seeing a clear demand for such content. A demand for services, for applications, for efficiency, for data but not a demand for point of view or reporting or discernment or entertainment. And why should there be such a demand? Did we need more media? I found myself wondering. More entertainment? The Internet was, possibly, just a communications system. One that people controlled; they could do whatever they wanted with it. That was good. Except that I had no particular plan for exploiting it.

5. My wife. It wasn't really a question of having to choose between my wife and my get-rich-quick schemes. It was never presented like that. But philosophically and temperamentally she had a lot of difficulties with the pyramid schemes that cyberspace was founded on. While the pure excitement of the mad dash toward quick money could generally deal with my reservations—and sometimes even hers—the reality of Jon Rubin and the Patricof boys was a sobering one. If I had to choose, it was an easy choice.

6. AOL. If you were going to be in the Internet business, a portion of your life— a greater portion than you wanted and likely a greater portion than you could stand—would be spent dealing with AOL. That seemed to me a certain order of hell.

7. The money. The need for ever more capital meant that the entrepre-

neurial impulse—the impulse to own your own business and direct your own fate—would soon be exhausted. Your share would be reduced to a minimal ownership of the whole. Your future then would be to make the transformation from entrepreneur to professional manager. That is, I think, the goal for some entrepreneurs. For others, it is not.

8. Starting over. For some people, even some entrepreneurs, this is terrifying. But to me, in fact, the most interesting time is the time before you've convinced anybody that what you're doing is smart. I could go back to the beginning.

9. Profit taking. I had not made the $15 million Bob Machinist said I'd need to be free from ever having to work again. Perhaps I was not, by both temperament and destiny, meant to be a rich man. But the Internet had been a profitable experience for me. For a writer (which, however hard I tried not to be, I seemed to remain) it had been a wonderful payday. What's more, I was due a check. For the better part of a year, I had floated my own salary to ease the cash flow pains. It was due to me now and could finance, well, for instance, the writing of a book.

10. It was spring. There was a wonderful sculpture show at the Guggenheim. Jasper Johns was at the Modern. And there was a new Chinese wing opening at the Met.

But in the end it came down to money.

Jon Rubin continued to assume that I was negotiating. No matter how sincerely and earnestly I said to him, "I'm really trying to figure out what I want to do; it doesn't make sense for me to try to run this company if I'm just too burnt out" (even though this was true, I was aware, saying it, that I could really squeeze him if I wanted, that I had, wholly inadvertently, turned the tables), he continued to come with new enticements for me to do the deal with Little One and Big One.

At one point, he even offered to return the company to me. To entirely relinquish his position, to hand it back. Good riddance. But then Jesse said that what Jon was really offering was a new structure turning equity into debt which seemed to mean that the Rubin family would not only own my business but my apartment as well. So I passed on this opportunity.

Where we got to then was to no more Mr. Nice Guy.

Negotiations turned from carrot to stick.

"You understand that there is no possibility that you will fuck me. I would never allow that to happen," Rubin said, meaning, certainly, to be menacing.

He *was* menacing, too—sort of.

It unfolded, with some degree, no doubt, of predictability, that on the day I was expecting the check for my back salary—my freedom pay—no check was forthcoming.

"Jon wants to speak to you first," was the message.

We had, then, a choreographed conversation in which Jesse was Balanchine and Jon the dancer. In the State of New York an employer (in this instance, Rubin, as the controlling shareholder), cannot withhold, or threaten to withhold, an employee's (which was me) accrued salary. He can, however, make it clear that you'll have to go through fire to get it.

Except, of course, if I did the deal with Little One and Big One. Then I could have my money.

Nausea held me. This wasn't money that I thought I had a good chance of getting. This was money I had banked. This was savings account money, by another name. This money was my escape from Jon Rubin and from the Internet.

My own stupidity turned my stomach. I had had this conversation with Alison a hundred times. "Don't worry about it," I had said. "I have an understanding with Jon. The money's not at risk."

Oh yeah.

The two lawyers Alison produced to pick at the problem seemed almost amused that I would, in fact, have let my money ride like this. "Some businessman *he* is," they were gently saying.

"How many signatures does a payroll check require?" one of them asked.

"One."

"Just Rubin?"

"No. Either I sign the payroll checks or the CFO does."

"Not both?"

"No. Either or."

"Really?" said one.

"Mr. Rubin," said the other, "doesn't have a great deal of interest, apparently, in the details."

"You can say that again," I laughed.

The lawyers looked at each other.

"Would there be a problem with that?" one asked the other, cryptically.

"Not legally," said the other, the employee specialist.

"Well, then," said the first lawyer, "just write yourself a check."

"Just write myself a check?" I was taken aback.

"It's a payroll obligation. You're the paymaster."

"Can I do that?"

"Sure," shrugged one.

"Not if you want to preserve a relationship with Mr. Rubin," said the other. "But if you want to say fuck you, you most certainly can."

At that moment, they became the two most beautiful words in the English language.

Books continued to fly out of our office. We were recycling our $30 high-end computer books in $6.95 mass market editions. In three years' time, the Internet had gone from a purely tech interest with big, expensive tome-like books to books on drugstore racks. Our new electronic product, NetClock, a list of the Web's daily real-time events, a true *TV Guide* for the Net, was featured on Infoseek's opening page. That is, we had achieved meaningful distribution. We could look forward to millions of impressions a day—and God knows the traffic we could expect when (and if) there was something on the Net worth tuning in to. We had recently spawned a mini-industry with a novelty book we'd published called *Net-Spy*: "How to Find Out Anything You Ever Wanted to Know About Anybody Online" (largely a list of telephone, e-mail, and business directories on the Internet). As *NetSpy* became one of the hottest-selling books in the country, it started to suggest some of the ways in which the Net would capture or titillate the imagination of the ordinary consumer: we would use the Net to invade each other's privacy—and we would love it. I began to think about turning *NetSpy* into an electronic product—that was a Ginsu knife if I ever saw one.

While I was sorry that the Internet might not immediately elevate mankind, it was still hard for me not to get wrapped up in a business that somehow, amazingly, puts its finger on America's pulse.

I could, certainly, have matched my ten reasons to leave with ten compelling reasons to stay. But I wasn't arguing anymore. Whether wisely or not, I knew what I was going to do.

Business, at least if you are not precisely a businessman, is about romance. And you know when a romance is done.

I wrote myself a check.

I wrote a press release.

I wrote a letter of resignation.

I began to clear out my desk.

Rubin, it turned out, had slipped off for a few days of skiing in the Alps, so I was deprived of the moment, of even imagining the moment, when he was handed my fax. In fact, there was, I could sense, an hour or so of confusion about who was in charge and who would take what steps.

But then the locksmiths arrived; all the doors were secured against me. A guard took up duty to inspect my belongings.

And my last phone call was put through: "Jesse Meer for you," Ann said.

"Jesse," I said, surprised to find my heart beating suddenly very fast.

He spoke low. "I just want to give you some prior notice about what's going to happen to you. I really don't think you have any idea who you are dealing with. Well, you're going to find out now. Because now," he said, his voice starting quickly to rise, "you're going to reap the whirlwind."

"Jesse, as I said in my letter, I've resigned. It's no longer appropriate for you to be speaking with me."

"You're telling me what's appropriate, you little fuck? You're telling me? We're going to bury you in litigation. We're going to be all over you until you cry for mercy. You and your family will never know what hit you. You're dead. You're fucking dead. You little shit! You little fucking shit! I'm going to get you! I'll get you!"

"I'm going to terminate this conversation now, Jesse."

"YOU LISTEN TO ME . . ."

My laptop was spirited out through the women's room under the eye of Jesse's guard.

Chapter Ten

Past as Prologue

I briefly waited for summons and complaint to arrive and a life of litigation to begin.

"Deep pockets don't sue shallow ones," Alison kept saying, which seemed like something important to understand about late-twentieth-century life and business.

I stewed a little and decided that we should clearly go after them, that I owed it to myself, that I had been robbed of my business and fortune.

We took ourselves and the kids to Italy on my back salary instead. Lavender bushes bloomed beside the house we rented in Tuscany and down along the path through the olive trees to the pool.

By increments, we began to lay the business to rest.

"Just the expectations . . ." Alison would look up and say, and we would shake our heads.

"What were they thinking?"

"Everybody is such a bullshitter."

"The VC mind-set is all short term."

"They were bastards."

"If you give a preference, you'll always be fucked."

"People go into the technology business without knowing anything about technology."

"I never even wanted to be in the technology business."

Under the olive trees by the pool on the plain where Hannibal slaughtered an army of Romans, I began to fit the details of my experience into the larger picture. Several years before all this started, Louis Rossetto had said to me that not much changes over a year or two but everything changes over ten years, a notion I've recently heard Bill Gates propound and take credit for. Partly what Louis meant, as I considered it now, was that the present, the workaday present, is necessarily concerned with the fear of failure, the challenge of surviving, the balance of setbacks and moves forward, the temperature of the burn rate—the only things on my mind during my entrepreneurial sojourn. But out of those concerns assumptions change, sensibilities are altered, dearly held beliefs are discarded, paradigms shift, and power is taken. In other words, life is what happens when you're making plans, as my old friend Weird Stan was fond of pronouncing, dyspeptically. Which is not at all to justify the failure to take a longer view or a susceptibility to the temptations of get-rich-quick schemes or my believing in ridiculous promises but to accept all those things as part of a larger process of transformation.

Then I started to brood about whether or not this was true. Because mightn't it be that the future you get when you build it on pure opportunism and shortsightedness and the promise of immediate gratification and the age-old tricks of a pyramid scheme is a future that's going to make a lot of trouble for you? Do we have to look further than television to make that case?

The browser creators, Java programmers, and push inventors seem happy with what they have wrought, however transitional their accomplishments will come to be in the long run. On the other hand, I don't know any "content" creators who aren't wrestling with what to do with the Internet, who aren't embarrassed with what they've so far been able to offer. I don't know anybody seriously thinking about this thing as a content medium or publishing system or entertainment platform who won't admit that contentwise it's 99 percent dross.

In the early 1960s, Newton Minow, the chairman of the FCC, threw up his hands and memorably pronounced television a "vast wasteland."

Were we already in the 1960s of the Internet?

Surely we were headed there.

Daily, I crept off from the pleasures of the Tuscan sun to read the reports that flowed in over the Internet to my laptop, which was propped up on an Etruscan (perhaps) wall. The industry, from my rarefied view, seemed headed into a perilous state. Virtually all of the primary traffic sites—AOL, Yahoo, Excite, Lycos, Infoseek—had put their real estate up for sale. Not just discreet avails either, but every single square inch of space. If you were an advertiser or a Ginsu knife dealer or a content creator, you could buy a position in front of this traffic. You could stage your own news, you could offer your own search engine, you could, actually, do anything you wanted, without even having to make clear who was doing it.

Was this so shocking?

Yes. It was shocking. The ordinary conventions of context—that is, this is an ad, this is news, this is produced by us, this is produced by a third party whom we cannot vouch for—the reliability of provenance, the one generally constant point of pride in the media world, were being sacked. The inherent problem of the Internet, that it lacked clear authorship and responsibility, was being compounded instead of solved.

I resolved that I was going back to the reliable and trustworthy media world. I had a magazine concept I wanted to develop, a possible PBS series to explore, this book to write. I had things to say, after all. Messages to send. That was the business I was in.

We are back in New York by Labor Day, in time for the children to start school.

"How's the Internet?" ask the investment bankers who are the parents of my children's classmates.

"Chugging right along," I reply, waving.

I survey the landscape.

Faces have changed.

Louis has agreed to step down as Wired's CEO. Jane has stepped down as president. TV projects at Wired have been canceled. The book division is all but defunct. Two new magazine start-ups have been tabled. The focus of the online group has been narrowed. A search has started for new management (the scuttlebutt is that the search isn't going very well). The new CEO will have to deal with the Louis issue. Kill the king. Then prepare the company for sale. Louis and Jane, however, have had a son.

Bruce Judson has left Time and Pathfinder. He went to CellularVision, a wireless cable company that's figured out how to use wireless satellite technology to provide consumers with inexpensive high-speed connections to the Internet, where he dazzled me with a demo. It is very fast. "Speed is the killer app!" he announced. But shortly thereafter he left CellularVision to form the Judson Group and to write a book.

CMP has gone public. But not before getting rid of its Internet businesses. After spending $25 million or so, CMP closed *NetGuide* magazine. I felt a pang of something.

Infoseek and Robin Johnson have parted company. I send him e-mail at his Infoseek address, but it is unceremoniously bounced. The reports are that all the faces are different out at Infoseek and that Johnson and his family have headed to Europe.

Seth Goldstein, my former assistant turned cyber ad agency CEO, confessed to the *Wall Street Journal* that he had spent 20 percent of his investor's money on ergonomically correct chairs. This, he confides to me, might not have helped him in his efforts to raise a second round of financing. For months we had followed each other in and out of VC meetings. With weeks to go before his burn rate consumed him, he did a fire-sale deal with a West Coast firm, getting paid in stock. Unexpectedly, the stock rose and Seth was suddenly worth a couple of million dollars—not the pot of gold but nice work when you're twenty-six. But then, in a sudden correction, the stock lost 65 percent of its value in a day.

David Hayden no longer speaks to Christine Maxwell and is divorcing his wife, Isabel Maxwell. He has started a new company, CriticalPath, an e-mail back-end company. If you're an ISP, CriticalPath will wholesale you e-mail services.

Pat Spain, at Hoover's, completed another $4 million of financing and is preparing to take his company public—with the help of the people at Patricof (on my introduction).

Jon Rubin's company, First Virtual, which went public at $9 per share, has sunk to $.75 per share.

Our EVP is now the EVP at Starwave, perhaps the most successful Internet content company

Our AOL Exec is still going strong.

A headhunter calls to see if I might be interested in Wired's CEO job. I say, restraining my laughter, that I would not, but I suggest Bruce Judson, Robin Johnson, Seth Goldstein, David Hayden, Pat Spain, the EVP, and our AOL Exec.

I am back having lunch in Manhattan. Reporting projects. Publishing projects. Movies. Television. This is where I want to be. I say to Alison, "This is where I want to be." I call up everybody I know and say, "This is where I want to be." Except that I cannot get over the certainty that all this—this well-heeled, self-satisfied, tried-and-true way of putting together sentences and sentiments and of sending messages out to an impatient public—is doomed. Possibly, we will be lesser for it, too. The world, however, is as it is. It infuriates me that the people I'm having lunch with don't get it, don't care about it, don't see a personal interest in the end of what we do. "If you eat lunch you are lunch," feels like an extraordinarily powerful analysis of the time we live in when you're sitting in a midtown Manhattan restaurant.

"Do you have any plans to be out here?" inquires someone in San Francisco whom I know from the "early days" of the Internet. We've been exchanging e-mail. We've been tossing around a few ideas. Speculating about what might be next.

"I'm thinking I should do a trip. There're a few people I'd like to see. I'm curious about a couple of things."

"Well, we should keep talking."

"No harm in talking."

I am, I realize, restless in New York, discomfited by the sense of missing something.

I would not say necessarily that I am thinking of doing it again, but I would not say that I would not do it again either.

"Why would you ever want to do this again?" Alison asks.

"I don't want to do necessarily the same thing again," I rationalize.

I have been to the West Coast more than thirty times in the past two years, but now, heading out once more after a few months' respite and no longer a cyber warrior CEO, I'm nervous, uncertain, forgetful. Will the car come? Can I get my upgrade? Should I check my bag or not?

I am heading out to Seattle because . . . well, no explanation necessary. It's the new capital of the new world.

The assumption, in October 1997, is that the Internet is a Microsoft game.

I have been here—Seattle, Redmond, Bellevue, the Campus (they all merge)—several times before. Once, after a long and involved e-mail correspondence with a Microsoft manager about how we—our company and Microsoft—could "work together," I came out for a face-to-face meeting. The manager said he would call my hotel and leave instructions about where I should meet him on the Campus. There were, however, no instructions when I arrived. No word at all. Nor any calls the next morning. Nor a record of him when I called Microsoft. I have never resolved what happened here. It still seems *X-Files*-ish to me. But when I've described this incident to people at Microsoft, they don't seem weirded-out or even that surprised. "It's a pretty dysfunctional place, actually," is the prevailing explanation for much of the difficulties the outside world has communicating with Microsoft.

It's creepy, too, I think, the way everyone in Seattle—literally everyone—talks about Mr. Gates, or BillG (his e-mail address), as though this is someone we share, someone whose significance and place in our lives we all accept and understand (and are thankful for). The Seattle obsession with Gates must be at least as extreme as Detroit's once was with Henry Ford.

The other thing everyone talks about in Seattle is the traffic. As though no one there had ever had to deal with traffic before.

Apparently, the traffic has grown over the past few years as Microsoft has grown and as Seattle and environs have become a mecca of Internet-related start-up companies. Still. Not just creepy but provincial, too.

I'm sniffing around.

I'd like to know if working in the Internet industry means working for Microsoft.

I've come out to see one of Microsoft's princes of content. A crown prince, some say.

A force to be reckoned with if Microsoft becomes a major media conglomerate—if the Internet becomes major media.

Michael Goff, now in his standard issue Microsoft office in Building E on the RedWest Campus, worked for Roger Black, the magazine designer and now the creative director of @Home, back when Black and I shared an office on lower Fifth Avenue in New York in the early 1990s. Black assigned Goff to work for me on a magazine start-up Black and I were collaborating on.

At twenty-five, Goff, who had grown up in Washington as the child of CIA parents and had gone to Stanford, was handsome, tall, glib beyond his years, gay, and remarkably self-confident—unnaturally so. He was smart, too. And domineering. Even at such a young age, a shouter.

While Black and I, with a handful of other experienced magazine hands, had been trying to get a difficult and ambitious project off the ground, Goff was using the combined experience and counsel of this team to put together, in his off-hours, his own business plan.

A year or so later, long after Black and I had abandoned our development efforts, Goff's magazine, an upscale, lifestyle, fashion-oriented, we-spend-money gay magazine, originally called *Rogue* but, on my more tempered suggestion, renamed *OUT,* launched.

Goff, who would turn into one of the more notable self-made media meisters of the decade, was very much self-styled. He had no particular expertise or professional point of view. He wasn't a journalist per se. Or a publisher. Or even an advocate, gay or otherwise. He was, proudly, an opportunist. A marketer. A name dropper. A big thinker. A publicity hound. A mogul (manqué).

I admired him at the same time I made fun of him (behind his back). He was a gay Sammy Glick. A would-be David Geffen. A young man without a doubt.

I had said to him in mid-'95 or so, "You ought to be doing what I'm doing. Magazines aren't for you. You should try the Internet. It's all about big ideas, marketing stuff. You'd be great at it."

But Goff's sense of timing was significantly different from mine. I preferred to arrive early whereas Goff preferred an entrance.

"It doesn't work," he said. "What am I going to get out of this? I've looked at it, there's nothing there. It's all, like, for techies. What does it do for me? I have AOL. It's shit."

"It will get there."

"Well, call me."

Long before I ever heard the name (and halcyon days they were) *Jon*

Rubin, Goff had enlisted Rubin to back him in a series of steps to make *OUT* magazine something more than a magazine and to make Goff something more than a magazine publisher. Goff saw the magazine as a higher order of marketing concept: He saw its direct marketing potential. He saw the power of "the list." He saw product lines. He saw a gay-related empire.

His big idea was a gay casino.

But his ambition and grandiosity put him on a collision course with his investors, who, in fact, wanted just a magazine.

"I think it's fine," he said after he got the boot from *OUT,* "if they just want a magazine, but that's obviously not something that was going to hold my interest. Nor do I think that a magazine, just a magazine, is sustainable in this business climate."

"What will you do?" I asked.

"I'll be assessing my opportunities."

His first opportunity, unfortunately, was to get hired by Jon Rubin to advise him on what I was doing wrong.

We were peppered with memos. Why not turn each of our Web pages into a slot machine? Every time the page comes up, the user has the chance to be a winner? Yes, every page a winner! That was an idea both Goff and Rubin were particularly fond of.

By the summer of 1996, Microsoft was coming to terms with its first substantial blunder in cyberspace. Or, actually, in fact its second. Its first was to ignore the Internet altogether, to dismiss its potential as a consumer and business application. Its second, which it faced that summer, was to have built a stand-alone, proprietary online system, MSN, to compete with AOL and CompuServe and even Apple's eWorld long after it was clear to anyone in the business that online systems would not survive. Now, having abandoned its closed-system strategy, Microsoft was looking out to the Web for a new business and technology model. It had two big ideas: hire real (i.e., old) media talent, and corner the market for local advertising on the Web.

Microsoft's big coup was hiring Michael Kinsley, the former editor of the *New Republic* and a television personality on CNN's *Crossfire,* to start an online opinion magazine called *Slate.*

Then, after an exhaustive search of New York editors, Microsoft hired Michael Goff to run Sidewalk, its local-city-magazine-type network of Web sites. "I told them that everything they were doing was wrong! They loved that," Goff reported back about his experience being interviewed at Microsoft.

"Gone Windows: Duo system for sale. Who would have ever thought?"

he e-mailed his friends, bidding farewell to his Macintosh roots upon his arrival in Redmond.

It was hard to imagine Goff—almost a caricature of a New York media personality: gay, in black clothes, hyperopinionated, celebrity-fixated—out in rainy, geeky Microsoft land. But soon enough the reports came back that he had ascended to BillG's right hand. That Goff was the King of Content out in Redmond. That he had ascended to some spectral plain at Microsoft so mighty and rarefied that no one actually reported to him, he just advised Gates and delivered opinions.

"Oh, he's perfect out there," laughed Roger Black. "He's as aggressive and arrogant as they are."

"I'm really surprised that he's lasted. The people, the weather," I noted.

"He's going to Hollywood. He's going to be Gates's man in L.A. when Microsoft makes its move."

Wired reported as much shortly thereafter.

This was the question: How far and how deep would Microsoft go into the media business? Into entertainment? Into content? By the spring of 1997, there were many media people who were truly freaking out about Microsoft (and others who were frantically and eagerly trying to get Microsoft jobs). "Wait'll Goff comes," I took to teasing people. "He's a shouter, you know."

Still. When I started to see what Microsoft was doing, took a look at the first launches of Sidewalk (in Seattle and in New York), hung around a bit at MSN, watched MSNBC, went to be interviewed a few times at the highly decorated studios in Englewood, I thought, There's something wrong here. If I'd picked up anything in my cyberspace sojourn, it was a certain sensitivity to when companies were fucking up.

This is why I came out to see Goff. Because the world is potentially a much more interesting place—at least for me it is—if Microsoft isn't running it.

In my e-mail I spoke of meaning anyway to get out and see him. I said I was trying to figure out what I would be doing next. And that I was working on this book and thought it might be appropriate to end it with what was going on at Microsoft. "One theme of the book is the transition of traditional media and editorial people into this new media and technology environment. I'd love to come and talk to you about your experience. Would you be game for that?"

He wasn't. He wouldn't see me.

He was adamant. Resolute.

It was the Microsoft thing: Don't talk. Loose lips sink products that haven't shipped.

Creepy.

The more Goff resisted, though, the more curious I became.

Hey, remember, we're friends, I wrote.

"I'm deeply involved with where Microsoft is going—and like every-thing on the Internet, that is changing, and I don't really want to speak of it at this juncture." He tried to face me down in an e-mail.

I said I was coming anyway.

"Come on, for old time's sake," I cajoled.

"I'll put you in the book anyway," I threatened.

"You're hiding something," I accused.

He agreed, finally, to have lunch.

Shortly before I arrived to see him, I got word that Goff was making in-quiries about buying the company I had left behind. I wondered if this wasn't a knee-jerk Microsoft response to someone who they thought might have a hostile interest or bad attitude. Suggest that Microsoft might be a buyer. Or was it a more benign reflexive interest? Oh yeah, him, that company. Hey, why don't we buy it?

But it didn't matter to me. I was a free agent.

A cab drives me through the rain and traffic (the cab driver tells me he has driven Mr. Gates two different times: one time he slept, the other time he was very nice, a regular guy) to the RedWest Campus and Building E.

As I arrive, a bus pulls up from another end of the campus to dump off a team of programmers for a meeting in a Building E conference room. I think, I could follow them in, slip behind secure doors, peek at white boards, learn secrets.

I've seen that movie.

When I first met Goff in the early 1990s, he dressed in gay grunge style (work boots, tight jeans, and flannels); later he took to black gabardine suits (an expensive, ascetic, flattering, high-fashion look); now, in Red-mond, he is in relaxed and unprepossessing Gap and other catalogue attire.

I get a warm greeting. His disinclination to see me wasn't personal. He is just Microsoft and I am not.

But soon enough we are two guys from New York and this is some kitschy place for not our sort of people.

"The water feature," Goff says, acidly, indicating the highly artificial waterfall on our brief tour of the RedWest Campus.

"It looks like America," I say, gesturing to the boxy buildings and the template landscaping.

"It looks like a minimum security prison," he says as we head over to the ski-chalet-looking dining room.

I prod him a little, friendly-like, solicitously, about missing New York.

"This is a vacation, being here," he says, more than a shade defensively. "It's time-out. It's easy." He laughs. "I'm still thinking about developing my gay casino."

So he is hedging his bet. I think to myself, It is certainly possible that he is the new man. Micro-Superman. That he is the person at the crosshairs of convergence. His personality is right. He is fluid enough and confident enough. He could do it. He could be whatever is required. Obviously, too, with Gates behind him he has all the leverage and credibility and force that ought to be needed. It's a pure play opportunity. The only variable is, well, destiny. Is this Microsoft's destiny?

For the past year Goff has shepherded Sidewalk, perhaps the single largest project yet undertaken on the Web—as much as $100 million sunk during 1997. It is now launching around the country (and in Sidney, Australia): Seattle, New York, Houston, San Diego, Washington, D.C. Its fundamental premise has been to take for Microsoft a piece, ideally the lion's share, of the $60 billion-a-year local advertising market. Retail. Banking. Classified. National brand. Direct. The advertising that now goes to newspapers, radio stations, local TV, cable, and yellow pages. In its grab for this market, Microsoft's Sidewalk represents the most direct confrontation yet between old media and new media.

That, at least, was the original, sweeping, Sidewalk vision.

But that vision has, so far, been tempered by factors as grand as the Justice Department and as annoying as the fact that most local advertising is targeted at people who don't use computers.

So the reality is that rather than competing with the local daily newspaper franchise or network affiliate, Sidewalk, whose present focus is entertainment, dining, and soft features, is positioned to compete with the local alternative weekly.

Still, this is supposed to be part of a stealth plan. This is Version 1.0. "Remember," people at Microsoft say, "Windows wasn't much in the beginning." The point is to get into the market. Indeed, in each market, Sidewalk has tried to hire the top old-media restaurant critic, movie reviewer, and name editor.

Were it not for the notion of versions—that you can always do it again and make it different, better—and for the fact that Microsoft will support development until the right approach is discovered, it would be easy to conclude that Sidewalk is a catastrophe. A $100 million wipeout.

Its editorial foot is leaden. Even with experienced, name-brand editors, Sidewalk has that PTA-prose feel. It's definition-less, identity-less. Dull. It doesn't juice you, like a good alternative paper. It doesn't make you feel, "Hey, I'm missing something," as a good city magazine does. It doesn't, in other words, send a message, a fragrant "come a little closer" message, and perhaps it isn't capable of sending one.

And it's disorganized. Disorganized in an interesting way, because the version in each of the cities is organized differently enough from the others so that you start to think, well maybe it isn't Sidewalk, maybe the one thing the Web, with its hyperlinks and nonlinearity, doesn't offer is—well, organization. The Web might be naturally, inevitably, disorganized—anarchic. Without a doubt, picking up the morning paper or using a Zagat's restaurant guide is easier and quicker than logging on and using Sidewalk.

But more damaging, from Microsoft's point of view, is the fact that Sidewalk has no traffic. Nobody uses it. Nobody visits it. It's a ghost town—despite big advertising budgets. It has no traffic because it has no distribution. Microsoft made that wonderful, classic hubristic business mistake: rather than harness the existing behavior of the consumer, it thought it could make people behave the way it wanted them to behave. Remember MSN on your desktop? You'd go to the Net through MSN just because it would be so easy, so "transparent." Tell it to the Marines—or AOL. While changing behavior isn't impossible, it is very difficult, quite unlikely, and will take a lot more time and money than you bargained on. A sound lesson.

"I can't help feeling," I say, after Goff and I sit down with our trays, "that Microsoft is running about a year behind the curve, that it's learning things that I learned a year ago."

"What? Like that it takes a lot more people and requires a lot more money to do daily edit than anybody ever imagined? That it's hard to keep things fresh and up-to-date?"

I laugh. "For starters. But I was thinking more generally, too. Microsoft got into the online service business when everybody knew such services were an endgame business. Then it got into creating Web magazines well after a lot of people understood that people weren't using the Web the way they use other media, especially print media. Then it counted on getting traffic without aligning with a distribution system."

Goff is blasé. "Nobody's claiming victory. I don't know what works. Do you know what works?"

"Sex," I shrug. "AOL sex chat. Does Microsoft want to go into the sex business?"

"MSN's sex chat is just as good as AOL's," he says, competitively.

"But is Microsoft really interested in building a sex-based business?"

"It's not something I would be interested in," he responds haughtily. As the publisher of a gay magazine, he had banned from his pages sex-related classifieds. "Cyber sex doesn't, personally, get me off."

"Yes, but—"

"No. Microsoft is not going to emphasize that business." That sounds not only like common sense but like policy, too. "But you're right," he says. "Other than sex, there are no hits." He means hits in the show business sense. "There are no hits anywhere in the medium. I obviously hope that we're developing hits. But there aren't any now.

"Okay, hits," I say, focusing on the notion. "That's a mass media concept, hits. Here's something I've been thinking about. We got into the Internet business, at least I did, because the assumption was, 'This is a new communications technology, so it must be media.'"

"Yeah?"

"Well, what if it's not media?"

"What's media?"

"Media. Media as we know it. The business that you and I have been in. Media: the means by which we send a coherent message to a more or less large and diverse group of people."

"So? Maybe it isn't media. Big deal. Anyway, I don't want to argue about definitions. I don't think that's interesting, whether it's media or not. Maybe it's not media. It's not media alone. I'd certainly agree with that. It's new media. When we've brought in writers and they just want to concentrate on their story and are still thinking about the story in the same way they would if they were writing for their newspaper or magazine, I know they don't get it. This isn't media. One thing it is, is tools. It's like Excel or like Word."

I know that I'm hearing revisionism. Because the one thing Sidewalk is not like is Excel or Word. Sidewalk is media. Sidewalk is like a magazine. Sidewalk has media ambitions. Sidewalk is content. Editorial. Sidewalk is Microsoft's effort to show that it can do what the media business does, to show that it can not only process information but create it and present it, too. What Goff is saying—let's go back to applications, to software, to what Microsoft knows how to do—is a substantial retreat from content.

"Like traffic," he says.

"Getting traffic?" I say, meaning succeeding in attracting a large number of surfers to a Web site.

"No. Real traffic. Cars. It's a big problem here! It really is. But online we have a solution. You can come online, or call your secretary from the car, and find out which bridge is clogged. That's invaluable. And that's a real use of the medium. You can't get that from a newspaper or magazine."

I don't immediately know what to say or how to react to the idea of a traffic report being a breakthrough.

"Who does Bill take on his boat?" Goff asks—or, rather, almost demands.

"Excuse me?"

"If there's a flood or something."

"Bill Gates as Noah," I nod.

"First, he takes the programmers. Because you can't do anything without programmers. Then he takes the product managers, because they have to be able to market the product. Then he takes the testers, because you have to deliver performance. And then, if there's room left, he takes the people who write the documentation."

"It's not immediately clear," I say, after a moment's consideration of this view of the world, "what I'm supposed to take away from that."

"Just that the writers are not the most important people here," he says partly, and pointedly, for my benefit. "Microsoft makes software. Applications. It doesn't create content, it doesn't send messages. That's not what Microsoft wants to be doing."

"Well, I'm talking about advertising messages, too. If you can't send a message, you can't sell an ad."

"There are no hits. What can I tell you?"

"Your model, though, remains an ad revenue model."

"And transactions. Transactions," he nods, and says it again, like a mantra. "Transactions."

I tell him about the newspaper editors, about how I've had the feeling they want to throw over their newspapers and become retailers. I say that it seems to me important that we keep in focus what it is that we really do.

He takes this personally: "I'm an entrepreneur. The Internet appeals to my entrepreneurial side."

"Michael, you work for Microsoft."

"So? I'm still an entrepreneur. I'll learn what I can here and take it with me."

"Sure."

"Remember my gay casino?"

"Anyway, transactions," I say, getting us back to the Internet.

I know where Microsoft is. I know the point they've reached in understanding the medium. Transactions. Approximately where I left off.

"So transactions are where you're at?"

◼◼◼

We wrapped it up shortly thereafter. I had confirmed, albeit quite unscientifically, what I had come to confirm: that Microsoft could not see the future, either; that they would, more expensively, make the same mistakes as everyone else; and that, in the manner of most large enterprises, they would make them later than everyone else.

Over the next several days, as I plied a little reporter's trade through the Microsoft organization, it wasn't hard to find pockets of discontent among Microsoft's Internet editors—many had left old media organizations, and all had gone through the Microsoft indoctrination process. A new version of Sidewalk, Version 3.0, was coming, and it was likely that many of the content jobs would be going. The editorial conceit was done with in the 3.0 release of Sidewalk—no more restaurant reviews, no more service features—and the transaction model was moved to the forefront. It was about selling cars and travel services and financial products.

Still.

Given Microsoft's expressed ambition to take over the medium, how could anyone doubt that the industry would soon be trapped in a Microsoft infrastructure and governed by Microsoft assumptions?

Well, I was sanguine.

Because it was déjà vu all over again. Microsoft was making the same mistakes with the billion dollars it was sinking into the Internet as I had made with my $5 million. At the end of the day, their burn rate would be as consuming as mine.

How did I know this? How could I be so unthreatened?

You had to have been there.

Except the real point was, there was no there there.

An ever-transforming technology and audience meant, simply, that all bets were off.

The Internet would defeat everybody—except the very, very quickest to alight and then be gone.

It was a speeded-up version of culture itself, a series of fads and trends mixing with social and historical and economic forces and technological advances and roiled by constant upheaval and sudden reversals.

Maybe.

I had dinner in Seattle with our former EVP. He had left New York to join Starwave, the Paul Allen–funded company that had partnered with

ESPN to create the Web's leading sports site. The EVP had been looking for the security provided by deep pockets and national brands. But, meanwhile, control of Starwave had passed to Disney, ESPN's parent, and Starwave appeared to be headed for a move to New York. He was as unsettled now as he had ever been since leaving the packaged goods business for the Internet.

I felt somewhat less guilty. I was not the sole cause of his turmoil and discontent. He could blame it on the Internet.

In transit, as I headed down the West Coast, jacking into airport modem ports and in-flight telecommunications panels, the rumors were pouring in:

Disney would buy Excite.

Time Warner would bid for Infoseek.

AOL was scrambling fast because its advertising revenues—the great new engine of its growth into a major media giant—were way below expectations.

Pointcast, the leader in push technology, which, six months before, had spurned a $400 million offer from Rupert Murdoch, was in a tailspin, its management in disarray and its purpose in doubt.

This level of rumor, however, was not different from any other forty-eight hour period in the growth of the Internet.

I went on to San Francisco.

∎∎∎

With some trepidation and excitement, too, I picked up on my conversation with my friend from the Net's early days.

In truth, we'd been having this conversation for a couple of years now, on and off, in the background, shadow ideas, other-path businesses. My interlocutor had an easy familiarity with technology and the assumptions of the digital age. He had pioneered many of them. But he had a proud skepticism, too.

Skepticism, certainly in my experience, is the most useful point of view for imagining the future. The opposite of any expectation will always be true; every contrarian position taken with regard to the Internet has proved to be a smart position.

"The Web," he said, fondly and nostalgically, "will be a joke. We're really going to laugh about this. A few years from now, if you say "dotcom" to someone, they'll break up. The Web is a well-meaning but painfully awkward construct. Remember Automats in New York? Every dish was behind a different window—a piece of pie here, a ham sandwich there—and you put in your money in a slot by each window and took out the food that you wanted. The Web and the Automat."

Most conversations like this—conversations about what will happen, about what's next—encounter their own naïveté or foolishness or lack of imagination sooner rather than later. In fact, so many conversations like this are occurring simultaneously in so many places that the notions you're struggling with will, quite likely, be old hat by the time they are articulated.

But some go on.

This conversation, and others of its type, are a set of what-ifs. What if we bring this point of view to these particular assumptions? Now what if we change the assumptions just so? What if we could get the capital to develop this, how much difference would that make? Now what if we could make this happen at this speed? How many people would we need? What would our burn rate be on that?

Yes.

You can imagine the world out a bit—six months, a year, maybe two years (no more, though)—and then try to plot the logic of how to get there and how to stake out a bit of that logic for your own.

Or you could take developments from one part of the world and anticipate their effect on another part of the world. Perhaps you might supply the connection, shepherd the relationship, anticipate the transformation.

Or you might focus closely on cause and effect: We know this is happening, so what are the implications? How will people cope with such a development? Will they pay you to help them cope?

Certainly, you could look at the people with money, the Time Warners, the Microsofts, the Murdochs, and anticipate what answers they will need to what questions. That is always a good strategy: dangle the future in front of large corporations. Pose a question and answer it.

Or you can play the VCs. They move in packs, after all, so it shouldn't be that difficult, if you really sit down and analyze it, to figure out where the lion's share of investment dollars will be two or three quarters out.

Or you can do a little bit of all of the above.

Just so you're not too far ahead, but far enough.

Maybe it will be . . .

The split screen. The process by which we merge old, passive broadcast media onto the same monitor with new, digital interactive media. This is Microsoft's WebTV hope, the reason for its investments in cable. There is, people are starting to say, a big pot of gold for someone who can figure out the right approach for integrating TV with the universe of information, passivity with interactivity, sports with a virtual sports bar. And just think of the sex stuff!

Or the bots. Information robots. Soon–sooner than you think–you'll never go to a Web site again. My friend is right: we'll laugh at the idea. Instead, your bot will be out there working for you. That dream of every student, of someone or some*thing* to do the reading for you, has come true. Yes. Try this for a content play: Bots as informed and as intelligent as books, roaming the universe of information, accepting, rejecting, editing for you.

Or how 'bout this: the world beyond the Net. After the deluge. Just think about what happens to us when we live in a world—one fast coming—in which no information is more than a few seconds away. All knowledge accessible, instantly, to everyone. Think of that. How will we deal? What will we become?

I once had a teacher—long, long ago, long before PCs, networks, digital memory—who gave this as a due-for-tomorrow assignment: Describe in a one-page essay a completely new medium. Not television. Not radio. Not records. Not movies. Not magazines. Not newspapers. Not books. Something else. Did she know what she was saying? What she was asking? I have wondered since. Did she have any idea?

The thing about technology is that, with a little imagination, you can get ahead of it. And you can be there when it catches up with you. To profit, gloat, or have the chance to spin it—just a tad is all you'll get the chance to do—in the direction you'd like to see it go.

Ahead, you, as an entrepreneur, will encounter financiers, promoters, and all manner of opportunists wanting to open kimonos with you. And having been there, having done it, having had the experience of being ahead of the pack, of having imagined the future specifically enough and vividly enough to sell it, I would certainly advise you that it's inevitable— they're going to screw you.

But I can give it another spin, too:

Nobody knows what's going on. The technology people don't know. The content people don't know. The money people don't know. Whatever we agree on today will be disputed tomorrow. Whoever is leading today, I can say with absolute certainty, will be adrift or transformed some number of months from now. Whosoever screws with you will get screwed with, too. It's a kind of anarchy. A strangely level playing field. The Wild West.

And here I am, making plans again.

To find more information, links,
and a complete index to *Burn Rate*, go to

http://www.burnrate.com

Acknowledgments

Neither the company described in this book, nor this book itself, would have been possible without the manifold contributions of my esteemed colleagues Peter Rutten, Chip Bayers, Kelly Maloni, Ben Greenman, and Jay Sears. They have carried me.

There are numerous people thoughout the Internet industry whose views have informed this book. I am particularly grateful to Pat Spain, Bruce Judson, Seth Goldstein, Jim Morouse, Rosalind Resnick, Joshua Quittner, and David Hayden for sharing their perspectives and recollections with me.

Simon & Schuster has been a supportive and enthusiastic publisher, and Marion Maneker a deft and artful editor. I also want to thank Eric Rayman for his considerate reading of the manuscript.

I owe a debt to Peter Ginsberg, my agent, for suggesting this book at exactly the right moment.

In addition to standing by me, and mostly keeping me out of trouble, my wife, Alison Anthoine, has been my most faithful reader.